AF560254

W. B. YEATS

AN EVALUATION OF HIS POETRY

W. B. Yeats

AN EVALUATION OF HIS POETRY

[Including Background of Author and His Times, Aspects of His Poetry, Critical Analysis, Study Questions and Critical Essays]

Aditya Nandwani
B.A. English (Hons) , Delhi University;
M.A. (English), IGNOU; Print Journalism (English) YMCA

ANMOL PUBLICATIONS PVT. LTD.
NEW DELHI - 110 002 (INDIA)

ANMOL PUBLICATIONS PVT. LTD.

H.O.: 4374/4B, Ansari Road, Darya Ganj,
New Delhi-110 002 (India)
Ph.: 23278000, 23261597
B.O.: No. 1015, Ist Main Road, BSK IIIrd Stage
IIIrd Phase, IIIrd Block
Bangalore - 560 085 (India)
Visit us at: www.anmolpublications.com

An Evaluation of His Poetry

First Published, 2009

PRINTED IN INDIA

Printed at Mehra Offset Press, Delhi.

Contents

Preface

William Butler Yeats (1865-1939), Nobel Prize winning Irish dramatist, author and poet wrote The Celtic Twilight (1893).

As one of the founders of the Irish Literary Revival, along with J. M. Synge (1871-1909) [whom he met in 1896], Sean O'Casey (1880-1964), and Padraig (Padraic) Colum (1881-1972) Yeats' works draw heavily on Irish mythology and history. He never fully embraced his Protestant past nor joined the majority of Ireland's Roman Catholics but he devoted much of his life to study in myriad other subjects including theosophy, mysticism, spiritualism, and the Kabbalah.

At a young age he was reading Dante Alighieri, William Shakespeare, John Donne and the works of William Blake and Percy Bysshe Shelley, recommended by his father and inspiration for his own creativity, but fellow Irish poets Standish James O'Grady (1846-1928) and Sir William Ferguson (1818-1886) were perhaps the most influential. A devoted patriot, Yeats found his voice to speak out against the harsh Nationalist policies of the time.

His early dramatic works convey his respect for Irish legend and fascination with the occult, while his later plays take on a more poetical and experimental aspect: Japanese Noh plays and modernism being major influences. While his works explore the greater themes of life in contrast to art, and finding beauty in the mundane, he also produced many works of an intimate quality especially in his later years as father and aging man of letters. We make out of the quarrel with others, rhetoric, but of the quarrel with ourselves, poetry—"Anima Hominis," Essays (1924). Yeats spent most of his life between Sligo, Dublin, and London, but his profound influence to future poets and playwrights and theatre, music and film can be seen the world over.

Author

Chapter 1

Introduction

William Butler Yeats (1865-1939) is regarded as not only the most important Irish poet, but also as one of the most important English language poets, of the 20th century. He was a key figure in the Irish Cultural Revival, his later poems made a significant contribution to Modernism, and he was awarded the Nobel Prize for Literature in 1923.

Yeats's life, and his poetry, bridged the late 19th and early 20th centuries. As a youth he studied art in fin de siècle London and absorbed the prevailing outlook of aestheticism, which was also expressed in the writing of Oscar Wilde, and the painting and poetry of the Pre-Raphaelites. He was also influenced by the French Symbolist poets, and developed a lifelong interest in mysticism and the occult, which fed into his poetry, lifting it above the concerns of everyday life.

His early poems, the first being published when he was twenty, are characterized by a dreamy romanticism in both their form and content. He was interested in the Gaelic language, song, and folklore, and used effects borrowed from Gaelic literature in his own poems. He wanted to reawaken Ireland to its ancient literature. According to an article written a year before his death, his efforts had a mixed reception. On the one hand, these evocations of Celtic beauty, heroism, and strangeness wakened... Ireland's ears to the sound of its own voice speaking its own music.

While on the other, political societies and the press turned against his aesthetic purposes. The poems in The Wind among the Reeds (1899) were termed "affected," "un-Irish," "esoteric," "pagan," and "heretical."

Yeats's poetic style underwent a number of transformations as he grew older, becoming leaner and more direct. Unusually for a poet, he wrote his best work late in life, between the ages of 50 and 74. His greatest period is generally said to have begun with the publication of *The Wild Swans at Coole* in 1919, and by the end of his career he was ranked along with Ezra Pound and T. S. Eliot, as a foremost modernist poet.

Yeats's grandfather and great-grandfather were Protestant rectors, but Yeats himself rejected Protestantism because of the materialism with which he felt it to be associated, and in London he joined the Theosophical Society, having met its co-founder, Madam Blavatsky. He was also a member of the occult Order of the Golden Dawn. He considered himself to be a visionary, like William Blake, whom he admired, and devised his own mystical view of life, which owed more to paganism and oriental religion than to Christianity, which he set out in *A Vision* (1925, revised 1937).

In *A Vision* he developed his theory of 'gyres', which lies behind the concept of the 'widening gyre' in the opening lines from 'The Second Coming' (quoted above). 'Gyres' were spirals of cyclic time which widened to the point of collapse, and in those lines Yeats expressed the idea that world history was spiralling out of control towards the end of an era, and that an apocalypse was drawing close. He returned to the theme in 'The Gyres', from *Last Poems*, expressing his view that the approaching end of our civilization was not necessarily a matter for despair. In fact it was an inevitability about which we could 'laugh in tragic joy', and 'Rejoice!'.

Hector is dead and there's a light in Troy;
We that look on but laugh in tragic joy.
What matter? Out of cavern comes a voice,
And all it knows is that one word 'Rejoice!'
['The Gyres']

Throughout *Last Poems* Yeats faces the decline of his own ageing body, as well as that of civilization, but finds ample reason to rejoice in response to art, dance, nature, and sensual pleasure.

Yeats lived through a turbulent period in Irish history, including the rise and fall of Parnell, the Easter Rising of 1916, and ultimately, in 1922, independence from Britain. He joined the Irish Nationalist cause as a youth, and in 1922 became a senator in the Irish Free State. But although he was a 'fiery young Nationalist', and his work was embedded in, and drew upon, the politics of his day, his writing is far from being overtly political. He was opposed to literature being used as a vehicle for political propaganda, feeling that:

The danger to art and literature comes today from the tyranny and persuasions of revolutionary societies and forms of political and religious propaganda.

Yeats said of the dramatist J. M. Synge, whose plays he put on in the Abbey theatre:

He was the man that we needed because he was the only man I have ever known incapable of a political thought or of a humanitarian purpose... he was so little a politician that the world merely amused him and touched his pity.

Irish politics was a theme to which Yeats frequently returned, particularly in the middle phase of his career, but he was responding as an individual to the turmoil and violence which was on the one hand tearing his country apart, and on the other hand setting it free. In his poem 'Easter 1916' his concern is to commemorate the individuals who suffered and died in the struggle to bring about what he calls 'A terrible beauty', and in his Nobel lecture he drew attention to the 'monstrous savagery' perpetrated on both sides of the conflict.

A trumpery dispute about an acre of land can rouse our people to monstrous savagery, and if in their war with the English auxiliary police they were shown no mercy they showed none: murder answered murder.

The themes of Yeats's poetry transcend political argument, and the Ireland we see in his poems owes as much to the ancient myths and legends which had fascinated him during his visits to his grandparents in Sligo, as to the political events of his day. He expressed his Nationalism through a passionate desire to revive the Irish literary tradition, and worked towards this end by founding clubs and societies, and by setting up an Irish national theatre. He wanted to revive the spirit of the ancient oral tradition of Gaelic folklore and song, to bring the imagination and speech of the country, all that poetical tradition descended from the middle ages, to the people of the town... It seemed as if the ancient world lay all about us with its freedom of imagination, its delight in good stories, in man's force and woman's beauty, and that all we had to do was to make the town think as the country felt; yet we soon discovered that the town could only think town thought.

He felt it important to promote literature through theatrical performances, he says, because the great mass of our people, accustomed to interminable political speeches, read little with the help of Lady Isabella Augusta Gregory, a fellow Nationalist who was also interested in Irish traditional folklore, and was herself a playwright, he set up the Irish National Theatre Company, which took up residence in the Abbey Theatre in Dublin. The plays they put on brought them into frequent conflicts with the public, the press, and the religious establishment. The most notorious was J. M. Synge's *The Playboy of the Western World*, presented in 1904, which initially had to be performed under police protection because it caused riots due to its implication that the rural Irish tend to glamorise lawless thugs, but later became a regular part of the theatre's repertory. In 1923 they produced *The Shadow of a Gunman* by Sean O'Casey, which drew directly upon the conflict between the Irish and the British and stirred up a lot of Irish feeling.

Yeats's own plays drew on the same sources of inspiration as his poems. He was also fascinated by Japanese Noh plays, to which Ezra Pound introduced him while working as his secretary, and was influenced by them in the writing of a number of short plays, such as *At the Hawk's Well* (1916), *Four*

Plays for Dancers (1921), *Wheels and Butterflies* (1934), and *The King of the Great Clock Tower* (1935).

Another important source of inspiration in Yeats's life and writing was his unrequited love for the actress and Irish Nationalist activist Maude Gonne, who played the leading role in his most successful play *Cathleen ni Houlihan* (1902), and to whom he proposed, only to be rejected. It is generally accepted that it was this love which inspired the passages about love and passion in his poems and plays. He later proposed to her daughter, but was rejected by her too.

Yeats's poems frequently took mystical flight, into regions where it was not easy for the reader to follow, but he also had a 'balancing streak of common sense' and he could bring us down to earth with a bump with stark honest lines such as these:

I have found nothing half so good
As my long-planned half solitude,
Where I can sit up half the night
With some friend that has the wit
Not to allow his looks to tell
When I am unintelligible
Fifteen apparitions have I seen;
The worst a coat upon a coat-hanger.
['The Apparitions', from Last Poems, 1936-1939]

In those lines we see the direct, colloquial, modern voice, which influenced later poets of the 20th century. His mystical temperament is still present in his reference to 'apparitions', but the worst being 'a coat upon a coat hanger' is surely a reference to the stark reality we all have to face - the fear of death; his coat is there, but he isn't in it. We also see the change Yeats's style and tone had undergone when we compare those lines to the romantic opening lines of his best-known early poem:

I will arise and go now, and go to Innisfree,
And a small cabin build there, of clay and wattles made
['The Lake Isle of Innisfree']

He had come a long way from his original stance of 'a romantic exile seeking, away from reality, the landscape of his dreams'.

Yeats's ardent pursuit of the occult and spiritual was idiosyncratic, and cannot in itself be said to have been a major influence on the generation of poets to come, but in leaving behind the escapist romanticism of his youth and developing a stronger, leaner, more direct style in response to the changing times, he became a leading figure in modernist literature, and could be said to have opened a door through which later British, Irish, and American poets followed.

In Yeats's old age, in 'Under Ben Bulben', (a hill in Sligo, near which he was buried), he addressed future Irish poets:

Irish poets, learn your trade,
Sing whatever is well made,
Scorn the sort now growing up,
All out of shape from toe to top,
['Under Ben Bulben', from Last Poems]

Chapter 2

W. B. Yeats: Biography

In 1888 Henry James recalled his first sight of England, twenty years earlier. He had arrived by ship and he remembered how 'the sense of approach was already intolerably strong at Liverpool' and how 'the perception of the English character of everything was as acute as a surprise'. Many Irish men and women have shared this experience of the foreignness of England on first disembarking at that same port. The young W. B. Yeats frequently made the journey to Liverpool on his grandfather's craft, though perhaps because he first set foot in the country as a very young child, we have no description of a sea voyage to the neighbouring island as Irish rite of passage, to set beside those of various other Irish writers. *Reveries Over Childhood and Youth,* by contrast, records the excitement of a return journey to Ireland through Liverpool. In fact the England in which Yeats was to spend much of his life plays surprisingly little part in his writings and is specifically referred to only three times in his poetry.

Yeats as a schoolboy in London seems to have been almost completely immune to the undoubted atmospherics of the world's largest metropolis. The city in which his family settled in 1877 for sufficient time for the future poet to attend a school, the Godolphin in Hammersmith, was unquestionably a challenge to the imagination. The paintings of Turner had opened English eyes to the beauty of an urban sunset. Whistler did for London's famous fogs what Turner had done for sunsets. And it was in 1877 that Whistler's *Nocturne in Black and Gold; The Falling Rocket*, that distillation of an urban mood, inspired by a fireworks display on the Thames, led to Ruskin's denunciation of his talent and a famous libel trial. London as artistic subject was available and controversial. In the 1890s Yeats's friend Arthur Symons would evoke it as an art object in its own right: 'continually changing, a continual sequence of pictures, and there is no knowing what mean street corner may not suddenly take on a glory of its own'.

The young Irish schoolboy Willie Yeats, who spent over three formative years in London in the late 1870s and early 1880s does not seem to have been affected by such urban aestheticism. The pages in *Reveries Over Childhood and Youth* dedicated to this period of his life are marked by the settled distaste with which he had viewed most things English, as if he had in part been responding to the world though his mother's jaundiced eyes. For it is she who had taught him, on noticing how the English kiss at railway stations, 'to feel disgust at their lack of reserve'. Since she hated London and longed for Sligo, so her son for some days told himself 'that whatever' he 'most cared for had been taken away'. No identification with his surroundings, normal in childhood, filled this vacuum.

Rather, a developing sense of his own distinctiveness as an Irish son of an artist overcame him and anti-Englishness began to coalesce, indeed, into a distinct sense of the individual and his world. Where another imaginative and sensitive child might have developed a romance of the city, Yeats began to respond to the glamour of a country whose name was danger. At school, he tells us: 'Anti-Irish feeling was running high, for the Land League had been founded and landlords had been shot, and I, who had no politics, was yet full of pride, for it is romantic to live in a dangerous country'.

One part of London did, however, offer some attractions: the garden suburb of Bedford Park where the family, as we saw, took a house in the spring of 1879. Yeats remembered that 'for years Bedford Park was a romantic excitement' and how when they lived there he and his siblings 'could imagine people living happy lives as we thought people did long ago when the poor were picturesque and the master of a house could tell of strange adventures over the sea' ; almost as he would have done in an ideal Sligo.

The London of the 1870s and 1880s in which Yeats spent part of his boyhood and young manhood was a city undergoing rapid transformation. Its ancient 'agglomerating habit' had, since the the 1860s, become a kind of mania. Indeed the population in the greater London conurbation grew by 125 per cent in the period 1861 to 1911 when the population of England as a whole grew by 80 per cent. A huge public housing crisis developed and by the 1880s there was a widespread sense that London, a city increasingly of migrants and immigrants (from a depopulating countryside, from various parts of the Empire, including Ireland, and from repressive regimes in Europe), was becoming dangerously overinhabited. There was a reactive fear that the city was becoming overpopulated by undesirable elements. Voices were raised to express an apocalyptic premonition of imminent urban degeneration, there were social commentators who suggested the forced removal of unwanted people. One less drastic response was for capital to flow to the periphery of the city, where new middle-class housing estates sprang up to meet the demand for salubrious dwelling-houses with rail links to the city, secure from the threat posed to daily life by the immiserated urban poor. The era of the speculative builder had arrived with a vengeance.

Where Sligo had not been immune to the forces of Victorian change, in London the Yeats family was close to the heart of the monster. And its power was not only extending in tentacles of suburban blight — it was changing the social environment and the psychic landscape. For the nature of city life was altering, as one social historian reports: 'Between 1870 and 1900, there was a sterilisation of public space as activities moved into specialised and purpose-built locations: the music hall, sports ground and department store. Streets were not used in the same way as they had been in the past in British cities, or as they continued to be used in most European cities'.

The era had dawned when privacy would be a prime value in the world of Pooterism and the semi-detached villa on a suburban line. The city Dickens had celebrated, in which public and private intermingled in the thronged streets of a socially variegated capital, was rapidly disappearing. Class and location became instinctively associated in a universally comprehended mental map, with the working class East End as a version of the inferno.

Bedford Park was purpose-built in the era of the purpose-built; but, paradoxically, its purpose was to resist the spirit of the times. The district which G. K. Chesterton dubbed 'the fantastic suburb' and described as a 'queer artificial village' had been deliberately envisaged as an artists' colony by its architect, Jonathan Carr. When the Yeatses moved in it was still very new and worthy of comment. In 1881, for example, *Harper's Monthly Magazine* featured it in a lengthy illustrated article which caught the atmosphere of the place, where in little more than three years, 350 houses had been constructed.*Harper's* commended its sanitary efficiency (which deteriorated swiftly), its elegant lack of fussy ostentation, its air of instant antiquity, its adjacency to the city by rail, its co-operative stores, club-house (built in 1879 and progressively open to men and women 'on a perfect equality') and a tavern named after Chaucer's Tabard Inn.

The journalist reckoned that the suburb met two needs. It offered a solution to the problem that 'the people who most desired beautiful homes were those of the younger generation whom the new culture had educated above the merg pursuiv of riches, at the same time awakening in them refined tastes which only through riches could obtain their satisfaction'. In other words, affordable chic. And in as much as it functioned co-operatively, it did not mean that an exquisite environment and domestic regime had to be bought at the cost of destructive personal toil. The Yeats family should have thrived.

To a limited extent it did. The children enjoyed the garden and the adventure of living in so new a place. A governess was employed for the young ones, while Willie continued to attend the Godolphin. There was a cheerfully complete Devon family holiday in 1879, when Willie was fourteen. There, Jack's talents as an artist began to show themselves in a family of sketchers. Willie even started to excel in school, though he hated its bullying and English complacency. He exhibited great promise in scientific subjects. His father was gratified when in his son's last year at the school the 'reports were written in rose-water'. He recalled: '"Of exceptional ability" was a blessed phrase that once occurred, and I said to myself, "He will be a man of science; it is great to be a man of science"'. J. B. Yeats remained true to Comptean positivism.

Perhaps the family's comparative happiness in these years, despite the chronic money worries, can be explained by the simple fact that they were occupying a house that they liked. For in the Anglo-Irish way, houses were a measure for the Yeatses not only of social standing but of how well life was being lived, a tribute paid to ideals of amplitude and traditional hierarchy. Their home at this time 'was the biggest and most elegant house the Yeatses ever lived in alone as a family' so perhaps there was an underlying familial satisfaction that, in a world of suburban mediocrity and privacy, the Yeatses were living with stylish creativity among talented people in the Bedford Park collective (as well as artists, there were professional men and retired military types), as befitted the family of the Irish gentleman John Butler Yeats believed himself to be. For although the house lacked grandeur of scale, it was very charming and airy, its formal rooms giving on a well-designed garden that extended the living space in the integrated fashion William Morris had originated when he had built his own house at Upton, near London, in 1859/60.

Certainly Yeats as poet was to take 'the house' as theme. He would discover in the metaphor of a country house in its landscape, dynastic and cultural lessons for a degraded present. His ideal was to become a complex blend of memories of the long avenues of the Big Houses in County Sligo, Lissadell pre-eminently, from which his essentially middle-class family had been excluded in his childhood years, of images drawn from the poetry of Jonson and Marvell, and his own social experience of country-house life as a guest, in Ireland and in England, when he was a mature man. Anything approaching an actual, secure personal hold on even an approximation of such a residential ideal was not to be his until after his marriage, in his fifty-second year.

Yeats's parents were never again really to enjoy a sense of being at ease in an appropriate house with their children around them. For in 1881 the family returned to Ireland and domestic uncertainty reasserted itself. Perhaps one may account for Yeats's preoccupation in his work with the ideal of the house as not only a consequence of a characteristic caste concern, but as a compensation for what had been so absent in his own immediate background. There was no Yeats house, for memory and legend to mythologize, until the poet purchased a Norman keep at Thoor Ballylee in County Galway in 1917 — only a series of addresses. And these (the Sandymount villa, a long, low cottage on the cliffs at Howth, a villa overlooking Howth harbour, the Bedford Park residences) symbolize the social precariousness of a family existing between the rooted, customary life of the country-house ideal, with, in Ireland, its estates and agreeably collective life of farm, stable-yard, horse-boxes, well-run kitchen and the modern anonymity of a suburban villa in such a place as Dublin's Rathgar, to which the Yeatses must at times have felt themselves ignominiously reduced. Yeats himself recalled in a letter written in 1922 'that Rathgar villa where we all lived when I went to school, a time of crowding and indignity'. The offence still rankled after almost forty years.

The return to Ireland in 1881 meant a new school for Willie — the Erasmus Smith High School in Harcourt Street in central Dublin. It is from this period that we begin to have records of the poet-to-be as he was seen by people other than his immediate relatives and to gain an impression of the young person beginning to emerge from the family chrysalis. The scientific bent, already noted in London, blossomed, in the way of boyhood's obsessional hobbies, into a fascination for entomology. His capacities and curious incapacities began to reveal themselves too. His school-fellows sensed his reserve and observed his distracted air. He could not spell and had no talent for foreign languages. What may have been a mild form of dyslexia and a tone-deaf ear made it always difficult for Yeats to rectify these deficiencies in later life. He was also very shortsighted. However at school, as one acute fellow pupil recalled, he evinced strong ability in Euclid and algebra. Arcane geometric and mathematical interests would resurface in later life.

Yeats was in fact somewhat older than his fellows in the High School classroom and was already displaying in elaborate conversations the wide reading he had done and his commitment to the discussion of general issues of life and art. He spoke of T. H. Huxley and Herbert Spencer. He seemed to come and go as the fancy took him, as if attendance was a matter for himself alone. Shortly after he left the school in December 1883, he loaned one senior pupil A. P. Sinnett's *Esoteric Buddhism*, a book to which his Aunt Isabella Pollexfen had introduced him.

By his own admission, Yeats departed school with 'small Latin and less Greek'. It scarcely mattered, for his real education had been going on elsewhere. Daily he and his father left Howth for the train journey to Dublin, where J. B. had his studio just off St Stephen's Green in the centre of the city. They breakfasted together there and Yeats returned from the nearby school at midday for a light meal. Edward Dowden frequently joined them; he was now a distinguished professor at J. B. Yeats's old university and author of a popular study of Shakespeare which had made his academic name in 1875. There was much wide-ranging talk. Charles Johnston, another High School boy, who shared Yeats's burgeoning interest in theosophy and the occult — which dates from this period — recorded his impressions of that studio, where the poet experienced his intellectual awakening:

Many of the finer qualities of Willie Yeats' mind were formed in that studio on St Stephen's Green, in long talks on art and life, on man and God, with his sensitive, enthusiastic father. One remembers the long room, with its skylight, the walls of pale green, frames and canvasses massed along them; a sofa and a big armchair or two; the stout iron stove with its tube; and, filling the whole with his spirit, the artist stepping forward along a strip of carpet to touch his work with tentative brush, then stepping back again, always in movement, always meditating high themes, and now and then breaking into talk on the second part of 'Faust,' or the Hesperian apples, or the relation of villainy to genius.

It was hardly surprising that Yeats preferred the studio to the High School, where the headmaster measured the worth of his pupils solely by examination prowess.

The Dowden who came visiting in those Dublin days was no longer the impecunious young man who had looked on a Trinity chair with trepidation. The Professor's stipend and fees for the diverse literary tasks he performed (as well as income deriving from the family business in Cork) had brought him a large house in the prosperous suburb of Rathmines. His mild bohemianism found occasional expression; he irritated the Board of his college by lecturing on risky literary topics. He was an advocate of Whitman, with whom he had corresponded. He was becoming too a pronounced Unionist. Although his marriage was less than happy, he must have seemed an object lesson to the young Yeats in how it was possible to shape a cultivated life in the Ireland in which his own future might lie.

For a time Yeats seems to have hero-worshipped the elegant, ironical older man until, as is the way with such youthful enthusiasms, he began to suspect feet of clay. J. B. Yeats had always reckoned Dowden a traitor to his own poetic nature, one who had forsaken the cause of art for security (though he was not averse to borrowing money from his old friend, who never pressed for repayment). He told Dowden that all his poems had 'a furtive look', as if Dowden were ashamed to confess himself a poet. W. B. Yeats, later, when his own personal identity as the distinctive kind of Irishman he became, was more secure, was to indict the professor and family friend as the chief representative of an intellectual Unionism which in Victorian Dublin had betrayed Irish possibility.

In the autumn of 1882, in Howth, Yeats caught sight of a red-headed girl driving in a dog-cart. He was smitten. She was in fact a distant cousin, so a meeting came easily enough with the Laura Armstrong for whom Yeats wrote some of his earliest verses. In 1889 he remembered her 'wild dash of half insane genius'. Perhaps he was recalling her performance in *Vivienne and Time*, a play he had written for her. It was put on in a local judge's house in Howth, in the home of the family's landlord in fact.

Armstrong was engaged to be married when Yeats fell for her. She would scarcely have taken his poetic suit too seriously. The daughter of an army sergeant, she had set her cap higher than the son of an impoverished portrait painter. For in the stratified, genteel world of Protestant Dublin Yeats's status was unquestionably anomalous. Trinity College would have helped to clarify that uncertain marginality which made him a somewhat solitary figure as a Dublin schoolboy, even when putting on a play he had written in Judge Wright's imposing redbrick house overlooking the sea at Howth. At Trinity he could have mixed with the scions of Ireland's Protestant middle class (the Ascendancy proper preferred Oxbridge for their sons) and, by his gifts for debate and conversation, have made a name for himself in the Historical Society, where many an Irish lad of parts had caught the public eye and established the contacts which in later life could compensate for lack of family means.

Yeats's paper qualifications, when he left school in December 1883, were too poor to allow matriculation. Instead, in May 1884, he enrolled in Dublin's Metropolitan School of Art, Kildare Street, in sight of his father's *alma mater* but different in tone and social composition for it was less conventional politically, with a touch of bohemian eccentricity among its students. There he met George Russell (AE), just the kind of person Trinity would scarcely have produced for him as a possible soul-mate. They shared a dislike of the School's teaching methods, which Yeats later characterized as 'destructive of enthusiasm'.

Russell was a native of Lurgan, County Armagh. He was the son of an accountant who had settled in Dublin when George was eleven. When Yeats met him, he had been attending the art college in a desultory way since his arrival in Dublin. He had a fluent, facile style with the brush, but (much more significantly for Yeats) he painted the visions which rose up before him like emanations from some alternative reality. Russell was one of those people (William Blake, whose work Yeats was to edit in the 1890s, was another) who have what can only be described as the capacity for waking dreams. He truly 'saw' the mythological personages, the angelic or fairy folk, who appeared before him as in some mysterious tableau. For Yeats, who was beginning to revolt against his father's materialism and the realistic Rembrandt-inspired art he had turned to after his Pre-Raphaelite phase, Russell was like a messenger sent to set him on a true path. He was a godsend to a dreamy youth who was beginning to make poetry, not painting, his avocation.

Russell was not the only acquaintance outside the social circle of the family whom Yeats was developing at this crucial point of his development. There were others as involved in heterodox speculation as Russell who were ready to explore occult possibilities. Among them were Charles Johnston (son of a Unionist MP and fanatical Orangeman from the North of Ireland) and Charles Alexandre Weekes, another High School boy who sought occult illumination. Yeats also became a regular attender at the Contemporary Club, which met initially in the college rooms of a Trinity don, C. H. Oldham, and then took a more public address in Grafton Street, near the college but distinct from it. The Club for Yeats was an introduction to political, social and cultural debate superior to anything the college's Historical Society could have supplied, with its essentially undergraduate atmosphere. For under the Protestant Home-Ruler Oldham's liberal-minded regime, its meetings attracted some of the most energetic and persuasive of contemporary public speakers. The ethos was one of freedom of speech, with no holds barred. Yeats encountered a range of Irish opinion, the kind of thing the Unionist-dominated university would not have offered. And he was challenged to overcome innate shyness and personal insecurity when confronted by polemical opposition. He remembered it as a test of his 'self-possession'. His experience in the Club meant that Yeats put himself to the hard school of public debate, seeking out controversy where he could find it, as a means of honing his own rhetorical skills.

The principal orator at the Contemporary Club and Yeats's chief antagonist was John F. Taylor, in whom the young poet faced the force of histrionic authority in the service of a windy, essentially pious Catholic nationalism (James Joyce rescued Taylor from obscurity, only to immortalize him as a Victorian windbag in the 'Aeolus' chapter of *Ulysses*). In the figure of John O'Leary, another Club disputant, he met a man whom, he believed, exerted a more effective and profound (because moral) authority in the Ireland of his day.

John O'Leary (1830-1907) was a Fenian (the revolutionary Brotherhood that had risen in 1867 to assert Ireland's right to independence by force of arms), an associate of those who had provoked alarm in the Sligo of the poet's childhood. For the Yeats who was beginning to suspect Dowden of an artistic bad faith disguised in an ironical pose, and whose own father must at times have seemed a loquacious but ineffectual dilettante, O'Leary was a new mentor. And where Taylor was loudly contentious, O'Leary was courteous and noble in demeanor. He had been sentenced to twenty years' penal servitude in 1865 for treason-felony, which added romance and danger to his record for the impressionable youth inebriated by the headier passages of Shelley's romantic and revolutionary verses.

O'Leary had been released from prison in England in 1871, on condition that he would not live in Ireland. His protracted Parisian exile invested his return to the country in 1885, when Yeats met him, with further glamour. Here was a man who had suffered and had kept the faith. That he was bookish and cultivated added to the appeal of a figure who began to occupy the rôle of a substitute father for the poet.

In *Reveries Over Childhood and Youth* O'Leary is represented as a foil for Dowden, the one's austere, classical dignity rebuking the other's suave, condescending provincialism. With O'Leary came his politics, the antithesis of Dowden's and apparently more hard-edged than J. B. Yeats's unfocused if good-hearted national feelings. He was anti-clerical, suspicious of Parnell and, as a landlord himself, his attitude to tenant rights was decidedly cool. O'Leary believed that ultimately 'a people who are not prepared to fight in the last resort rather than remain slaves will never be made free by any sort of Parliamentary legerdemain whatsoever'. But he combined this with a conviction that a country must be worth fighting for. It must, accordingly, have a cultural life of its own and its citizens must be the epitome of the moral virtues.

There was something Robespierre-like in O'Leary's sense of the revolutionary as just man, and his *obiter dicta*, brief and stoical, in a country of garrulous overstatement, impressed Yeats enormously: 'There are things a man must not do to save a nation' ; 'I have but one religion, the old Persian: to bend the bow and tell the truth'. Yeats judged that O'Leary had 'the moral genius that moves all young people' and deemed him 'the one indispensable man'. Late in life he reflected in valedictory self-assessment that he was 'a nationalist of the school of John O'Leary', as if to remind himself that he had never abandoned the curious blend of public spirit with individual hauteur in the service of a revolutionary elitism, which O'Leary had preached verbally and represented in what Yeats had regarded as his dignified person.

O'Leary, so different in his austere single-mindedness, which Yeats subsequently was to find abstract and uncreative, shared with Yeats's father a pecuniary problem. Although he had embarked on a medical education, he had no actual profession. He depended on the rents from his property in

County Tipperary, which dried up during a bitterly fought rent strike that lasted from 1889 to 1891. A man who counselled that it might be better to wait 100 years before Home Rule lest it be 'an altogether wrong sort', was directly affected by the more pragmatic revolutionary energies which had been released in a swiftly modernizing Ireland by the Land War of the 1880s. Agitation and consequent land reform were transferring power from the ascendant landowning Protestant caste, with its ecclesiastical, legal and professional penumbra (in which decent, even ample, livings could be achieved), to an emerging class of former tenant farmers who believed they had at last come into their national inheritance. They were flexing their political muscles in a demand for Home Rule, of a kind which O'Leary the landlord found distinctly threatening.

In June 1885 Yeats met a Miss Katherine Tynan to discuss with C. H. Oldham plans for the recently founded *Dublin University Review*, at her father's residence in Clondalkin, then a village to the west of Dublin. Tynan's father was a prosperous Catholic farmer and entrepreneur, who had seen to it that his daughter, one of twelve children, had been provided with a genteel, convent education. His hopes for his daughter were well founded, for not only did she share her father's strong support of Parnell's crusade for legislative independence, she displayed distinct literary gifts. In 1885, through a fatherly subvention, she published a first volume of verse; it met with a gratifying critical reception. Seven years older than Yeats (though she claimed she was only four years his elder), she already had the self-confidence to conduct a regular 'evening' of literary conversation in her Clondalkin home. For Yeats, this was an introduction to the middle-class Irish Catholic world that hitherto would have been closed to him in Sligo and Dublin. Friendship developed. Tynan would stay with the Yeatses in Dublin and the poet corresponded frequently with her on his family's return to London in 1887. It is in these letters from the English capital that we find the young poet trying out ideas about poetry and, with Tynan (whom he feared, rather presumptuously, might wish to marry him) as confidante and sounding-board, dealing surprisingly frankly with the insecurities of late adolescence amid minor illnesses and frequent debilitating nervous crises.

Among the pressures provoking these distresses were a father's financial inadequacy and a growing awareness that, by finding employment himself, he could ameliorate the family's exiguous circumstances. To make matters worse, his father disapproved of his literary son seeking regular work. In a letter of 12 February 1888, this anxiety about work, and the conflict with his father, comes to a head. Yeats felt caught in a 'web of thoughts': 'To me the hope of regular work is a great thing for it would mean more peace of mind than I have had lately but Papa see all kinds of injury to me in it'. Things did not improve. In June the family finances reached a crisis. Yeats was at work, with a July deadline, on a collection of Irish folk tales for the Camelot Classic series which he hoped would bring ready cash. Still his father disapproved, yet the poet bowed to practical literary industry. Over the next two months the word 'work' recurs in his letters in the context of the lists and prospectuses of a young man desperate to establish himself in a career or its literary equivalent. It all took its toll. As usual the motherly Tynan received the *cri de coeur*: 'I have had three months incessant work without a moment to read or think and am feeling like a burnt out taper'. He had been reduced to a job of mere transcription to raise some ready cash.

Autumn was a rush of proofs and scrabbling for new commissions, with 'as much work' as he could manage, 'only badly paid'. In mid-December he began to compose 'The Lake Isle of Innisfree', with its longing for 'peace... dropping slow'. A year of literary drudgery reached its ironic conclusion when Oscar Wilde, then thirty-four years old, invited Yeats for Christmas dinner at the elegant home he shared with his wife in Tite Street. He thought the young man alone in London. The poet was impressed by the precious interior of the house beautiful, by Wilde's studied act of self-fashioning and by his commitment, in disdain of the market-place, to art as a form of moral vision. It was this latter aspect of his fellow Irishman's experiment in living that was to mean most to Yeats. He would remember how Wilde in his person and in his critical writings had espoused a doctrine which made the aesthetic a force for the spiritual transformation of human consciousness. After dinner Wilde read aloud to Yeats from the proofs of his iconoclastic treatise 'The Decay of Lying'.

Yeats's conflict with his father was not only about the conventional employment which J. B. Yeats believed was inimical to creative freedom. It was, even more seriously, a religious conflict. The mature Yeats recalled the religious crisis he had experienced as a youth in the following terms:

> I was unlike others of my generation in one thing only. I am very religious, and deprived by Huxley and Tyndall, whom I detested, of the simple-minded religion of my childhood, I had made a new religion, almost an infallible Church of poetic tradition, of a fardel of stories, and of personages, and of emotions, inseparable from their first expression, passed on from generation to generation by poets and painters with some help from philosophers and theologians. I wished for a world where I could discover this tradition perpetually, and not in pictures and in poems only, but in tiles around the chimney-piece and in the hangings that kept out the draught.

This passage, despite Yeats's claim of generational uniqueness, seems to recall a quintessentially Victorian crisis of faith — the dogmas of orthodox Christianity melting in contact with Darwinian evolutionism and scientific humanism. Yet there was little in his immediate family background to suggest that he was so earnestly instructed in Christianity that he would have found its abandonment psychologically disturbing. For although he had been baptised and confirmed and had been taken to church by his mother, religion played little part in his upbringing, despite the clerical tradition of the Yeats family. In fact Yeats as a man and writer shows few signs that his developing imagination was much affected by religion as he could have experienced it in church service and school teaching as a child and youth. His religious feelings in childhood were expressed in private prayer and an overly scrupulous conscience. In as much as Christian liturgy and symbology surfaces in his poetry, it is the iconography of a more Catholic faith that fires his imagination (the true cross, the Madonna with Child, the image of the Holy Family), rather than anything redolent of the low-church, Biblically earnest piety of the nineteenth-century Church of Ireland. Losing orthodox Christian faith can scarcely have been traumatic.

What Yeats may mean in the passage cited above is that for him religion is related to his perennial sense that life must be comprehended systematically. For the poet refers there to his first attempt to construct a religious system of his own. And, as we shall see, religious speculation and system-building are inseparable in Yeats's mature intellectual processes, in a way which makes his spiritual nature not at all one that deals in piety, faith or good works, but in systematic knowledge, structured ritual and organized power. In this, of course, the no-nonsense scepticism of Huxley and Tyndall and his father's Comptean rationalism were just as much the enemies of what he sought to build as of the childhood Christianity he had shed.

So religious ambition meant that he was seriously at odds with his father. In the early months of his friendship with Russell, both paternal parents, in a nice irony, disapproved of the new relationship. Russell's father deprecated Yeats as an influence luring George away from orthodox faith; J. B. Yeats feared that Russell would encourage his son in the foolish irrationality, towards which he seemed attracted like a moth to a flame. Oddly enough, though, it was Dowden's account of Shelley's diabolism at Eton College, in his biography of the English poet, which prompted the friends to try raising spirits. The fundamental conflict between Yeats and his father, however, was about much more than a parent's concern at a son's youthful follies among dubious companions. A clash of outlooks and of ways of being in the world was in the making.

How intense this conflict became is clear in the disturbing incidents that the poet described in the first draft of an autobiographical account (it remained unpublished in his lifetime) of the years following the family's return to London in 1887. The poet remembers a quarrel over Ruskin which turned physical. Ruskin 'added to [the poet's] interest in psychical research and mysticism', enraged J. B. Yeats. One night he broke the glass of a picture with the back of his son's head as he put him out of the room. Another night he ended a similar argument in a challenge to fisticuffs.

'I was much among the Theosophists, having drifted there from the Dublin Hermetic Society', recalled Yeats of his early years in London as a young man. The Dublin society had been founded on 16 June 1885, with Yeats as the president of a small group of spiritual neophytes. George Russell, no joiner of groups, disapproved of their aims and kept himself apart. It was an early hint of the controversy Yeats would discover in the worlds of occultism and Theosophy where disagreements were endemic. It was also an introduction to the way in which leadership and conflict are inevitably joined in human affairs.

When Yeats wrote to John O'Leary in 1892 that 'the mystical life is the centre of all that I do and all that I think and all that I write. It holds to my work the same relation that the philosophy of Godwin held to the work of Shelley and I have all-ways considered my self a voice of what I beleive to be a greater renaisance — the revolt of the soul against the intellect — now beginning in the world',, he was identifying what had been his principal preoccupation since he had left the High School: the occult. And the occult was to remain a controlling, energizing obsession throughout his life.

Yeats's fascination for and deep interest in the possibility of occult reality and powers which might be acquired through esoteric knowledge, had, by 1892, brought him into contact with some individuals whom his rationalist father must have found alarming in the extreme. They were individuals who fed on a diet of controversy in a world of claim and counter-claim to magical authority and of scandalous revelations of fraud and deception. The Dublin Hermetic Society itself had been founded in 1885 in emulation of a branch of the Theosophical Society in London. One of the most extraordinary of the many extraordinary figures who made late Victorian

London an emporium of exotic cults, creeds, social experiments and outright religious lunacies was the presiding genius of Theosophy.

Madame Helena Petrovna Blavatsky (1831-91) was a native of southern Russia. Following a life of colourful international gypsydom, marital confusions and (or so her followers were required to believe) religious initiation in the tenets of what came to be called Esoteric Buddhism, at the hands of occult masters in Tibet, she fetched up in London in 1887. She had founded the Theosophical Society in 1875 and had communicated her religious discoveries to the world in general through her treatise *Isis Unveiled* (1877). From 1879 to 1885 she had been in India where she established the headquarters of her movement. One of her main, if not unambiguously loyal, advocates in Europe was A. P. Sinnett, author of *Esoteric Buddhism* (1883).

Sinnett's book, together with his earlier more anecdotal text *The Occult World* (1881), was Yeats's introduction to a way of thinking about reality that retained the supernaturalism of Christian faith, but in a totally different doctrinal context. Sinnett's writings revealed that there were living in the world, in the secret land of Tibet or in inaccessible northern India, a group of spiritual masters, or Mahatmas, who shared their occult knowledge of the very nature of the universe with selected individuals with whom they could communicate at a distance. Madame Blavastsky was one such privileged messenger, who was empowered to inform all who would listen of the truths vouchsafed to her.

High romance indeed for the young poet already entranced by Shelley's Neoplatonism, full of revolt against scientific positivism. In his early poetry, India, the India to which Sinnett's writings had introduced him, became indeed a version of the Sligo of his dreams, a secret place apart, where, as on an isle in a western lake, the modern world could be escaped in a transcendental eastern peace. As 'An Indian Song' (subsequently 'The Indian to His Love') had it: 'there we will moor our lonely ship/ And wander ever with woven hands'.

Yet it is also a place, like the west of Ireland, where immemorial folk wisdom has its roots in deep antiquity, of great spiritual power, where the gods 'dwell on sacred Himalay — / On the far Golden Peak; enormous shapes — /Who still were old when the great sea was young'.

Sinnett's books, moreover, offer a thoroughgoing system, albeit one that comes from oral sources. Yeats, who esteemed his mother's innocence of literature in her direct contact with the 'folk', must have been pleased to hear that the Mahatmas were the custodians of an unwritten tradition. It was a system too that claimed to take account of science, even that of Darwin. The opening sections of *Esoteric Buddhism* seek indeed to defend the new creed as a higher form of evolutionary theory, one that avoids the scientific reductionism of the Darwinian version. Sinnett attacked what he termed 'Dense materialism which cannot conceive of consciousness as anything but a function of flesh and blood'. And in letters in *The Occult World*, purportedly from a very Mahatma himself, Yeats heard a refreshing counter-voice to his father's philosophical complacency — 'Full always of Mill and humanitarianism'. Here was secret doctrine, anti-materialistic and reserved for the privileged few:

> The mysteries never were, never can be, put within the reach of the general public.... The adept is the rare efflorescence of a generation of enquiries; and to become one, he must obey the inward impulse of his soul, irrespective of the prudential considerations of worldly science or sagacity.

Sagacity, whether prudential or not, was something Yeats, in his lifelong quest for occult knowledge and power, never quite abandoned. His sensibility was always to be marked by extremes of enthusiasm, held in check by a canny circumspection, and his intelligence, in a curious dialectic, was simultaneously credulous and sceptical. Throughout his life he remained hungry for belief, but inveterately the investigator who seeks demonstrable proof of the supernaturalism he could not live without. When in 1886 the Dublin Hermetic Society, which he had sought as president to direct towards metaphysical rather than ethical concerns, became a branch of the Theosophical Society, Yeats disassociated himself. Theosophy as a body of esoteric doctrine appealed to him to be sure, but not the atmosphere of pious moral uplift and vaguely progressive self-improvement its initiates also encouraged.Nevertheless when an Indian missionary, Mohini Chatterjee, had arrived in Dublin in 1885 to instruct the members of what would become the new branch, Yeats had begun to waver. And Blavatsky worked her curious magic too.

Chatterjee, from whom, the poet later testified, he learnt more as a young man than from any book, was an Indian associate of Blavatsky. Yeats recalled him as a 'handsome young man with the typical face of Christ' and as 'beautiful, as only an Eastern is beautiful'. This orientally glamorous personage was helping HPB, as Blavatsky was known to her acolytes, to recover in London from the damning report on her activities in India, which the Society for Psychical Research had commissioned in 1884. That report had concluded that HPB's repertoire of mediumistic tricks — flowers mysteriously falling from ceilings, 'precipitated' letters which inexplicably arrived bearing messages from the Mahatmas, astral bells, music, moving bodies — was wholly fraudulent. Its conclusion managed to be both damning and oddly celebratory. It had determined of HPB that she was 'neither the mouth-piece of hidden seers, nor... a mere vulgar adventuress; we think she has achieved a title to a permanent remembrance as one of the most accomplished, ingenious, and interesting imposters of history'.

It was the impact of Chatterjee and especially that of Blavatsky herself that for a time made Yeats a member of a section of the Theosophical Society. From Chatterjee he had acquired that pose of world-weary longing for a reality where will is forsaken for dream, which invests such early poems as 'The Song of the Happy Shepherd' and 'Fergus and the Druid'. Blavatsky offered information about that reality. The poet, it seems, fell under the spell of her extraordinary, even mesmeric, personality. It was not that he disregarded the evidence of the

Psychical Society's report For as Peter Washington has observed of Theosophy's attractions: 'it appeals to passionate amateurs and spiritual autodidacts'. Yeats as a young man was assuredly both and, essentially motherless, was vulnerable to the authority of a powerful woman (though he detected something masculine in her, the spirit of a female Dr Johnson) who unabashedly sought to dominate through the force of her legend and her bizarre, psychologically uninhibited personality. In 1889 Yeats dubbed her in an American newspaper 'the pythoness of the Movement'. Still in the coils of her strange hold on him, he tried in a flippant tone to assert his intellectual independence as he reports how HPB 'holds nightly levees at Lansdowne Road. She is certainly a woman of great learning and character. A London wit once described her as the low comedian of the world to come'. 'Great learning' was accompanied by ample girth. Her favourite dish was fried eggs floating in butter and on this diet she weighed in at over seventeen stones.

Madame Blavatsky's learning was not in fact as substantial as her person. It was almost completely second-hand, even plagiarized. An early critic of her book *Isis Unveiled* assessed that volume as a 'rehash of Neo-Platonist and Kabbalistic mysticism with Buddhist terminology'. A proven charlatan, she yet managed to influence individuals whose distaste for the materialism of much Victorian science made them ready to grasp at spiritual straws. Derivative as it was, her system of doctrines did, nevertheless, amount to a largely coherent account of reality which could command credence among the susceptible. They were doctrines which Yeats was to embrace and hold to with great tenacity. For, as Graham Hough has argued, they were, when stripped of much nonsense and a farrago of mystificatory mumbo-jumbo, the elements of what can be deemed a perennial occultist philosophy, which has found expression in a variety of religious traditions. Ignoring for the most part the complex cosmology of the Society itself, Yeats took from Theosophy the doctrines which can be made readily comprehensible in Hough's succinct summary:

The idea of an age-old secret doctrine, passed on by oral tradition from generation to generation. He found a God seen only as the boundless, Absolute, impassible, unknowable, indescribable. He found a world consisting of emanations from this Absolute, and souls who were sparks or separated fragments of the same substance. Their object was to return to the One from which they came, but to accomplish this they have to make a long pilgrimage through many incarnations, live through many lives both in this world and beyond.

The concept of each soul experiencing many lives meant much to Yeats. It appealed at the outset, one may surmise, to his own youthful crises of identity, as his early encounters in Dublin and London offered him a range of possible modes of life and challenged the shy, insecure youth to acts of social self-definition: in 1933 Yeats remembered how in his youth 'sometimes the barrier between [himself] and other people filled [him] with terror' and recalled how he had in 'an extreme degree the shyness... that keeps a man from speaking his own thought'. The doctrine of many lives allowed that the self was not an absolute but a site of possibility. The principle of *karma,* also annunciated in the Theosophical creed, implied too that a spiritual destiny would work itself out in many times and places, in many human guises. Perhaps Yeats's mature belief in the dramatic mask as a self-fashioned expression of a complex, polar human identity, has its source in the occult doctrine of the soul's reincarnation, which he espoused as a young man under the tutelage of the redoubtable HPB. For in both conceptions the self is denied singularity, is subject to change and reconstitution. In the one it experiences dramatic duality; in the other plurality.

In Theosophy Yeats also met with the idea that reality is antinomial, that, in Hough's words, there are 'two alternating phases in the self-unfolding of the one — active and passive, objective and subjective; called in *Isis Unveiled* "the days and nights of Brahma"'. Such a teaching must have touched a chord in the youthful poet whose verses were beginning to exhibit a fascination for a world imagined in terms of ubiquitous oppositions and polarities — between the domesticated and the wild, between the quotidian and the claims of fairyland, between sun and moon, between reality and romance.

There was more to Yeats's membership of the Theosophical Society in London than a desire for religious truth. Theosophy itself had emerged alongside the rich Victorian sub-culture of Spiritualism. That movement offered to those who put their faith in mediumship more than a metaphysical account of the universe. It promised direct experience of the supernatural, contact with the dead and with spirits. It was an era of table-rappings and spirit manifestations. Spiritualism had indeed almost achieved the status of a religion in its own right as belief in orthodox Christianity waned in a climate of middle-class speculation about such topics as mesmerism, phrenology, clairvoyance and faith healing. The young Yeats was avidly curious about all such matters. Madame Blavatsky, who had begun her strange career as a religious teacher in the increasingly competitive world of mediumship, had by the 1880s abandoned its practice and she discouraged her disciples from experimentalism in the spiritualist field. No doubt as a proven fraudster, she had good reason to direct acolytes to the doctrinal content of her teachings, rather than to her discredited 'powers'. She told Yeats that 'mediumship and insanity are the same thing'.

Yeats was not to be curtailed. As if to give him his head, while keeping the reins in her own hands, HPB allowed the formation in 1888 of an esoteric section of the London lodge, in which Yeats sought to expand his knowledge of practical magic, whatever the personal risks. In January 1888 he had attended a seance in Dublin at which he had been forced to rely on the opening lines of *Paradise Lost* (he could remember no prayer) to protect himself from a terrifying experience. Then his 'whole body', already depleted by bouts of anxiety, depression and by chronic minor infections, 'moved like a suddenly unrolled watch-spring'. He was 'thrown backward on the wall'. 'For years afterwards', he confessed, 'I would not go to a séance or turn a table and would often ask myself what was that violent impulse that had run through my nerves. Was it a part of myself — something always to be a danger perhaps; or had it come from without, as it seemed?'

The following month he heard from one of HPB's disciples of the even more terrible things which can happen at a seance. He reported to Tynan who had been present with him at the Dublin 'occurrences'. His tone in this letter is chastened; he is at pains to set her tender Catholic conscience at rest by assuring her that he has learnt his lesson: 'When she heard I had been to a spiritualistic sceance, she told me she had gone to many till Madame Blavatsky told her it was wrong. So you need not fear for spiritualistic influence coming to me from that quarter. She told me of horrible things she has seen or beleives she has seen at sceances. She has seen the medium thrown down by a spirit and half-stifled, the marks of fingers coming on his throat and finally his clothes set on fire'. Yeats's curiosity conquered his caution, however, in other branches of occult experiment, even if his hold on mental health occasionally seemed tenuous. At the end of 1888 he wrote to Tynan of one of his 'collapses' and of how a 'single vigerous conversation, especially if any philosophic matter comes up, leaves me next day dry as a sucked orange'.

Yeats was clearly living on a knife-edge in these difficult years of his young adulthood. But he pressed on, whatever the psychological and social risks, with attempts to disprove the Victorian materialism he found so threatening. In February 1890 he wrote to Tynan once more, whom he had earlier assured that mesmerism held no appeal, of recent experiments in mesmerism and clairvoyance he had made with colleagues and of their shattering implications: 'To prove the action of man's will, man's soul, outside his body would bring down the who[le] thing — crash — at least for those who beleived one but then who will beleive'.

It was perhaps inevitable that the young Yeats should have been intrigued by the experimental aspect of the material he was studying (and his commitment to such study provoked his expulsion from the esoteric section of the Theosophical

Society in 1890). His sister 'Lily' was gifted with 'second sight' in the Irish way. Uncle George Pollexfen's servant, Mary Battle, also had 'the gift'. The folklore of the Irish countryside too, with its hauntings, revenants and changelings, its Hallowe'en games to placate the walking spirits of the dead, was an integral part of everyday awareness, even in the middle-class world of Yeats's childhood. What seems like an innate Gothicism in the Ascendancy caste's preoccupation with dynasties, misalliance, ancestral houses — repeated motifs in their nineteenth-century fictions — meant as well that spectral matters were never far from a social consciousness that anticipated, but feared it could not prevent, imminent ruin. The uncanny and the weird often broke through the surface of polite Irish convention, as spiritualist obsessions, and like the prevailing hypochondriasis, found ready soil as the political unconscious maybe sensed seismic, threatening shifts. In an Irish setting, the young Yeats, who on reading a work of astrology persuaded fellow esotericisms to seek to summon the phantom of a flower from its ashes under a bell-glass, is certainly no singular figure. There is something characteristic, even traditional, about his Irish instinct for the spooky and the domestic supernatural.

There were, however, implications in the mid-Victorian occultism, which quickly became an obsession with Yeats, that were anything but traditional; for more was at stake than the scientific world-view which Yeats thought could come crashing down if his kind of experimentalism could gain a hearing. The role of woman was intimately bound up with the emergence of Spiritualism and of occultism as a kind of counter-culture in a society governed by ideals of empiricism, scientific validity and material, technological progress.

The great majority of the mediums who had made Spiritualism a fashionable craze and something of a religious cult in Britain since the 1840s were women. A historian comments of the period: 'the typical spiritualist experience involves a female medium and a male spirit or control'. A census of hallucinations by the Society for Psychical Research in the years 1889-92 confirmed this gender difference when it found that women were twice as prone as men to mediumistic experiences. In one way this gender imbalance among the Spiritualists simply tended to consolidate conventional Victorian estimates of female character. For the irrationalism of the Spiritualist and occult movements, their opening up of zones of bizarre experience and belief beyond the purview of empirical philosophy, could readily be dismissed as forms of pathology, hysteria, at the further reaches of typical feminine psychology. Theoretically such an analysis might have seemed satisfactory to a certain kind of rationalist; in experience, however, more complex relations and exchanges between the sexes were being actualized and figured in the worlds of mediumship, magic and occult adeptship.

For although the image of female medium and male spirit control might appear to replicate in the supernatural world the social relations of the actual one, the feminized spirituality vested in mediumship gave to women a symbolic power as desire, insecurity, religious doubt and sexual ambivalence circulated in the foggy late Victorian cultural atmosphere. Woman, as Alex Owen has argued in *The Darkened Room*, became a site of divinatory, almost priestly energy, at the point in Victorian culture where medicine, law, and science vied with religion for authority over the human body (much was made of corporeal manifestations, even to the point of eroticism, in the Spiritualist repertoire).

As a version of female power, Spiritualism and its sister, the Victorian flowering of occult magic, became a handmaid of the vigourous contemporaneous crusade for female emancipation. Indeed, a religious fashion which may have had its roots in the 'frustrations experienced by uncounted mid-Victorian women barred from gainful and stimulating employment by social conventions, with horizons limited by the predictable routine that domestic responsibilities imposed', in time became one inspiration in an emancipatory movement that sought a social order in which such frustrations would be a thing of the past. For Spiritualism and occultism offered a mode of behaviour for women which signalled that they would no longer accept the prescribed roles that society had determined for them in suburban isolation from political and social power.

For Yeats, occultism was a way of defining himself as a man who had revolted against his father's materialism. It did not, by contrast, offer him any stable vision of masculinity as he sought to carve a role for himself as an adult in the insecure space between the Ireland he considered his home and the England in which he tried to make his way. Indeed in stepping into the the world of occultism, he was entering a psychological zone in which sexuality and gender, the role of woman, and correlatively, the role of man, were set in question in the eddying confusions of power relations and of gendered identity itself. It was not a world for a young man whose own sense of selfhood and of masculinity were inchoate. In a poignant, even distressing letter of 6 September 1888, written from Blenheim Road to Tynan, Yeats, on the day on which he received a first proof of his first volume of verse, *The Wanderings of Oisin and other poems* (1889), admits to the terrible self-consciousness that he fears has made him an inarticulate victim of his own nature. It is a letter which betrays the anxiety of the man who is not as yet assured of a self, who has tried to make that uncertainty the stuff of his art:

> Some thing I had to say. Dont know that I have said it. All seems confused incoherent inarticulate. Yet this I know I am no idle poetaster. My life has been in my poems. To make them I have broken my life in a mortar as it were. I have brayed in it youth and fellowship and worldly hopes. I have seen others enjoying while I stood alone with myself — commenting, commenting — a mere dead miror on which things reflect themselves. I have buried my youth and raised over it a cairn — of clouds.

There is in this fraught confession a history of self-inspection, of repeated assessments of many selves which seem to be mere reflections of an external world. The self is incoherent. That was something the worlds of Spiritualism and occult experiment confirmed. For not only were the two movements loaded with ambiguous messages about sexual difference and power exchanges between the sexes, but their intimacy with altered states of consciousness, trances, visions, out-of-body experiences, astral-travel, mediumistic possession, challenged the very basis of individual personality. As Owen astutely observes, mediumship in particular (and her words hold good for the other phenomena encountered in occultism and magical experiment) 'helps to lay bare the paucity of any analysis based on the often unacknowledged notion of the unified subject. Mediumship, because it so often involved the disclosure of a multivalent and disruptive unconscious, revealed the inconsistency, heterogeneity, and precariousness of human identity'.

For the immature Yeats Theosophy and occultism performed one signal service. It offered social acquaintanceship with a range of spirited women for whom respectable domestic life in a Victorian marriage offered few attractions. Mrs Annie Besant, for example, the socialist activist and progressive advocate of women's rights, turned to the oriental creed in 1889. She had separated from her boring, authoritarian clergyman husband in 1873 to travel a well-publicized route that took her from secular atheism to Theosophy and prophetic leadership of a section of the movement after HPB's death in 1891. Yeats found her a 'very courteous and charming woman'. She became one of his occult experimental coterie, whose dabblings in practical magic led to Yeats's expulsion from the esoteric section of the movement in October 1890.

Florence Farr, the actress, and sexually free spirit, who in 1894 produced and acted in Yeats's *The Land of Heart's Desire*, also shared Yeats's occult interests. They began their friendship in 1888 and by May 1889 he trusted her sufficiently to read a scene of an earlier play *The Countess Kathleen* to her for comment. A year later she appeared in one of the two main roles in Todhunter's pastoral romance, *A Sicilian Idyll*. This had its première in the Clubhouse on an early summer evening in Bedford Park, where the residents were much given to fancy-dress balls, amateur theatricals and masques. The play itself, with its Alma-Tadema classical poses in self-conscious expression of a titillating sexual modernity, was of a piece with such cultivated entertainments for relaxed, mildly bohemian, metropolitan suburbanites at leisure. Fashionably progressive attitudes were aired amid the wine-glasses, the flower-boxes and good taste of a slightly precious night out. Farr, in the person of Amaryllis, a classical prototype of the New Woman, got to denounce marriage (her own had ended after four years, though she still employed her former husband's name). The ambiance was one of vaguely realised Sapphism (the published version of the play has an epigraph from the poet of Lesbos).

Yeats was enraptured by Farr's beauty and the enchantment of her voice. For on stage she and her fellow actor Heron Allen sought to speak verse with 'a passionate austerity that made it akin for certain moments to the great poetry of the world.'. Farr possessed for the youthful Yeats 'three great gifts, a tranquil beauty like that of Demeter's image near the British Museum Reading-Room door, and an incomparable sense of rhythm and a beautiful voice, the seeming natural expression of the image'.

Yeats understood that the occult was a feminized spirituality. In the revised and enlarged edition of *The Celtic Twilight* (1902) he averred that 'women come more easily than men to that wisdom which ancient peoples, and all wild peoples even now, think the only wisdom'. Furthermore he was entering on manhood in a era when the concept of masculinity was undergoing the sea-change which in the 1890s would allow the epicene heroes of Wilde's boulevard comedies to situate the androgynous dandy at the apex of a decadence that had its many layers of ambivalent and inverted sexuality. In 1873 Walter Pater had published *The Renaissance: Studies in Art and Poetry*, in which a series of impressionistic meditations in art history and literary criticism were an elaborately disguised paean to an equivocal aestheticized eroticism, at its most narcotic in his prose poem on the famously enigmatic smile of the *Mona Lisa*. It influenced a generation for whom the idea of the beautiful in the 1880s and 1890s came charged with a bisexual voltage, when it was not in direct contact with socially repressed homoerotic energies.

For Yeats 'beauty' was quintessentially a female attribute. Although he had entered a milieu in 1880s' London where sexual difference had been made problematic in all sorts of ways (Farr wore her hair short in the deliberate fashion of New Womanhood), his own sexual nature was positively heterosexual. Heterosexual, but not uncomplicatedly so. For constitutional shyness and social insecurity, together with a touch of Protestant Irish prudery (he was uncomfortable with friends' crude conversation), together with his sheer impecuniousness as a prospective suitor, meant that his sexual initiation was delayed until his thirty-first year. Some of the most anguished passages of the autobiographical draft which he began in 1915 recount with raw adult pain how the shock of sexual awakening in his teens inaugurated a lengthy period of unbearable sexual starvation and nervous tension. There he recalls how his struggle with his senses made him dread the subject of sex and 'the almost unendurable strain' of his chaste life. His confession in that text to the effects of masturbation on his overwrought sensibility is a reminder that he lived at a time when, for all the sexual *frisson* of its art and social experimentalism, self-relief was regarded as moral pollution. It was 'plain ruin' and filled him with self-loathing.

However difficult Yeats found the demands of the flesh, the object of his desire was the opposite sex. None of the friendships of his early youth seem to have involved the kind of homoerotic intimacy with another young man that had reached its Victorian apogee in Tennyson's regard for the short-lived Arthur Hallam and which had characterized the male-bonding atmosphere in which Pre-Raphaelitism had its inception. Yeats himself, in what he identified as an 'incredible timidity' found it easier to make intimate intellectual contact with women, since in a man he always found 'some competing thought'. For him, however, sexual desire was strikingly modulated by a sense of female beauty which art had stimulated, for all its urgent, bodily imperatives and frustrations. He was not necessarily unusual as a young man in the way he read the world in terms of literature and painting. Many literary-minded people instinctively do so.

That, in as immediate and pressing a dimension of experience as the sexual, he so readily turned to iconographic representation as a means of coping with such a disturbed aspect of his life tells us, nevertheless, in a markedly distinctive way, something crucial about his sensibility. And it is something which offers a guide to the peculiar quality of his own artistic procedures, the governing principles of his *oeuvre*.

When Yeats remembered how Farr had seemed a very Demeter to his youthful eye, like a statue he saw frequently, he was recalling how, even as a young man, life and image were for him in complex relationship. A habit had established itself early whereby experience was interpreted in terms of its iconographic potentiality, its tendency to approximate to pre-existing forms, to enter relationship with its own dynamic capacity for taking on significance. An agenda had begun to be set, in which the poet's own life could be rescued from mere individual inconsequence and become the stuff of an exemplary, formal art. It could do so in an artistic transcendence as image among the many images which tradition and certain contemporary writers and artists had bequeathed to a world rapidly losing any significant form in the incoherence of urban modernity.

Images of women nevertheless had their direct effect on the young Yeats, as he confessed in 1915: 'women filled me with curiosity and my mind seemed never long to escape from the disturbance of my senses, I was a romantic, my head full of the mysterious women of Rossetti and those hesitating faces in the art of Burne-Jones which seemed always anxious for some Alastor at the end of a long journey'. In the poetry he composed in the 1880s Yeats was willing to represent himself as just such a Shelleyan figure, in thrall to an ideal of female beauty that represented sexual desire as a quest romance. The intensity of sexual longing finds expression in an erotically inspired dedication. Its object is unambiguously female, though Yeats does derive from the art and poetry of Morris, Swinburne and Rossetti, if not its equivocal images of sexual difference, then its acknowledgement of the unsettling power vested in the beauty of woman. For as Nina Auerbach has shown, in *Woman and the Demon*, Victorian culture, for all its attempts to restrict woman to the domestic sphere, was granting her, in its poetry and art, symbolic power as enchantress, sybil or goddess. The courtly hero on his quest (the Arthurian cycle of tales was a constant source of imagery) may be a figure of noble ardour, but he is captive to a power — his own desire — that the woman in her beauty provokes. She becomes masterful, dangerous, sinister, even mortally threatening, since her power so unmans the hero. Elizabeth Cullingford astutely comments on this process: 'Woman' is granted immense textual and symbolical significance in order to disguise (or to maintain against increasingly vehement feminist demands) her lack of social significance'. Yet the permission so granted for woman to enter iconographic and textual space in art and literature — paradoxically — unleashes her power.

Yeats's 1880s' apprentice verse is populated by figures of woman as enchantress and as agent of occult power in a context of quest and death. George Bornstein points out that: 'Female magicians' appear in all four of the verse-plays that Yeats published at this initial stage of his career. His masters as he set his hand to verse-making were the Keats of 'La Belle Dame Sans Merci' and the Shelley of 'Prometheus Unbound' and, especially, 'Alastor', as the images of Rossetti and Burne-Jones and the Pre-Raphaelite school gave flesh to literary imagining. In *Mosada* (published in 1886 and the most fully realised of these early dramatic experiments) a Moorish lady, who is to be condemned by the Inquisition as a witch and who dies at her own hand, summons

A phantom fair
And calm, robed all in raiment moony white.
She was a great enchantress once of yore,
Whose dwelling was a tree-wrapt island, lulled
Far out upon the water world and ringed
With wonderful white sands, where never yet
Were furled the wings of ships. There in a dell,
A lily-blanchèd place, she sat and sang,
And in her singing wove around her head

> *White lilies, and her song flew forth afar*
> *Along the sea; and many a man grew hushed*
> *In his own house or 'mong the merchants grey,*
> *Hearing the far-off singing guile, and groaned,*
> *And manned an argosy and sailing died.*

Woman is the enchanting, magically powerful alternative to the worlds of domesticity and commerce, but she can be deadly in her mesmeric 'guile'.

Woman as beautiful temptress reaches its apotheosis in Yeats's 1880s' poetry in the figure of the fairy Niam in his first major poem, 'The Wanderings of Oisin', which he completed in its earliest version in November 1887 after almost two years of dedicated work. The poem was the title poem of the poet's first collection. It was heavily revised in later publications. The question as to where it should stand in any collected edition of Yeats's poems became one of the many editorial cruces which have marked the publishing history of this most self-revising of authors (he came to fear that when placed at the head of his work, the poem tended to distract from what followed).

For from the first Yeats was conscious that a poem is more than an individual work, that it finds richer meaning and new kinds of life in the many contexts in which it appears, until it rests in the canonical finality of a posthumously established *Collected Poems*. This means that, from a very early stage in his career, Yeats had a clear and abiding sense of himself as a poet, for all his social insecurity and personal and sexual timidity. The fact that over the years he returned frequently in his writings to 'The Wanderings of Oisin' to comment on it, suggests that it was in this work that he felt he had come into possession of his own talent, had become sure of a poetic destiny. If so, he was assuredly right, for it was a truly impressive debut.

In 1931 Yeats offered what Harold Bloom has identified as 'the most illuminating of his many insights into his own poem'. In an introduction to his play *The Resurrection* Yeats wrote:

When I was a boy everybody talked about progress, and rebellion against my elders took the form of aversion to that myth. I took satisfaction in certain public disasters, and felt a sort of ecstasy at the contemplation of ruin, and then came upon the story of Oisin in Tir na nOg and reshaped it into my *Wanderings of Oisin*. He rides across the sea with a spirit, he passes phantoms, a boy following a girl, a hound chasing a hare, emblematic of eternal pursuit, he comes to an island of choral dancing, leaves that after many years, passes the phantoms once again, comes to an island of endless battle for an object never achieved, leaves that after many years, passes the phantoms once again, comes to an island of sleep, leaves that and comes to Ireland, to S Patrick and old age. I did not pick these images because of any theory, but because I found them impressive, yet all the while abstractions haunted me. I remember rejecting, because it spoilt the simplicity, an elaborate metaphor of a breaking wave intended to prove that all life rose and fell as in my poem.

Such a passage gives a critic leave to read the poem so summarized not only as autobiography, but as a poem of Victorian crisis, a revolt, couched as apocalypse, against the dominant myth of social progress.

Richard Ellmann took the autobiographical hint. He suggested that the three islands where Oisin spends 100 years apiece can be associated with the three phases of Yeats's early life: the isle of dancing and song with the Sligo of 'Sindbad's yellow shore'; the isle of battles with his unhappy years at school in London when he was locked in futile conflict with his English school-fellows; and the island of sleep with the idyllic days in Howth. He also recognized how such a pattern, which Yeats himself, in his late poem 'The Circus Animals' Desertion', saw as one of 'Vain gaiety, vain battle, vain repose', was that not only of youth, but of life as a whole. Other critics have sought not only to read 'The Wanderings of Oisin' as a social and human document, but as a work which gives insight into the poet's psyche. David Lynch makes much of the heavily charged eroticism of the work, with its crowded symbolic landscapes, which he finds all too open to a reading where the vain battle with a continually reviving monster in the second isle can be reckoned an oedipal conflict with the father which is repetitive, futile and issueless. Another critic finds the 'dusky demon' of the same book 'orgasm incarnate'.

The most admiring account of the poem is Bloom's (though he addresses the poem in its revised form). He prefers it to some of Yeats's later and more widely regarded works. For Bloom 'The Wanderings of Oisin' is a late and notable entry in the tradition of romantic quest poems in which the epic action of a major narrative becomes the vehicle for a subjective spiritual history. In this, Yeats observes the emotional trajectory of his high romantic precursors (Blake and especially Shelley) but makes his poem, for all its commitment to the direct expression of transformative feeling in the person of the poet/Oisin, subject to the implacable, divisive forces of nature. The poem ends with Oisin, who has abandoned his fairy-bride for love of his old warrior companions, arguing with the St Patrick who has conquered pagan Ireland with a new faith. When Oisin touches the earth, the weight of the ages falls on him and he perishes. It is an ambiguous victory, which allows Oisin's poetic imagination only the consolation of nostalgia. He will 'go to the house of the Fenians, be they in flames or at feast'. For Yeats, if not for Oisin/Yeats (and the poem is the one where the poet and his hero are the least distinct) however, the ambiguity was potentially more tragic than nostalgic, since in entering so Shelleyan a subjectivity, he was forced to embrace 'the quester's natural defeat as a victory... of a man divided against himself, natural against imaginative, neither capable of final victory over the other'.

Such a formulation for all its force lacks, it is necessary to add, a sense of history. Bloom is so anxious to set the text in the ideal dimension of a literary tradition that history — which is represented by the querulous voice of St Patrick in the poem — is ignored. For Patrick speaks to Oisin not simply as the voice of the reality before which the timeless world of vision in the land of youth must wither, but as a force for the very progress that Yeats had rejected in the poem's defiance of his own social world. In fact in Victorian Ireland St Patrick was not simply a figure in an antique source text from which Yeats took the matter for a poem, nor indeed just a folkloric motif (the debate between Oisin and St Patrick was extant in contemporary Irish folklore) but a living presence in national self-understanding.

The Catholicism which was transforming Yeats's Ireland in the post-Famine period regarded the coming of St Patrick to the country in the fifth century as a progressive event, which had resulted in its own increasingly hegemonic if benign power over the social order. The centre of that power was St Patrick's College, Maynooth, the national seminary founded in 1795. Yeats, by contrast, offers in this initiatory work a vision of apocalypse in which the concept of progress itself seems paltry and sacrilegious in face of a Celtic *Götterdämmerung* in which old age consumes the pride of life, and death is preferable to mere existence among 'a small and a feeble populace stooping with mattock and spade,/Or weeding or ploughing with faces a-shining with much-toil wet' in the land of St Patrick's 'bell-mounted churches'.

It is these historical implications of Yeats's text which also make Richard Ellmann's negative critique of the poem wide of the mark. Ellmann reckoned that among the work's weaknesses were inconsistencies in its symbology: 'a powerful contrast which Yeats draws in the poem between Oisin and Patrick, as representatives of pagan and Christian Ireland, seems irrelevant to the timeless portrait of life in the three islands'. In fact that contrast is of the essence since the pagan world of fairy is rendered in terms which make it seem non-teleological, non-purposive, ahistorical. It is repetitive, patterned as if obeying typological imperatives, cyclical. Yeats himself indeed, in his introduction to *The Resurrection*, as he thought of the image of life as a process of rising and falling, continued: 'How hard it was to refrain from pointing out that Oisin after old age, its illumination half accepted, half rejected, would pass in death over another sea to another island. He would be free not only of the biological and human facts of life, but of the progressive history over which St Patrick and his followers assume they have authority.

Presumably he would be led onwards by the fairy Niam. For she is the poem's female presiding genius. And 'The Wanderings of Oisin' is a poem which, as Yeats told Tynan, contained nothing in 'clear outline', and things 'under disguise of symbolism', to which only he possessed the key, where a tapestry, a 'cloud and foam' of interrelating images of bird, tree, water, sea, glimmers with indeterminate implication, like shot-silk in changing light. It is a poem which sets the magic power of enchantment against history; secret lore, the hermetic, against what is conventionally known of life and destructive time.

Yeats as he worked on this poem sought to comprehend much he had experienced and felt in his life. His mother had suffered her first stroke in the late summer of 1887, so it was also a time of anxiety. Both personal life and the work of creation took their toll. That autumn in Sligo he finished the poem and brought the last part round to read to his Uncle George. He could hardly read so 'collapsed' he felt, his voice 'quite broken'. Subsequently he endured a period of weeks when his voice deserted him and he suffered a series of minor nervous collapses. That part of the poem, he told Tynan a year after he had finished it, 'really was a kind of vision it beset me night and day'. The poem as a whole has a dreamy visionary quality, and perhaps no moment seems more the stuff of dreams than that when Oisin first glimpses Niam:

Her eyes were soft as dewdrops hanging
Upon the grass-blades' bending tips,
And like a sunset were her lips,
A stormy sunset o'er doomed ships.
Her hair was of a citron tincture,
And gathered in a silver cincture;
Down to her feet white vesture flowed,
And with the woven crimson glowed
Of many a figured creature strange,
And birds that on the seven seas range.
For brooch 'twas bound with bright sea-shell,
And wavered like a summer rill,
As her soft bosom rose and fell.

A Rossetti temptress, with Burne-Jones colouration and William Morris costuming. Yet a vibrant erotic longing energizes the verse with youthful desire, despite the obligatory gesture, in such conventional Victorian imagining of alluring womanhood, to the female as death-dealer. This is the poem of a young man anxious to meet his own amatory destiny. He had not long to wait.

The Abbey Theater and the Irish Revival

In 1904, Yeats, along with Lady Augusta Gregory and Annie Horniman, founded the Abbey Theater. At the Abbey, and with his educational pamphlets, Samhain, Yeats sought to create an Irish theater and educate the Irish public by offering a place for the performance of works by Irish dramatists. This laudable goal met with difficulties. The 1907 Playboy Riots, in response to supposed indecency in John Millington Synge's The Playboy of the Western World, infuriated Yeats, who supported Synge's play in the face of pushes for censorship. After discovering ancient Japanese Noh Drama in 1916, Yeats began to incorporate Noh conventions (little scenery, heavy symbolism, stylized movements) into his own drama. The Abbey Theater and Yeats's poetry made important contributions to the Irish Revival, a resurgence of Irish drama, poetry and prose from the Victorian period to the 1920s.

Politics and Marriage

Though frustrated by the Dublin reaction to Synge's Playboy of the Western World, Yeats's attitude to Ireland changed again in 1916. The Easter Rising of 1916, when roughly 700 Irish Volunteers took over parts of Dublin and proclaimed an Irish Republic, inspired in Yeats a new nationalism. His elegy for those executed by the British, "Easter 1916," eulogizes the dead while retaining an ambivalent attitude toward violent resistance. In 1917, Yeats married Englishwoman Georgie Hyde-Lees. Yeats believed that his wife was capable of acting as a spirit medium, and based much of his mystical work, A Vision (1925), on her automatic script. The couple had a son and daughter and lived in a Norman Castle, Thoor Ballylee. From 1922 to 1928, Yeats served as a Senator for the Irish Free State, and was awarded the Nobel Prize for Literature in 1923. Yeats died in the South of France in 1939, and was buried in 1940 in Sligo.

Chapter 3

Timeline of Yeats

A BRIEF CHRONOLOGY

1865	(June 13, at 10.40 pm) William Butler Yeats born in Dublin, the eldest child of John Butler Yeats, a lawyer turned painter, and Susan Yeats, née Pollexfen.
1867	(July) The Yeats family moves to London.
1868-71	Family holidays in Sligo.
1872	(July) Susan Yeats takes WBY and her other children to her parents' house in Sligo, in the west of Ireland, for two years.
1874	(October) The family returns to London.
1881	(Summer) The family returns to Ireland, living in Howth, near Dublin
1884	(May) WBY enrolls at Metropolitan School of Art, Dublin
1885	(April) First poems published in the Dublin University Review (June) Founds Dublin Hermetic Society with AE (George Russell) and Charles Johnston. WBY meets Douglas Hyde, Katharine Tynan and John O'Leary.
1885-1886	WBY attends his first séance; arrival of Mohini Chatterjee to help found Dublin Theosophical Lodge
1886	(April) Leaves Metropolitan School of Art (October) *Mosada, A Dramatic Poem*, is published privately
1887	(April) Returns with family to London (May) Visits Madame Blavatsky, who has just arrived in London. WBY first meets MacGregor Mathers (Samuel Liddle Mathers).
1888	WBY meets George Bernard Shaw at William Morris's house, and Lady Wilde, Oscar Wilde's mother.

(September) *Fairy and Folk Tales of the Irish Peasantry* (ed.) published. (November) Joins the Esoteric Section of the Theosophical Society (December) Christmas Day with Oscar and Constance Wilde in London.

1889 (January) *The Wanderings of Oisin and Other Poems* is published. WBY meets Maud Gonne.

1890 (January) Maud Gonne has a son, George, by her lover Lucien Millevoye (WBY unaware). WBY founds Rhymers' Club with Ernest Rhys.(March) WBY initiated into the Hermetic Order of the Golden Dawn (October) WBY asked to resign from Esoteric Section of Theosophical Society.

1891 (March) *Representative Irish Tales* (ed.) is published. (August) WBY proposes to Maud Gonne for the first time but is refused. MG's son dies. (September) WBY and John O'Leary organise meeting of Young Ireland League to unite various literary societies. (October) Death of Charles Stewart Parnell. (November) *John Sherman and Dhoya* (short fiction) is published.

1892 (May) *Irish Fairy Tales* (ed.) is published; Irish Literary Society founded in Dublin, with its inaugural meeting in August. (August) *The Countess Kathleen and Various Legends and Lyrics* is published. (October 16 at 8.25 am) Bertha Georgie Hyde Lees born at Fleet near Aldershot. Her birth-certificate gives 17 October, but she always celebrated her birthday on 16th.

1893 (January) WBY enters the Second Order of the Golden Dawn. (January/February) *The Works of William Blake* (ed. with Edwin Ellis) is published. (November) *The Poems of William Blake* (ed.) is published. (December) *The Celtic Twilight* (stories) is published

1894 (March) *The Land of Heart's Desire* is produced in London. (August) Maud Gonne's daughter by Lucien Millevoye, Iseult, is born.

1895 (March) *A Book of Irish Verse* (ed.) is published.(August) *Poems* is published

1896 (February) WBY takes rooms at Woburn Buildings in Bloomsbury, London. He begins an affair with Olivia Shakespear. (August) WBY meets Lady Gregory at Tillyra Castle, Galway, home of Edward Martyn, a cousin of George Moore. (December) WBY meets J. M. Synge in Paris.

1897 (April and June) *The Secret Rose* and *The Adoration of the Magi* (stories) published. (July) WBY stays at Coole Park, Galway, Lady Gregory's house. He discusses the foundation of a Celtic Theatre with Lady Gregory, Edward Martyn, and George Moore.

1898 Working on 'Celtic mysticism', with Maud Gonne and members of the Golden Dawn. (December) WBY and Maud Gonne contract a mystical marriage.

1899 (February) WBY visits Maud Gonne in Paris and proposes marriage again, and is refused again. (April) *The Wind Among the Reeds* (poems) is published. (May) *The Countess Cathleen* is performed as the first production of the Irish Literary Theatre in Dublin

1900 (January) The death of WBY's mother, Susan. (March) Protest riots in Dublin at Queen Victoria's Jubilee visit to Ireland, Maud Gonne involved. (April) Mathers sends Aleister Crowley to seize Golden Dawn headquarters but WBY and others manage to repel him.

1901 (October) *Diarmuid and Grania,* originally planned with George Moore, is produced in Dublin.

1902 (August) WBY meets John Quinn and, at some point in summer, James Joyce. (April) *Cathleen Ni Houlihan* is produced, with Maud Gonne in the title role. (October/ November) *The Pot of Broth* is produced by Irish National Theatre Society. (November) *Where There is Nothing* published

1903 (February) Maud Gonne marries John MacBride, who had fought against the British in the Boer War (May) *Ideas of Good and Evil* (essays) published. (August) *In the Seven Woods* (poems) published. (November) Leaves for first lecture tour in USA, returning following March.

1904 (June) *Where There is Nothing* produced by Stage Society. (December) The Abbey Theatre opens with *On Baile's Strand.*

1905 Theatre business dominates.

1906 Theatre business and lecturing.

1907 (January) J. M. Synge's *The Playboy of the Western World* opens at the Abbey to riots. (March) Death of John O'Leary. WBY's father settles permanently in New York

1908 (January) Fays resign from the Abbey company (Spring) Affair with Mabel Dickinson (September-December)

	WBY's *Collected Works* published by Shakespeare's Head in 8 volumes (November) Mrs Patrick Campbell in *Deirdre* in Dublin and London
1909	(March) J. M. Synge dies.
1910	(August) WBY granted Civil List pension of £150 per annum(Septmeber) George Pollexfen dies.(December) *The Green Helmet and Other Poems* published.
1911	(April) Meets Ezra Pound in Paris(September) WBY accompanies Abbey Players on tour of USA (May) Meets his future wife, Georgie Hyde Lees, for the first time
1912	(November) *The Cutting of an Agate* (essays) published
1913	(October) *Poems written in Discouragement* published (November) Rents Stone Cottage in Ashdown Forest, Sussex, with Ezra Pound as secretary
1914	(January) Leaves for USA lecture tour (May) *Responsibilities* (poems) published (July) Home Rule Bill for Ireland passed but suspended because of European situation (July) Georgie Hyde Lees joins the Hermetic Order of the Golden Dawn, with WBY as sponsor (August) First World War begins
1915	(January-February) At Stone Cottage with Ezra and Dorothy Pound (May) Hugh Lane, Lady Gregory's nephew, drowned when S.S. Lusitania is torpedoed in the Atlantic(December) Refuses a British knighthood
1916	(March) *Reveries over Childhood and Youth* (autobiography) published (April) *At the Hawk's Well*, the first of his Noh dramas, produced in London (April) Easter Rising in Dublin (May) Execution of leaders of Easter Rising, among them John MacBride (July-August) WBY visits Maud Gonne in Normandy, where she again refuses his proposal of marriage; he also discusses marriage with her daughter, Iseult.
1917	(March) WBY buys Thoor Ballylee, a Norman tower near Coole Park in Galway (August) Proposes marriage to Maud Gonne's daughter Iseult and is refused (September) Proposes marriage to Georgie Hyde Lees and is accepted (October) Marries Georgie Hyde Lees. Honeymoon in Ashdown Forest. Georgie, now known as George Yeats, begins automatic writing. (November) WBY and GY move to Stone Cottage. Automatic writing almost daily; first drafts of Michael Robartes dialogues (November) *The Wild Swans at Coole* is published

	(December) In London, but leave for Sussex because of zeppelin raids; Yeats meets Sir Edward Denison Ross to discuss Arabic for Michael Robartes dialogues
1918	(January) WBY and GY move to Oxford (January) *Per Amica Silentia Lunae* (essay) published (January) Robert Gregory, Lady Gregory's son, killed in action in Italy (May-September) Yeatses in Galway to supervise restoration of Thoor Ballylee, ready in September; automatic writing continues throughout (September) Yeatses rent Dublin house from Maud Gonne (November) End of First World War (December) In the General Election, Sinn Fein wins a majority of seats in Ireland but does not sit at Westminster and sets up Dáil Éireann (Assembly of Ireland), at the first meeting of which, in January 1919, Ireland's independence is declared
1919	(January) *Two Plays for Dancers* (February) Daughter, Anne, born in Dublin (June) Gives up London rooms at Woburn Buildings (Summer) At Thoor Ballylee; automatic writing continues (October) Civil unrest in Ireland
1920	(January) Yeatses leave for USA for lecture tour; automatic writing continues (August) GY has miscarriage (Autumn) Guerrilla war in Ireland intensifies
1921	(February) *Michael Robartes and the Dancer* (poems) published (July) Truce in Ireland (Spring-Summer) Moves within Oxfordshire; almost no automatic writing, but 'sleeps' continue (August) Son, Michael, born at Thame in Oxfordshire (October) *Four Plays for Dancers* published (December) Anglo-Irish Treaty signed in London, for the establishment of the Irish Free State (December) *Four Years* (autobiography) published
1922	(January) Dáil Éireann ratifies Treaty, leading to civil war in Ireland (February) J. B. Yeats dies in New York (March-September) At Thoor Ballylee, while civil war rages; sleeps coming to an end, working on *A Vision* (July) WBY receives Honorary degree from Trinity College, Dublin (October) *The Trembling of the Veil* (autobiography) published (December) WBY appointed to the Irish Senead (senate)
1923	(April) End of the Civil War(November) WBY awarded the Nobel Prize for Literature, which he receives in

Stockholm in December (November) *Plays and Controversies* (plays and essays) published

1924 Working on *A Vision* (May) *Essays* published

1925 Working on *A Vision* (January-February) In Italy, where he finishes 'The Gates of Pluto' and 'Dedication' for *A Vision*

1926 (January) First version of *A Vision* published by T. Werner Laurie (February) Sean O'Casey's *The Plough and the Stars* opens at Abbey Theatre to riots (November) *Autobiographies* (collection of earlier autobiographical writings) published

1927 (November) Yeatses winter in Algeciras, Seville and Cannes. WBY ill with congestion of the lungs, and in ill health for much of the rest of his life

1928 (February) *The Tower* published (June) O'Casey's *The Silver Tassie* rejected by Abbey Theatre (September) WBY resigns from Senead (October) *The Winding Stair* (poems) published (Winter) In Rapallo, revising *A Vision*, drafts first version of 'Seven Propositions'

1929 (June) *A Packet for Ezra Pound* published (Summer) Last visit to Thoor Ballylee (Winter) In Rapallo, revising *A Vision*

1930 (Autumn) At Coole

1931 Finishes revising *A Vision*, though the revised version is not published for six years(June) Delivers bulk of MS material for proposed 'Edition de Luxe' to Macmillans (September) Makes first radio broadcast for BBC in Belfast (Autumn-Winter) Lady Gregory in decline, WBY often at Coole

1932 (Winter-Spring) At Coole (April) Broadcasts for BBC from London. (May) Lady Gregory dies (July) Moves to last Irish home, Riversdale at Rathfarnham, near Dublin (October) Starts on last US lecture tour (November) *Words for Music Perhaps* (poems) published

1933 (July-August) WBY involved with fascist Blueshirts in Dublin (September) *The Winding Stair and Other Poems*, bringing together the poems from *The Winding Stair* (1929) and *Words for Music Perhaps and Other Poems* (1932), is published (November) *Collected Poems* published

1934 (April) Undergoes Steinach operation (vasectomy) for rejuvenation (November) *Wheels and Butterflies* (essays and plays) published (November) *Collected Plays*

	published
1935	(July) AE (George Russell) dies (November) *A Full Moon in March* (plays) published (December) *Dramatis Personae* (autobiography) published (December) In Majorca, working on translation of Upanishads with Sri Purohit Swami
1936	(January-April) WBY collapses, GY summoned to Majorca; WBY makes slow recovery (November) WBY's *Oxford Book of Modern Verse* causes controversy
1937	(April) *The Ten Principal Upanishads* published (October) Revised version of *A Vision* published by Macmillan (December) *Essays 1931-1936* published (December) Bunreacht na hÉireann (Constitution of Ireland) adopted, replacing Irish Free State with Éire.
1938	(May) *New Poems* published (August) First production of *Purgatory* at the Abbey Theatre. WBY's last public appearance (October) Olivia Shakespear dies (November) Yeatses leave for South of France
1939	(January) WBY dies at Cap Martin, buried at Roquebrune. (July) *Last Poems and Two Plays* published (September) *On the Boiler* published (September) Second World War begins
1941	Coole Park pulled down
1945	End of Second World War
1948	WBY's remains brought to Drumcliff, Sligo
1949	*The Republic of Ireland Act* establishes Éire as a republic
1953	Maud Gonne-MacBride dies
1968	George Yeats dies

Chapter 4

Yeats: List of Works

Poetic Works

1886: Mosada

1889: The Wanderings of Oisin and Other Poems

1891: John Sherman and Dhoya

1892: The Countess Kathleen and Various Legends and Lyrics

1894: The Land of Heart's Desire

1895: Poems

1897: The Secret Rose

1899: The Wind Among the Reeds

1900: The Shadowy Waters

1902: Cathleen in Houlihan

1903: In the Seven Woods

1910: The Green Helmet and Other Poems

1912: The Cutting of an Agate

1913: Poems Written in Discouragement

1914: Responsibilities

1917: The Wild Swans at Coole

1921: Michael Robartes and the Dancer

1921: Four Plays for Dancers

1924: The Cat and the Moon

1927: October Blast

1928: The Tower

1929: The Winding Stair

1933: The Winding Stair and Other Poems

1934: Collected Plays

1935: A Full Moon in March

1938: New Poems

Prose Works

1888: Fairy and Folk Tales of the Irish Peasantry

1891: Representative Irish Tales

1892: Irish Faerie Tales

1893: The Celtic Twilight

1907: Discoveries

1903: Ideas of Good and Evil

1916: Reveries Over Childhood and Youth

1918: Per Amica Silentia Lunae

1921: Four Years

1925: A Vision

1926: Estrangement

1926: Autobiographies

Chapter 5

Yeats: Background Context

The Ideological Odyssey of W.B. Yeats

In December 1923, William Butler Yeats, the first Irish writer to be awarded the Nobel Prize for literature, seized upon the occasion of his lecture to the Royal Academy of Sweden to present his literary career in political terms. Noting with irony that an English committee had almost certainly forwarded his nomination to the academy, Yeats cast himself as a standard-bearer of Irish nationalism and a champion of Ireland's cultural independence.

"The theatres of Dublin," he recounted in his speech on "The Irish Dramatic Movement," "were empty buildings hired by the English travelling companies, and we wanted Irish plays and Irish players. When we thought of these plays we thought of everything that was romantic and poetical, because the nationalism we had called up—the nationalism every generation had called up in moments of discouragement—was romantic and poetical."

Yeats had reason to regard himself as a political figure of national, even international, importance. He was at the time of this address a senator of the newly established Irish Parliament. Moreover, he spoke not long after the conclusion of a violent guerrilla war waged by the Irish Republican Army against British imperial rule in Ireland and a subsequent civil war, fought between the newly formed army of the Irish Free State and a breakaway wing of IRA irregulars, over the terms of the peace treaty that concluded the Anglo-Irish War of 1919-21. While Yeats could not boast of having fought in the streets against the British, he nonetheless used the occasion of his literary success to claim, retrospectively, a leading role in the national campaign that led to Irish independence in 1922.

But as a young man Yeats would reject the typically pro-British and pro-Unionist views of most Anglo-Irish Protestants and come to share the ardent nationalism of the Fenians. He counted among his closest friends and mentors the nationalist hero John O'Leary, who had been sentenced by the British to 20 years' penal servitude in 1865 for treason against the Crown. Some time after 1885, when he was 20 years old, Yeats himself joined the secret Irish Republican Brotherhood (a descendent of the Fenian Brotherhood of the late 1860s and a predecessor of the IRA).

Yeats' participation in an organization pledged to the violent overthrow of British rule in Ireland cannot be dismissed as a passing youthful indiscretion. Brown suggests that Yeats maintained contact with the banned organization as late as 1900, when a few of the more ardent Irish nationalists actively fought for the Boers against the British in South Africa.

Yeats' dreamy pre-Raphaelite poetry of the late 1880s and early 1890s, with its penchant for orientalist fantasy and Celtic mysticism, may seem innocent of political content. But for the young Yeats, who was self-consciously promoting himself to an English readership as an Irish poet, art was politics by other means.

Like so many other participants in the cultural revolution known as the "Irish Revival," Yeats believed that with the political collapse in 1891 of Charles Stewart Parnell (the leader of the Irish Party in the British Parliament and champion of Irish Home Rule), the ground on which the cause of Irish independence would be fought had shifted from the parliamentary to the cultural arena. By 1895, when Yeats had established himself as one of the leading Irish poets of his generation, he had already helped to found the Irish Literary Society of London and the National Literary Society in Dublin.

As the names of these organizations suggest, Yeats was pursuing in an active and public manner the cultural ideal of an independent Irish nation. Nor was this all. Yeats was deeply involved throughout his life in various occult, mystical, and magical pursuits, which included membership in the Theosophical Society and the Hermetic Order of the Golden Dawn. But even these occult interests could assume a political valence. In the mid-1890s Yeats, along with Maud Gonne, the woman for whom he yearned and rhapsodized for much of his adult life, hoped to establish a "Celtic Order of Mysteries" in a "Castle of the Heroes," located on an island in Lough Key in Country Roscommon. Yeats' aim, according to Brown, was to "infuse Irish reality, through symbolic rites and ritual enactments, with an ancient spirituality in which paganism and heterodox Christianity combined would help Ireland achieve a transcendent liberation from the crassly materialist world of England's commercial empire."

By 1902 Yeats had joined with other literary figures to establish first the Irish Literary Theatre and then the Irish National Theatre Society (later the Abbey Theater). The 1902 premiere of Cathleen ni Houlihan, co-authored by Yeats and Lady Augusta Gregory, celebrated and memorialized the 1798 rebellion of the United Irishmen against British imperial rule. It proved a popular and critical success, even among such Irish Catholic nationalists as Arthur Griffith, editor of the United Irishman and founder of Sinn Fein, who otherwise resented Yeats for what he regarded as the poet's misrepresentation of the political aspirations and cultural values of Gaelic Ireland's Catholic population.

Yeats' nationalism, like his politics more generally, was never orthodox, no matter how ardently pursued. As behooves a poet, would-be prophet, sometime magus, and political visionary, Yeats had the utmost difficulty adhering to any party line. He intended his brand of cultural nationalism to be an all-inclusive, big-tent movement that would welcome "Protestant and Catholic, Nationalist and Unionist, Parnellite and anti-Parnellite." Nevertheless, by the end of the first decade of the 20th century, Yeats had alienated not only most

Protestants, who favoured Ireland's remaining within the United Kingdom, but also the great majority of Irish nationalists, who envisioned an independent nation founded upon the twin pillars of Irish Catholicism and Gaelic culture. To his cultural antagonists and political enemies, the most famous Irish poet of the century was simply not Irish enough.

Yet "Easter, 1916," written in the aftermath of the unsuccessful nationalist uprising in Dublin against British rule, is arguably the most famous poem on the subject of Irish politics. Contrasting the gray conformist city of middle-class Dublin before the rebellion with the new world of heroic possibility ushered in by the guerrilla fighters and martyrs of Easter week, Yeats sounds out the names of the new Irish immortals: "I write it out in a verse—/MacDonagh and MacBride/And Connolly and Pearse/Now and in time to be,/ Wherever green is worn,/Are changed, changed utterly:/A terrible beauty is born."

Much to his subsequent embarrassment, Yeats had spent Easter week of 1916 not in Dublin but visiting the estate of Sir William Rothenstein in Gloucestershire, England. Yeats, like the vast majority of the Irish population, had been less than enthusiastic about the uprising, believing it to have been quixotic, careless of civilian lives, and perhaps even unnecessary. But Yeats quickly revised his view in the wake of the execution of the rebel leaders by semi-secret British court-martial.

In "Easter, 1916" he succeeded in casting himself as the bard who memorialized the Irish dead (many of whom were personal friends and acquaintances). Though physically absent on the days of reckoning, Yeats, through a poetic act of will, had in effect become the voice of Ireland, the militant prophet who named the founding fathers of the new nation.

Ever since 1965, when Conor Cruise O'Brien savaged Yeats for his apparent fascist sympathies, Yeats' political views have come in for much unfavourable scrutiny. Despite an early friendship with William Morris and his lifelong devotion to

Maud Gonne, both of whom embraced one form or another of socialism, Yeats detested all forms of communism and Marxism. But like his younger friend and fellow poet, Ezra Pound, Yeats was nevertheless a frequent and vocal critic of what he regarded as the crass materialism of the modern era. Notwithstanding his own entrepreneurial talents and ultimate financial success, Yeats often conceived of Ireland as an anti-materialist haven for premodern spiritual values. Moreover, Yeats was both by temperament and by ideological affiliation a great skeptic of pure democracy. In short, there is much to be said for the thesis that Yeats was a "radical" conservative, a reactionary critic of modern democracy, and a retrograde champion of the values of the old order. It is therefore all the more curious and surprising that Yeats' senatorial career should exemplify the ideals of classical liberalism.

Against the immediate historical background of a guerrilla war against British rule and the subsequent violence of the Irish Civil War, Sen. Yeats articulated a remarkably capacious, nonsectarian, and culturally heterogeneous concept of the new Irish nation. While he supported government funding of several cultural and scholarly enterprises dear to the interests of artists and intellectuals, Sen. Yeats was nevertheless wary of the powers of the newly created national Irish government.

Yeats opposed what he regarded as the gratuitous or imprudent use of the Gaelic language for official government purposes. He objected, for example, to the mandatory and exclusive use of Gaelic on street signs and on railroad tickets as a mere cultural pretense, or worse, "an attempt to force Irish on those who do not want it." Yeats opposed such linguistic forms of social engineering on practical grounds—the most important thing was for the overwhelmingly English-speaking population to be able to read the name of their destination on a ticket or for them to know with confidence where it was safe to cross a railway line. To institute a more ambitious scheme was to court a backlash against "all Irish thought, all Irish feeling, and all Irish propaganda." The latter sentiment was to prove prophetic.

Yeats seemed especially nervous that the new government might use its power to create a homogenous (and implicitly servile) citizenry. Critics of Yeats' politics have pointed to his growing enthusiasm in the 1920s for Mussolini's Italy. Yeats did indeed speak approvingly in the Senate and the press of Mussolini and Giovanni Gentile, the Italian minister of education. Nevertheless, in his speeches on the Irish educational system, Yeats worried that inferior compulsory public education might prove worse than no schooling. While admiring the Italian educational system, Yeats spoke out against the American and Japanese forms of public schooling on the grounds that they subordinated the good of the individual child to the good of the nation.

Never a systematic or rigorously coherent theorist, Yeats turned a blind eye to the totalitarian political foundation on which the Italian school system was built. Improbably, he persuaded himself that Gentile's philosophy was an elaboration of the thought of Burke and Berkeley, and that the Italian model offered a practical and holistic approach to education consistent with religious freedom and the cultivation of the individual soul.

Yeats' devotion to the rights and liberties of the individual stemmed in no small measure from his belonging to an increasingly beleaguered and vulnerable minority in the Free State: Irish Protestants. It is no accident that Sen. Yeats spoke eloquently and with conviction on behalf of what he hoped Ireland would become: "a modern, tolerant, liberal nation." In the course of his senatorial career, Yeats raised objections to increasing the powers of the constabulary to enter homes without warrant; opposed efforts to bar unaccompanied adolescents from attending the cinema; spoke in favour of official inspections of Irish prisons to ensure that political detainees were being humanely treated; sought to ensure that the Irish judiciary was shielded from the political influence of the executive branch; defended the rights of women to enter the civil service; consistently denounced all attempts to erode what we in America would call the separation of church and state; and vigourously supported copyright legislation designed to protect the property rights of artists, scholars, and writers.

In general, Yeats favoured the free exchange of intellectual and artistic products across national borders. With the exception of his support for measures designed to shield the fledgling Irish stained glass industry from foreign competition, Yeats inclined toward a doctrine of free trade—especially when it involved forms of international cultural exchange.

Most famously, Yeats spoke with great passion against an early attempt to abolish divorce in Ireland. Yeats' ringing and at times caustic rhetoric in defence of the rights of the Protestant minority constitutes his most memorable speech in the Senate: "I think it is tragic that within three years of this country gaining its independence we should be discussing a measure which a minority of this nation considers to be grossly oppressive. I am proud to consider myself a typical man of that minority. We against whom you have done this thing are no petty people. We are one of the great stocks of Europe. We are the people of Burke; we are the people of Grattan; we are the people of Swift, the people of Emmet, the people of Parnell. We have created the most of the modern literature of this country. We have created the best of its political intelligence.... If we have not lost our stamina then your victory will be brief, and your defeat final, and when it comes this nation may be transformed."

Alas, Yeats' rhetoric only served to inflame sectarian passions and failed to persuade his fellow senators. It is a pity, because elsewhere in his speech Yeats articulates a powerful and more broadly appealing reason to reject the proposed measure: It will make less likely the unification of the south and north of Ireland.

Yeats' defence of what he elsewhere referred to as "the liberty of minorities" and his excoriation of "fanaticism" reveal the liberal basis for his conception of Irish nationalism. Though his rhetoric may well have inflamed rather than dampened sectarian passions at the time, Yeats nonetheless articulated a principle of toleration, liberty, and the protection of religious and political rights that would make possible the unification of a diverse and culturally heterogeneous Irish people.

Brown gives rather little attention to Yeats' career in the Senate, but dutifully attends to Yeats' fascination with Italian fascism and his nearly lifelong hostility toward mass democratic politics. He draws attention, for example, to Yeats' brief enthusiasm in 1932 for Gen. Eoin O'Duffy's notorious, if short-lived, "Blueshirts," a paramilitary organization of Irish ex-servicemen that assumed fascist trappings. In fairness to his subject, Brown also notes that in 1929 Yeats took the trouble in print to warn his friend Ezra Pound against his enthusiasm for Italian fascism. Moreover, Brown suggests that in 1924 Yeats may well have played a small role in heading off a military coup d'etat against the fledging Irish Free State.

Brown argues that Yeats' infatuation with the Blueshirts grew out of the poet's "boredom with bourgeois democratic politics" and his "relish for drama, vitality, the heroic, the irrational, passion." Brown observes, however, that Yeats' very resistance to conformity and his love for agonistic struggle would almost certainly have soon made him an outlaw in any truly authoritarian regime.

For Brown, Yeats' poetic imagination was fueled by two countervailing psychic forces: a passion for drama, conflict, and heroic resistance on the one hand, and a profound fear of disorder and the breakdown of civility and custom on the other. Brown thus characterizes Yeats' peculiar crisscrossing of the political terrain of the '20s and '30s as an instance of his "instinctive libertarianism" at war with his "rage for order."

But it's also possible that Yeats' growing interest in fascist politics and eugenics in the 1930s stemmed not so much from an internal division in his character as from the external political developments of the day. Yeats seems to have become disillusioned by what he understood to be the increasing divergence of liberal and democratic principles in Irish political life.

While Brown suggests that Yeats was relatively untroubled by Eamon de Valera's election as prime minister in 1932, I would argue that the poet interpreted de Valera's victory as a sign that Ireland was on the road to an illiberal, albeit democratic, future. Offering a populist and nationalist vision of a rural, Catholic, and Gaelic Ireland, de Valera pursued a policy of cultural and economic protectionism that deepened the Irish economic malaise of the 1930s. As government interference with markets and morals increased, and economic and personal freedoms came under assault, emigration rose at an alarming rate. Though he never expatriated himself, as did such other writers as Joyce, Beckett, and O'Casey, Yeats in his later years spent much of his time nursing body and spirit beyond the confines of his native land.

Even in the late '20s, well before de Valera's election, there were unmistakable signs that a resurgent Catholic majority was prepared to curtail liberties that had been long granted to the Irish population. In 1923 the Irish Parliament passed the Censorship of Films Act, which stipulated that no film could be shown in Ireland without first having obtained a certificate of approval from an official government film censor. Five years later, just as Yeats was retiring from the Senate, a critical and far-reaching Censorship of Publications Act was brought before the Irish Parliament. The bill, which became law in 1929, empowered the Irish government to examine and approve all books and periodicals published or sold in Ireland.

The law granted the government explicit authority to censor materials deemed to be "indecent," which was construed as "calculated to excite sexual passions or to suggest or incite to sexual immorality or in any other way to corrupt or deprave." Even if a work was not judged indecent, it could be banned if it were found to "be injurious or detrimental to or subversive of public morality."

Provisions of the act effectively outlawed the advertisement of all forms of birth control. Assisted by the efforts of zealous customs officials, the Censorship Board banned or censored some 1,200 books and 140 periodicals in the 1930s alone. Those in violation of the law were subject to severe penalties, including fines, seizure of property, and imprisonment.

Such far-reaching curtailments of the traditional rights of free speech and free press were no doubt fueled by an increasingly powerful Irish cultural chauvinism; such acts in practice created an embargo on many "foreign" cultural commodities. As Yeats was well aware, these policies, while generally popular with the Irish Catholic majority, in effect discriminated against the tastes, cultural values, and religious practices and beliefs of a dwindling Protestant minority.

Yeats' anxieties concerning the looming threat of majoritarian despotism thus seem to have been well-founded, even prescient. The prospect of an illiberal Irish democracy may well have tempted Yeats, in turn, to take a more extreme and increasingly reactionary view of political and cultural matters in Ireland. It is worth considering that Yeats' political hopes were never founded on the conviction that democracy was the best guarantee of "a modern, tolerant, liberal nation."

Yeats found himself in the uncomfortable position of many political liberals in the 1920s and '30s. Despite the positive connotations of "democracy," the rise of mass political movements during the era by no means heralded the advancement of liberal political goals. Italian fascism, German Nazism, and Russian communism were, we should remember, mass movements that depended for their early success upon a broad base of democratic support. In Ireland, the populist (or at any rate popular) political movement of the day was far more humane and more respectful of the liberal tradition than the right-or left-wing mass movements to be found elsewhere in Europe.

Nonetheless, for Yeats, the power of a majority to effectively curtail even some of the rights and liberties long cherished by an increasingly vulnerable minority was disheartening and disturbing. In Brown's view, "the true foe" for Yeats "was neither of the two great political movements in conflict in continental Europe [fascism and communism], but obscurantist Catholicism, which in the name of democracy suppressed free thought" and "stirred up in him moods of frenzied prejudice against the common herd that have nothing benign about them." In this sense, Yeats' late and disturbing affinity for retrograde politics might well have marked not the fruition of his liberalism but rather the frustration of his liberal aspirations.

Of course, the interplay between the artistic imagination and political engagement is notoriously unpredictable. It is a disturbing paradox that several of Yeats' most inspired lyrics and plays emerged out of the political disillusionment and nihilism of his last years. Few 20th-century poems can rival the bitterness and poignancy of the declining poet's "The Circus Animals' Desertion," with its stark concluding lines: "Now that my ladder's gone/I must lie down where all the ladders start/In the foul rag and bone shop of the heart."

Even fewer modern plays can rival the sublimity and tragic power of Purgatory, which stages the fatal confrontation of a disillusioned man and his callous young son, a vagabond couple adrift amidst the ruins of a haunted Irish landscape. In a work that anticipates the minimalism of Beckett's drama, Yeats envisions a world in which the dead are more alive than the living, and in which all are condemned to repeat endlessly the purgatorial cycles of a malignant political history.

Chapter 6

Yeats, a Poet who Kept Trying Different Identities

Nothing turns a man into a statue more effectively than a combination of fame, death and the passage of time. Together they join hands and hoist him up on a high cold plinth. If the man is a writer, he disappears into the official editions of his work, all polish and (ideally) perfection, the fits and starts and wrong turns folded out of sight like the hem on a pair of dress pants.

There is always the biography. But in biography a man often undergoes a different sort of hardening: his turmoil, his inconsistency, his groping confusion are by necessity smoothed into a narrative whole. Even the most sensitive of biographers sacrifice throb and raggedness in the name of storytelling; their work would be unreadable otherwise.

For a sense of process — in the work and the life alike — exhibitions of manuscripts, books and related memorabilia can be extremely successful at getting the statue to come down off his plinth and take a breath or two. These exhibitions reverse time. They take a visitor back into the moment. Because of the inconsistency of materials available to a curator, they are not always comprehensive or in perfectly calibrated balance, but their subject is often palpable, paradoxical and animated.

Certainly this is very much the case with William Butler Yeats in "Such Friends," a rich survey of his work and life now on view at the New York Public Library.

Yeats (1865-1939) is a challenge to the curator, as he is to the biographer and in a different way to the reader of his verse, prose, memoirs and plays. He lived a long, complex, regularly self-reinventing life, and in his obsessions and enthusiasms he was sometimes, well, a little all over the place. His trajectory, of writing as of living, can be seen as one long attempt to build up, then to a degree break down again, a series of identities or preoccupations until he got closer and closer still to his true, authentic self and voice.

In his pivotal 1948 study, "Yeats: The Man and the Masks," which still remains fresh, Richard Ellmann saw these different identities as masks. Rodney Phillips, curator of the exhibition (and of the library's Berg Collection of English and American Literature, from which much of the material is drawn), highlights Yeats' use of doppelgangers, whom Yeats named variously Michael Robartes, Owen Aherne and Red Hanrahan. Many people have observed Yeats' lifelong self-division, which falls into two categories: Yeats the dreamer and Yeats the man of action.

Yeats the dreamer was variously attracted to the occult, spiritualism, fairy life and fairy tales, paganism, magic, seances, psychic phenomena, Eastern religion, Theosophy and Mme. Blavatsky, mysticism and William Blake. All of this culminated, famously, in his years-long preoccupation with the automatic writing of his wife, George, which was believed to give Yeats direct access to the spirit world and which led to "A Vision," Yeats' attempt to summarize and categorize all of human personality through "a system of symbolism."

Yeats the man of action, by contrast, worked for Irish nationalism, helped ignite the Irish literary renaissance, and was co-founder of the Abbey Theater, which encouraged the work of Irish playwrights. Mediating between — and arcing over — these two selves and drawing fully on their range of interests was of course Yeats the poet, whose lifelong directive, which he first articulated to himself when he was in his early 20s, was "Hammer your thoughts into unity."

Unity of thought is a tall, perhaps even an unreasonable, order for a man in his youth and his maturity both, and Yeats seems to have been only sporadically successful at achieving it. He was successful, however, at submitting himself to all these stimuli and all these interests, and out of them — and his knowledge of life, which age deepened significantly — he wrote magnificent verse whose meaning often remains accessible even when some of its inspiring symbols are obscure.

Yeats was supremely successful in another area as well. He made many profound and sometimes passionate connections to other people, and it is to these key human connections that Phillips has turned for the organizational tissue of his show.

Yeats' first connections were, like every human being's, involuntary, that is to say to his family, and in his, Yeats was both blessed and cursed. He was blessed because his family was artistic and accepting and encouraging of the pursuit of art and literature: his father, John Butler Yeats, was an intellectual and a painter, as was his brother, Jack; his sisters, Lily and Lolly, became printers who elegantly published many of Yeats' books at their Cuala Press.

Yeats was cursed, though, because his father was dominating, opinionated and often devouring of his gifted son. George Yeats told Ellmann that the poet brought a particular burden to their marriage: his lifelong tension with his father. And this when Yeats was already well into middle age. (He married at 52; George was 25.)

Little sense of the paternal burden comes through in the father's delicate and sensitive pencil drawings of the son, which like the best objects in this exhibition seem to live in a perpetual present tense, as though the artist had just lifted his pencil off the page minutes earlier and slipped the sketchbook behind glass for safekeeping. The notion is not so very far-fetched: John Yeats did in fact leave some of this work in Manhattan, where he lived for the last 15 years of his life, in a rooming house run by the Petipas sisters on West 29th Street.

Rather like Leopold Mozart, it would seem, John Yeats withdrew from his son's life (and country) once the poet achieved success, at least in person: daily letters continued to flow.

Yeats had both a father and a father figure. The latter was the Irish Fenian Brotherhood hero John O'Leary, who is represented here in an album of photographs of prisoners. An editor of The Irish People, he advocated overthrowing British rule and was convicted of treason in 1865. He spent two decades either in jail or exile before returning to Ireland in 1885 and becoming a major influence on the young, politically awakening, ever versifying Yeats ("Beautiful lofty things: O'Leary's noble head").

Also on display are O'Leary's copy of "Mosada" (1886), Yeats' first publication, and a famous letter in which he tells O'Leary that, next to poetry, he has decided to make magic "the most important pursuit of my life."

"The mystical life," he asserts, "is the centre of all that I do and all that I think and all that I write."

Among his friends Yeats was not alone in splitting his personality and trying on different identities. There must have been something in the air in the 1880s and '90s: Dr. Jekyll and Mr. Hyde and Dorian Gray (and his portrait) among the fictional schisms, George William Russell and William Sharp among the real ones. Russell, mystic, poet and artist, published under the pseudonym A.E.; he and Yeats intersected in their fascination with Theosophy, Irish matters and dreams. A.E. is represented here by manuscript material and a sketch by John Yeats.

William Sharp is an even more curious case. After publishing literary biographies under his own name, in 1893 he began to write poetry on Celtic subjects under the name of Fiona Macleod. Yeats said that Fiona was Sharp's "imaginary beloved," and that in her "all the heart, all the brain of the Celtic races shall be stirred." Fiona had her own literary style and feminine handwriting and conducted her own correspondence with Yeats and others.

As friends and lovers, or a mixture of the two, actual women were focal in Yeats' life. The poet Katharine Tynan, one of his earliest women friends, recalled that Yeats was "beautiful to look at with his dark face, its touch of vivid colouring, the night-black hair, the eager dark eyes." "He asked you to be profoundly interested in his poetry," said Tynan, whose work appears here alongside Yeats' in "Poems and Ballads of Young Ireland" (1888). "On the other hand, he was always interested in yours."

Yeats formed one of his most enduring friendships with Lady Augusta Gregory, a folklorist and a major figure in the Irish Literary Renaissance. Lady Gregory, whose papers became part of the Berg collection in the 1950s, is abundantly represented in "Such Friends." In her diary entry for April 14, 1894, for example, she records her first meeting with Yeats: "At the Morrises I met Yeats, looking every inch a poet." (That is the William Morrises, who also numbered among Yeats' friends.)

Then inevitably there is Maude Gonne, Yeats' elusive, longtime love and muse, who rejected his marriage proposals on five separate occasions. "I had never thought to see in a living woman so great a beauty," Yeats wrote of the first time he met her.

A radical Republican, Gonne conducted her personal life with more daring than Yeats initially grasped. In December 1898, after they kissed for the first time, she confessed to him about her affair with Lucien Millevoye, by whom she had two children. Yeats promptly wrote to Lady Gregory, in a letter on display here: "I have come to understand her and admire her as I could not have done before. My life is a harder problem to me than it was yesterday."

Two years later Gonne told Yeats: "I know that just now, perhaps, it is useless my saying to you 'love some other woman.' All I want of you is not to make up your mind not to."

In the cool marbled hall of the library, this century-old passion and the attempted thwarting of it flame fiercely.

They're visceral. They live in Gonne's crunched, sloped, rushed handwriting and in Yeats' more deliberate script. They live in the hastily folded paper and the envelopes the paper was hurried into and the flaps licked urgently shut. Above all they live in the words.

Life fairly exudes from these cases: this one man's one busy, layered life, which burst out in action and writing and friendship, decade after decade. Phillips referred to "the whole 'six degrees of separation' thing." Three, more like it. There's the Rhymer's Club, where Yeats and his poet friends met weekly to discuss one another's work. (Oscar Wilde stopped by.)

There is the Irish Dramatic Movement (its goal: Irish plays on Irish soil) and the eventual forming of the Abbey Theater. Here the links proliferate: to the actress and critic Florence Farr, to J.M. Synge, to George Bernard Shaw (who appears in three beautiful photographic self-portraits), to Sean O'Casey.

There are Yeats' encounters with the pricklier figures of 20th-century letters. When he met James Joyce, who was 17 years his junior, Joyce reputedly said: "I have met you too late. You are too old." "Deteriorating" is another word that slipped out that November day, but somehow Yeats' father sketched Joyce anyway, and Yeats was generous enough to recognize Joyce's gifts, telling him, "The work which you have actually done is very remarkable for a man of your age."

First Joyce, then Pound: for three winters a young Ezra Pound served as Yeats' personal secretary in a spare stone house in a tiny village in Sussex. He took dictation, read to "Uncle William," studied Japanese literature with him and, in a foreshadowing of his later relationship with T.S. Eliot, revised Yeats' work unbidden and published the revisions unapproved. Yeats was furious at first but later allowed most of them to stand.

"All life weighed in the scales of my own life seems to me a preparation for something that never happens," Yeats wrote near the end of one of his autobiographies, "Reveries Over Childhood and Youth." Alas something did happen to Yeats: in 1917, in middle age, he married.

Nearly 20 years earlier he had written to A.E. that "a poet, or even a mystic, becomes a greater power from understanding all the great primary emotions and these one only gets out of going through the common experiences and duties of life." This was very prescient. As a husband and eventually a father, Yeats grew to feel "more knitted into life." His work became more powerful. And he found in George, as Ellmann puts it dryly, that he had "married the Sibyl herself."

When Yeats panicked early in their marriage, George decided to soothe him by faking a few lines of automatic writing. Yeats was soothed and captivated and compelled, but the joke was on George, since she apparently had a talent for receiving messages from her various "communicators" or "controls" and in 450 subsequent sittings was to produce 3,600 pages of this "miraculous intervention," which became the basis for "A Vision." The first preserved page of George's automatic script (which has been lent to the library by their son, Michael Yeats) shows George's wobbly writing dropping off the page in an increasingly illegible slope. This is a document remarkable to behold: an obsession close to its original provoking moment.

All life prepared Yeats for marriage, perhaps, but it also seems to have prepared him for more life. To inhabit it, that is, and his art, more fully.

"I must lay aside the pleasant patter I have built up for years, and seek the brutality, the ill breeding, the barbarism of truth," he wrote in 1937. The barbarism of truth: his late verse is veritably racked with it; and with sharp, merciless, naked self-inspection; and with grief, as his friends began to die; and with an acute sense of his own approaching mortality.

Throughout "Such Friends," working holograph drafts, much-amended typescripts and revised proof copies of Yeats' verse are on display. In the end little makes the poet live and breathe so vibrantly as watching him do what he did best, fitting the words together like the shards in a mosaic, arranging and rearranging them until he achieved his exact and most radiant design.

In the final room of the exhibition the first continuous draft of "The Circus Animals' Desertion," Yeats' great retrospective poem of 1937, is laid out in all this searching evolution. It famously ends:

"Now that my ladder's gone,
I must lie down where all the ladders start,
In the foul rag-and-bone shop of the heart."

These words, some of the most beautifully conjoined in the English language, did not come easily to Yeats. He wrote and rewrote, he erased and he spliced and he sharpened. In looking back over his life as in anticipation of it, he worked hard, and he reworked hard. He was not a statue at all. He was a man.

Chapter 7

Haunting Image in Yeats Poetry

William Butler Yeats is considered to be one of the greatest poets in the English language, and his poetic achievement stands at the center of modern literature. In 1923, he was awarded Nobel Prize for literature.

He had a very long poetic career, stretching from the 1880s to the 1930s, and had experienced a slow and painful change in his poetic creation, starting in the romantic tradition and finishing as a matured modernist poet. After the age of 50 years old, an old-man image always haunted Yeats' mind, which made him pessimistic about life.

But the growth made him realise that eternal beauty could only live in the art. With the change from pessimism to optimistic eternality, a kind of philosophic thinking was reflected in his works, and this paper is just an analysis of theses changes in his poems.

William Butler Yeats is a great figure in the 20th century English poetry. His way is winding and complex. During his half-century's writing life, from mysticism to symbolism poet, Yeats had experienced great difficulties.

While sticking to Irish tradition and real life, he absorbed others' excellent poetry at home and abroad, and finally combines reason with feeling, symbol with reality and has become one of the most important and influential poets in this century.

Yeats was born in Sandymount, Dublin. His father is a poor businessman and becomes impoverished, then moves to London. Yeats' father practices the art as a painter, Thus, Yeats grows up in an atmosphere of art and culture. Young Yeats is very vague and dreamy. He has nostalgia for his past years in hometown. He dislikes London life around him, but loves countryside of Sligo (a beautiful, quiet small village town). As a poet, Yeats begins in the late romantic tradition. His poem is blue, melancholy, and his beauty is dreamy. Yeats is also much influenced by his lover, Maud Gonne, one of nationalist, extremist in politics. He falls in love with her, but they have different opinions in politics, which makes him always refused by her and finally separates. Especially in late years, Yeats tastes more bitterness. At that time, one of his eyes has been blind for several years, his ears begin to get deaf and many diseases become serious. The death nearly comes to him several times. Yeats finds himself feeble, weak, old and unable physically. This psychological event combines with Yeats' feeling, and this combination gives birth to an image — an old-weak-man image which haunts Yeats' mind in his late years even to his death.

Image is a concept not only in psychology but also in poetry. In psychology, an image is the recall or recurrence of past experiences in feeling and consciousness. In poetry an image can be raised to the level of symbol by association with a variety of contents and nuances until that image comes to represent and evoke the entire cluster of ideas and interrelationships of meanings whic h have been brought into being by the poem. Such an image may acquire this kind of significance on being repeated and utilized in many different poems over a long period of time or the symbol may be specifically created within a single work as, for example, the images of stone and stream in Yeats' "Easter 1916". Images which become a familiar feature of an author's works are already well on their way to becoming symbols because each new encounter carries with it the recollection and associations of past usage as well as meaning. And the images evoke indefinable and precise emotions, or call among us certain disembodied powers whose footsteps over our hearts we call emotions. Then the more powerful the emotions are, the clearer the images become.

In Yeats' poems, there is such an image — an old-lonely-bitter-man image over his late years. Over a long period of time, this image has been repeated and used by Yeats in many poems which express his spiritual suffering in mind, and his regret for old age and loneliness.

In "When You Are Old", old age is first mentioned. Though it's the description of his lover's old age, it reflects Yeats' feeling for old age — "old and grey and full of sleep. And nodding by the fire", "bending down beside the glowing bars/ Murmur, a little sadly". While describing Maud Gonne's old age, he is regretting for his own situation of being old, and being isolated from the outside world with lonely mind.

The old age is not a new theme for Yeats. He is always preoccupied as a poet with age and time especially after the age of 50 years old. And the event of being old gives rise to such feelings: weakness, loneliness, bitterness. The two aspects combine an image — an old-man image.

In "The Wild Swans at Coole", the feeling or the suffering in mind becomes more obvious. Yeats is beginning to speak out. Meanwhile, he has become aware of the confusion and incoherence of Maud's love. He is searching for what he calls "unity of being". This poem is inspired by swans Yeats has observed over a period of many years at Lady Gregory's estate. Swans are his favourite symbol, but the symbolic meaning changes here. He compares himself with natural animals — the wild swans, which are full of use and force, flying and playing unwearied and lover by lover. Compared with the energetic swans, he is old and lonely, like one of fifty-and-nine swans. Fifty-eight swans are in couple while only one is left lonely, isolated. Therefore this swan stands for constancy, immutability and permanence, especially the permanence of love.

The old-man image is just a symbol of Yeats himself. So, his heart is sore and he couldn't wander where he will with passion or conquest like wild swans. He thinks of the first time he "trod with a lighter tread hearing the bell-beat of their wings above his head at twilight". At that time, he was young and the step was light like the swan. But now the season of the year — autumn, which is described in the poem fits Yeats very well who is about 50 years old then and is coming to the autumn of human life. He is regretting for growing old. Early in the summer of 1897, Yeats once says in Yeats' Record "I must spend the summer of 1897 at Coole. I was involved in the miserable love affair. My heart was getting spoiled. My nerves had been wrecked. I was finding that I couldn't work, and think...." Now, in 1916, he is still in grief because of old age and also because of being refused by Maud Gonne. He knows this romantic love couldn't be re-kindled. Maybe this is his last try to propose, but in vain. So here his mood takes arm of a sour bitterness.

It's not difficult to find the hint of sad feelings in Yeats' many other poems. In "The Living Beauty", he sighs "Oh, heart, I'm old / The living beauty is for younger men/We cannot pay his tribute of wild tears". In "Subject for the Poem", he says "we singers have nothing of our own/ All our hope, our loves, our dreams/ Are for the young".

In "Sailing to Byzantium", Yeats says "that is no country for old men" and "an aged man is but a paltry thing/A tattered coat upon a stick". In "Among School Children, Yeats makes a striking contrast between a sixty-year-old public man and the young school children. We can strongly feel how nice to be young and how sad to be old. Such sad emotions can be felt in many lines of Yeats' poems. He has such a pessimistic attitude toward old men that he thinks once people are old, they become useless and there are no places for them in the world. While Narcissus enjoys watching his reflection in the water, old men like Yeats also admire themselves in the water. We only hear the old men say "everything alters/And one by one we drop away". Just as the old men say all that's beautiful drifts away like the waters, Yeats' youth and beauty go away with the time flying and he becomes old and ugly.

When the readers read his poems, a dominant sense of pessimism seizes their hearts until his last several years when Yeats makes a change in writing style regardless of life or death. Just like the last singing of a swan, he wants his last poems to be eternal and remembered by more people. In the history of English literature there is a common phenomenon that the older the poet is, the less energy he has and the worse his skill of poetry writing is.

But Yeats is different. In his last years, he loves life and praises life. Even though encountering some unexpected misery in life, he doesn't fall in despair. Instead he takes an active part in life activities and keeps writing and going forward. As an old man, Yeats, unlike most old men, doesn't like a quiet life in retirement. He thinks that craziness is the source of writing, which shows his eagle-like heart in old age. He puts all his heart on work and finally succeeds. This kind of spirit is shown in his "Long-Legged Fly": Like a long-legged fly upon the stream/His mind moves upon silence. In this poem the sentence is repeated three times in order to emphasize Yeats' unceasing hard work.

Although Yeats once shows his contempt on the old age in his poem to Olivia Shakespeare with such comments: "a fragment of my last curse on old age", which means that even the greatest men are owls or scarecrows by the time their fame has come. Now the scorn so pervasive before is gone even though the loss of youth and the waste of life still makes him feel bitterer and more disillusioned. He yearns to move away from the sensual world of growth and change, and to enter the timeless, eternal world of art and intellect. Yeats comes to realise that eternal beauty could only live in the realm of art.

His concern has turned to the great subjects of opposites or dichotomy such as youth and age. And this dichotomy has brought constant tensions in his works and revealed the human predicament. In his last period, Yeats has developed a tough, complex and symbolical style and tended to think about life problems in a philosophic way. In his opinion, life is a journey up a spiral staircase; as we grow older we cover the ground we have covered before, only higher up; as we look down the winding stair below us we measure our progress by the number of places where we were but no longer are. The journey is both repetitious and progressive; we go both round and upward. Through symbolic images of this kind Yeats explores the paradoxes of time and change, of growth and identity, of love and age, of life and art, of madness and wisdom.

In "Among School Children" Yeats makes a contrast between youth and old age and symbolizes the unity of the opposites in the poem. He writes: "Hollow of cheek as though it drank the wind/And took a mess of shadows for its meat/ Better to smile on all that smile, and show/There is a comfortable kind of old scarecrow." He calls himself scarecrow, but he tries to smile to show he is comfortable though he is old and ugly. Perhaps only by this way can his mind get comfort.

Then Yeats is not afraid of old age any more. Once "out of nature", or dead, the old man in "Sailing to Byzantium" will be gone into the "Monuments of unaging intellect," or the "artifice of eternity," where art arrests change. His great works of art, which are needed now to carry him beyond the sensual world, to transform him into a golden bird, would sing of time, "of what is past, or passing, or to come". On January 18th 1939, Yeats died of the heart disease. On his tomb stone carves his heroic lines which encourage us for ever. He is eternal with his lines.

Chapter 8

Yeats' Symbols: Cycles and Antinomes

In his 1901 essay "Magic", Yeats writes, "I cannot now think symbols less than the greatest of all powers whether they are used consciously by the masters of magic, or half unconsciously by their successors, the poet, the musician and the artist". Later, in his introduction to A Vision, he explains, "I put the Tower and the Winding Stair together into evidence to show that my poetry has gained in self possession and power. I owe this change to an incredible experience" (Vision). The experience he goes on to relate is the preliminary stage of the composition of the work itself. In A Vision, however, Yeats exhibits his poetic power as well, along with his knowledge of mysticism and affinity for symbology to illustrate the behaviour of the forces of human consciousness and history.

He ties these two cycles together into the overarching symbol of the work: the Great Wheel. This is a symbol that Yeats uses not only to explain the cycles of one individual's life, but also through the same motions, to explain the cyclical movement of the centuries, and the conjunction of certain historical events. When asked about the factual reality of his cosmological descriptions, he replies that they are "purely symbolical... [and] have helped me to hold in a single thought reality and justice" (Vision). Though to a large extent obscure and complicated, these symbols are paramount to an understanding not only of the ideas contained in A Vision, also the thought process Yeats conveys in much of his poetry.

The Great Wheel consists of and contains two opposing gyres, the primary and the antithetical, objectivity and subjectivity, which turn in opposite directions, the two opposing forces that govern the workings of the mind, life, and the universe. The two opposing gyres contain four more gyres, which symbolize what Yeats refers to as the four faculties: the Will and the Mask, or what is and what ought to be, and the Creative Mind and the Body of Fate, or the knower and the known. He then adds numbers to the symbol, corresponding to the phases of the moon, and is able to use them to designate every possible action of thought or life. He places these in a circular shape. "The whole system," Yeats writes "is founded upon the belief that the ultimate reality, symbolized by the sphere, falls in human consciousness... into a series of antinomies" (Vision).

The Byzantium poems are a prime example of the antinomies at work in the individual mind of man. In many of his poems, Yeats idealizes Byzantium, as a symbol of unity in spiritual and everyday life. He writes "I think that in early Byzantium, maybe never before or since in recorded history, religious, aesthetic and practical life were one, that architect and artificers... spoke to the few and the multitude alike. The painter and the mosaic worker, the worker in gold and silver, the illuminator or sacred books, were almost impersonal, almost perhaps without the consciousness of individual design, absorbed in their subject-matter and that the vision of a whole people" (Vision). "Sailing to Byzantium" expresses Yeats' longing to become a part of Byzantine art, to return to life as a golden bird, who transcends the temporality of the natural world. However, he is quick to criticize the idea of this transcendent state in the later poem "Byzantium". The two poems compliment each other, and together show the importance of the unavoidable contradictions that come with being human.

In the first stanza of "Sailing to Byzantium" Yeats writes, "That is no country for old men. The young In one another's arms, birds in the trees, - Those dying generations - at their song.

The conflicts in this poem are evident— between the temporal and the eternal, between the mortality of man's body, and the eternal existence of his soul through artistic creation. The speaker in the poem is concerned with his own advancing age, and is noticing the temporary state of everything around him. The song in this passage may signify the temporal world, in which "Fish, flesh or fowl, commend all summer long/ whatever is begotten born and dies." Everything speaks to him of its beginning which he knows will ultimately lead to its end. There is another song in the second stanza, that sung by the soul of an old man, and for Yeats this song is found in contemplation of Byzantine art.

"An aged man is but a paltry thing,
A tattered coat upon a stick, unless
Soul clap its hands and sing, and louder sing
For every tatter in its mortal dress;
Nor is there singing school but studying
Monuments of its own magnificence;"

This song arises out of the speaker's desire to transcend his temporary form, to contact that within him that which will continue after his mortal body has passed on. He no longer sees a use for the form he now inhabits, sees it rather as an obstacle to his advancement. The stanza that follows is an incantation, a song of sorts, addressed to the sages in a Byzantine mosaic. He bids them "purne in a gyre and be the singing masters of my soul". He continues:

"Consume my heart away; sick with desire
And fastened to a dying animal,
It knows not what it is; and gather me
Into the Artifice of Eternity."

He calls to the spirits of these sages in their own forms, carved in gold, and longs for an unchanging form of his own through which his soul can realise its own importance without the limitations of human desire and time. Yeats continues the bird/song symbology with his own longing to be transformed into a bird, though not of the nature of those he spoke of in the mortal world, but one:

"Of hammered gold and gold enameling
To keep a drowsy emperor awake,
Or set upon a golden bow to sing
To lords and ladies of Byzantium,
Of what is past or passing or to come."

Without the narrow limitations that time gives to vision, the speaker sees the opportunity to improve and isolate the song of his soul from the obstacles of his changing physical existence. He imagines that he will be able to see the past, present and future as they are, as a single, continual state of existence. In his poem "Byzantium" Yeats looks at his dream of immortality from another perspective. In this poem, the speaker has taken on the form of the golden bird, separated himself from temporality and his human, physical needs. Instead of the glorious idea of all inclusive vision he has previously conceived, he finds a dark, ghostly scenario, its only subjects immaterial phantasmic figures devoid of human flesh. He writes:

"A starlit or a moonlit dome disdains All that man is,

All mere complexities, The fury and the mire of human veins."

These "complexities" refer perhaps to the speaker's previous state, caught in the conflict between the needs of the human body and the aspirations of man's spirit. The state of existence he achieves in "Byzantium" however, Yeats likens to death, in that it transcends the physical, though at the same time has destroyed the possibility of contact with the physical world, as well as all the abilities that arise out of the conflict between man's spiritual ambitions and his temporal, physical vehicle. The poem continues:

"A mouth that has no moisture and no breath
Breathless mouths may summon;
I hail the superhuman;
I call it death-in-life and
life-in-death."

In A Vision, Yeats describes the state one is confined to after death as the domination of Spirit over Husk, or mind over physical body, in which in fact there is a widened perception, though there is only knowledge and no action. In this condition, "...there is only Spirit, pure mind containing within itself pure truth, that which depends only upon itself.... mind deprived of its obstacle can create no more and nothing is left but 'the spirits at one', unrelated facts and aimless mind, the burning out that awaits all voluntary effort". The bird that Yeats has seen himself become is still superior to the living birds in that it will never change, and lacks the survival needs of flesh and blood creatures. He writes,however,

"At midnight on the Emporor's pavement flit
Flames that no faggot feeds, nor steel has lit
Nor storm disturbs, flames begotten of flame,
Where blood-begotten spirits come
And all complexities of fury leave, Dying into a dance,
An agony of trance,
An agony of flame that cannot singe a sleeve."

Yeats sees the stagnancy in this representation, with the perspective of a living creature cast into the world of the dead. He allows his speaker awareness of what he is within a world where everything comes out of itself, and there are no necessary acts of will. Yeats points out in this poem the necessity of the conflict which he was earlier concerned with in "Sailing To Byzantium", that between the mortality of the human body and the aspirations of the immortal spirit. Without the conjunction of the two conditions, the value of knowledge is lost on a living mind. Yeats writes in A Vision that the spirit cannot understand all spirits in unity "until they have been perceived as objects of sense". In "Byzantium", the speaker has forsaken his physical senses for wider perception, but is unable to see the value in his newly acquired state. It is knowledge simply for its own sake, and he is unable to make use of it. The symbol becomes more complicated when applied to the cycle of history.

The Great Wheel and its numerical system, the phases of the moon and the movements of the gyres, become a vehicle for the interpretation of historical events, which conjunct and oppose one another. Yeats draws most of his parallels between two eras— the pre-Christian time period, and that after Christ's birth. Yeats begins the fifth book of A Vision with the entire text of his poem "Leda and the Swan". It is an introduction of sorts to his discussion of human history, and the nature of man's development. For Yeats, the rape of Leda by Zues in the form of a swan is his symbolic perception of the beginning of the first era he discusses, and perhaps the beginning of human civilization as we know it. Adams writes "In his placement of this poem and in what it dramatizes, Yeats seems to make the event stand for the beginning of human history, the history of a particularly human consciousness, the generating principle of what is mysterious... power born of the introduction of love and strife with perhaps a new knowledge and power, put together into life".

The birth of Helen brought to Greek civilization new ideals with regard to human beauty— the greater attention to the human body changed the perspective of Grecian artists, but along with it came the bloody battles of the Trojan war. Yeats begins, "A sudden blow. The great wings beating still/ Above the staggering girl, her thighs caressed/ By the dark webs, her nape caught in his bill,/ He holds her helpless breast upon his breast" (Vision). The encounter is both violent and sexual in nature, and the conjunction of these two motions are reflective of their results. Adams recalls that in the myth, this set of antinomies is personified in the two eggs that Leda produces— love, in the form of Helen, and strife in the characters of Castor and Pollux. Yeats writes "A shudder in the loins engenders there/ The broken wall, the burning roof and tower/ And Agamemnon dead." At the point of orgasm in the sexual encounter, the seeds of war, as well as those of love have been conceived. Adams writes, "In the Pagan era... religion is antithetical (gods being nearly human, in human images) and philosophy and secular life primary...In the Christian era, there is a reversal, and religion becomes primary". This is exemplified in the different conjunctions between man and God. In "Leda" it is direct and brutal— the human woman being physically overtaken by an actual creature.

The final lines, posing a question— "Did she put on his knowledge with his power/ Before the indifferent beak could let her drop?" imply a choice on Leda's part, though the rest of the poem makes it clear that the power and perhaps the knowledge as well was inflicted upon her more than accepted willfully by her. In the beginning of the Christian era, we will see another conception, which can be compared to the conception that takes place here. Instead of a violent direct one, Christ's conception is a mystical one— between a human woman and a distant, more overshadowing deity, taking place peacefully, and meekly accepted by its recipient due to her trust in the will of her God whose understanding she believes to be far greater than her own.

In book five, Yeats takes a scene from the Christian era, a vision of Salome "dancing before Herod and receiving the prophet's head in her indifferent hands." He continues, "Seeking images, I see her anoint her bare limbs with lion's fat, for lack of the sun's ray, that she may gain the favour of a king, and remember that the same impulse will create the Galilean revelation and deify Roman Emperors whose sculptured heads will be surrounded by the solar disk. Upon the throne and upon the cross alike, myth becomes a biography" (Vision). This "exultation of the flesh and of civilization perfectly achieved" (Vision) is a characteristic of the age begun with Leda's rape and is continued into the Christian era.

The two ages are essentially opposites in nature, though the operable forces within them overlap to a great extent. In the poem, "Two Songs from a Play", Yeats draws on the idea that time is cyclical and that the ages overlap and merge with each other using an allusion to Virgil's Fourth Eculogue to draw a parallel between the ritual death of Dionysis and the birth of Christ. In A Vision, Yeats quotes the passage: "The latest age of the Cumaean song is at hand; the cycles in their vast array begin anew.

The virgin Astrea comes, the reign of Saturn comes, and from the heights of Heaven a new generation of mankind ascends" (Vision p. 243). In this passage, Virgil prophesies the return of Astrea, who had ascended from the earth to become the constellation Virgo, to begin a new Golden Age. The work is seen as a foretelling of the birth of Christ: Astrea corresponding to the Virgin Mary, and the star Spica, the most prominent star in Virgo to the star of Bethlehem. In A Vision, Yeats also makes mention of the birth of Christ falling between the signs of Pisces and Aries, and the sun's transition between these two signs was also traditionally associated with the ceremonial death and resurrection of Dionysis (Finneran p.654). Yeats writes further, "Each age unwinds the thread another age had wound... all things dying each other's life, living each other's death"(Vision).

This conjunction begins to be evident in the second half of the poem: "Odour of blood when Christ was slain/ Made all Platonic tolerance vain/ and vain all Doric discipline." Yeats describes the age of Plato and Stoicism as having been overturned by the birth of Christ, ending the age of antithetical religion. Yeats mentions that it is said that the comeliness of the people began to decline, and the arts became more and more systematic after the crucifixion as religion became more fixed and influential in the lives of human beings (Vision p.271). He writes "the tradition is founded which declares even to our own day that Christ alone was exactly six feet tall; the perfect physical man. Yet as the perfect physical man He must die, for only so can primary power reach antithetical mankind" (Vision p.273). In the final stanza of the poem, we see the effects of this the interplay betweent the two symbolic forces. The cause of each result becomes also its end— the emotional, subjective part of each example is overpowered by the actual physical action that it originates from.

"Everything that man esteems
Endures a moment or a day,
Love's pleasure drives his love away,

The painter's brush consumes his dreams;
The herald's cry, the soldier's tread
Exhaust his glory and his might:
Whatever flames upon the night,
Man's own resinous heart has fed".

The pleasure of love deprives the lover of its source; the actual action of painting overrides the painter's vision; the action of war dominates over the soldier's ability and his intentions.

There is another era that Yeats begins to discuss, and that is the new age to come. He can only speculate on what may happen based on his system, though even that he finds to be nearly impossible. In "The Second Coming", written before A Vision's completion, he predicts some vast new revelation, though in vague terms, viewing it as something immense and threatening, perhaps because it is unknown. Yeats begins,

"Turning and turning in the widening gyre
The falcon cannot hear the falconer;
Things fall apart; the centre cannot hold;
The blood dimmed tide is loosed, and everywhere
The ceremony of innocence is drowned"

The beginning of Yeats' imagined revelation deals with the breaking down of all logical order and stability. Then, he describes the image of an immense fantastical, creature to embody the coming of this new ideal that mankind will embrace, and the essence of unforeseeable change: "A shape with lion body and the head of a man,/A gaze blank and pitiless as the sun,/ is moving its slow thighs, while all about it/ Reel shadows of indignant desert birds." His final lines are full of foreboding: "What rough beast, its hour come round at last now slouches toward Bethlehem to be born?" This is another reference to Christ's birth therefore connecting new era to the beginnings of other ages. It signifies a completion and a new beginning of the circuit.

At the end of his historical discussion in A Vision, however, Yeats contemplates the new revelation with as much interest, but less underlying dread, and a final realization that he cannot, in fact predict the direction mankind will take in its continued cyclical path.

He questions, "Shall we follow the image of Heracles that walks through the darkness bow in hand, or mount to that other Heracles, man not image— he that has for his bride Hebe 'the daughter of Zues the mighty, and Hera shod in gold'"(Vision) He contemplates whether civilization will continue along a primary vein, men worshipping idols of far away deities, or return to its antithetical predecessor, in which man's idols seen as are actual living beings captured in myth. Eventually, he resigns himself to not knowing for certain what the future of mankind will be. He concludes "The particulars are the work of the thirteenth sphere, which is in every man and called by every man his freedom. Doubtless, for it can do all things and know all things, it knows what it will do with its own freedom, but it has kept the secret" (Vision).

Chapter 9

Major Themes: Yeats Poetry

Age and Death

Though a young poet at the time of the composition of *The Rose,* Yeats is quite preoccupied with themes of aging and mortality. Imagining his old age served as an escape for the young Yeats, who found himself unsuccessful in love and imagined that later in life he would either have won his beloved or his beloved would have come to regret her rejection of him. "In Old Age" is particularly marked by the image of an older Maud Gonne (the woman with whom Yeats was in love) becoming wiser in old age.

Yeats also had an anxiety about death which was unusual in someone so young. He contemplated death less in terms of himself than in terms of his loved ones. When Maud Gonne traveled to France as a convalescent, a worried Yeats wrote "A Dream of Death." This meditation on Gonne's possible death is less of a nightmare than a dream come true, as Yeats envisions himself being useful to her in death as he could not be in life. Yeats, therefore, views both aging and death as more or less positive forces.

Images of Irish Nature

It is not surprising that a collection entitled *The Rose* draws heavily upon nature imagery. Yeats draws upon natural imagery both in terms of the symbols he employs and in the settings he summons. Indeed, natural imagery features in all of Yeats's poetry, even that which contains political themes.

Yeats's landscape descriptions are often obviously Irish, even if they do not include a specific place name. He highlights the rolling greenness and shifting light that characterize the Irish landscape. Additionally, some of his poems take a more specific approach to the Irish landscape. Many of them, including "The Lake Isle of Inisfree," treat a particular Irish place. Nearly all of these places are in County Sligo, Yeats' mother's ancestral home and the place on earth that he felt most connected to. Yeats was eventually buried in Sligo.

Yeats also references the natural landscapes of Irish legend and myth. Imaginary natural worlds like Faeryland or Tir na nOg, where people never grow old, provide a compliment to both the general and specific treatments of Irish nature. In all his poems, Yeats carefully chooses a natural backdrop - real or imagined - that captures his home country.

Irish Mythology

The Rose is rife with mythological references, from King Fergus to Conchubar to Diarmuid. Indeed, such mythic Irish figures populate nearly every poem in the collection.

Mythology operates as a theme in this collection in a number of ways. First and foremost it separates Yeats' poetry from British writing. British writers drew on Roman and Greek mythology - the mythology, in fact, of other (albeit ancient) imperialists. In choosing Irish mythology as his source of allusions and subjects, Yeats creates a poetry distinct from that of Ireland's long-time oppressors. This compliments Yeats' desire to cultivate a poetic language suitable to Ireland alone.

Moreover, Yeats' use of Irish mythological subjects allows him to avoid the political climate of his own day. Yeats, a moderate compared to his beloved Maud Gonne, found his political beliefs to be a burden in his pursuit of love. In treating legendary figures, Yeats avoids the problem of referencing the complicated political environment that so tormented him.

For a fuller discussion of the specific mythology that Yeats draws on, see the *Additional Content* section in this ClassicNote.

Irish Nationalism

Nationalism in Ireland in the 1890s was in a complicated stage. Many die-hard Fenians (Republicans), including Maud Gonne, were more than willing to take arms against the British to gain their independence. Another group, including Yeats, took the more cautious parliamentary approach. This political party, called the Home Rule Party, was led by John Redmund and held that Ireland could gain independence through legal means.

Because this collection focuses so much on Maud Gonne, Yeats inevitably touches upon his political differences with his beloved. These differences, needless to say, affected their relationship negatively. Yeats feared that Gonne was more repulsed by his moderate politics than by his person.

Thus, in some poems, such as "To Ireland in the Coming Times," Yeats seems to be willfully disassociating himself from the complex political fabric of his own era, instead hearkening to a simpler politics of ancient kings. Undoubtedly Yeats was drawn to these ancient mythic times anyway, but his interest takes on a sadness in the context of his relationship with the politics of his own day (and thus of his relationship with Gonne). Nationalist politics exist negatively in these poems, as the subject that Yeats doesn't want to address.

Maud Gonne

At the time that Yeats published this collection, Maud Gonne was the major focus of his life. He was deeply in love with her, and although Gonne did not return his romantic sentiments, she remained close friends with him. He saw her often enough to become obsessed with her. Most of the poems in the collection were written for or about Gonne.

The central image of the rose is a symbol of Gonne as well as Ireland. Gonne, an extreme nationalist, represents the Irish spirit in her politics as well as her beauty. Thus Gonne, Ireland and the image of the rose exist interchangeably in Yeats' poetic imagination. His beloved, with her violent desire to free her country from British rule, captures the ferocity of nationalistic pride with spiritual and physical beauty. She is the thorny rose, and the thorny rose is Ireland. Indeed, one of Yeats' fears is that he himself is not violent enough politically or personally to attract Gonne's attentions, a fear that seemed to be justified by her marriage to a military man.

Urbanization

Ireland is, historically, an agrarian land. For centuries it was a nation of farmers - often working under unfair conditions for their British conquerers. Thus, though Ireland's agrarian identity was complicated, it was central. A rapport with the change of seasons and with the harvest cycle was central to Irish life.

At the time of the composition of *The Rose*, however, urbanization had begun to encroach upon Ireland. Dublin was a major metropolitan area, for instance, in the heart of a traditionally rural society. This complex relationship between urban and rural existence is essential to Yeats' perspective in *The Rose*. Though he lived much of his life in London and Dublin, Yeats viewed cities as inherently negative and poisonous. Thus poems like "The Lake Isle of Inisfree," which romanticize the Irish agrarian landscape with breathless awe, largely express the poet's discomfort with his urban environment.

It is worth asking, then, whether Yeats' natural landscapes of Ireland are realistic or purely imaginative. They seem to exist largely in the poets remembrance and longings - to be places of escape from a modernity that Yeats finds discomfiting. Yeats invites the conclusion that, in fact, it doesn't matter whether his Ireland is the *real* Ireland: it is, nevertheless, a place of meaning for the Irish.

Thus Yeats expresses a desire to capture in imaginative verse the spirit of Ireland - its symbols, mythology, people, nature - that might well be lost in the encroaching press of nationalism and urbanization. Yeats, in short, writes against the city, but also from the city. He cultivates an imaginative place of escape that is only necessary because of the coming modernity.

Chapter 10

Text of Major Poems

NO SECOND TROY

Why should I blame her that she filled my days
With misery, or that she would of late
Have taught to ignorant men most violent ways,
Or hurled the little streets upon the great,
Had they but courage equal to desire?
What could have made her peaceful with a mind
That nobleness made simple as a fire,
With beauty like a tightened bow, a kind
That is not natural in an age like this,
Being high and solitary and most stern?
Why, what could she have done, being what she is?
Was there another Troy for her to burn?

THE SECOND COMING

TURNING and turning in the widening gyre
The falcon cannot hear the falconer;
Things fall apart; the centre cannot hold;
Mere anarchy is loosed upon the world,
The blood-dimmed tide is loosed, and everywhere
The ceremony of innocence is drowned;
The best lack all conviction, while the worst
Are full of passionate intensity.

Surely some revelation is at hand;
Surely the Second Coming is at hand.
The Second Coming! Hardly are those words out

When a vast image out of Spiritus Mundi
Troubles my sight: somewhere in the sands of the desert
A shape with lion body and the head of a man,
A gaze blank and pitiless as the sun,
Is moving its slow thighs, while all about it
Reel shadows of the indignant desert birds.
The darkness drops again; but now I know
That twenty centuries of stony sleep
Were vexed to nightmare by a rocking cradle,
And what rough beast, its hour come round at last,
Slouches towards Bethlehem to be born?

THE SONG OF THE HAPPY SHEPHERD

THE woods of Arcady are dead,
And over is their antique joy;
Of old the world on dreaming fed;
Grey Truth is now her painted toy;
Yet still she turns her restless head:
But O, sick children of the world,
Of all the many changing things
In dreary dancing past us whirled,
To the cracked tune that Chronos sings,
Words alone are certain good.
Where are now the warring kings,
Word be-mockers? — By the Rood,
Where are now the warring kings?
An idle word is now their glory,
By the stammering schoolboy said,
Reading some entangled story:
The kings of the old time are dead;
The wandering earth herself may be
Only a sudden flaming word,
In clanging space a moment heard,
Troubling the endless reverie.

Then nowise worship dusty deeds,
Nor seek, for this is also sooth,
To hunger fiercely after truth,
Lest all thy toiling only breeds

New dreams, new dreams; there is no truth
Saving in thine own heart. Seek, then,
No learning from the starry men,
Who follow with the optic glass
The whirling ways of stars that pass—
Seek, then, for this is also sooth,
No word of theirs—the cold star-bane
Has cloven and rent their hearts in twain,
And dead is all their human truth.
Go gather by the humming sea
Some twisted, echo-harbouring shell,
And to its lips thy story tell,
And they thy comforters will be,
Rewording in melodious guile
Thy fretful words a little while,
Till they shall singing fade in ruth
And die a pearly brotherhood;
For words alone are certain good:
Sing, then, for this is also sooth.

I must be gone: there is a grave
Where daffodil and lily wave,
And I would please the hapless faun,
Buried under the sleepy ground,
With mirthful songs before the dawn.
His shouting days with mirth were crowned;
And still I dream he treads the lawn,
Walking ghostly in the dew,
Pierced by my glad singing through,
My songs of old earth's dreamy youth:
But ah! she dreams not now; dream thou!
For fair are poppies on the brow:
Dream, dream, for this is also sooth.

THE FALLING OF THE LEAVES

AUTUMN is over the long leaves that love us,
And over the mice in the barley sheaves;
Yellow the leaves of the rowan above us,
And yellow the wet wild-strawberry leaves.

The hour of the waning of love has beset us,
And weary and worn are our sad souls now;
Let us part, ere the season of passion forget us,
With a kiss and a tear on thy drooping brow.

AT GALWAY RACES

THERE where the course is,
Delight makes all of the one mind,
The riders upon the galloping horses,
The crowd that closes in behind:
We, too, had good attendance once,
Hearers and hearteners of the work;
Aye, horsemen for companions,
Before the merchant and the clerk
Breathed on the world with timid breath.
Sing on: somewhere at some new moon,
We'll learn that sleeping is not death,
Hearing the whole earth change its tune,
Its flesh being wild, and it again
Crying aloud as the racecourse is,
And we find hearteners among men
That ride upon horses.

THE BLESSED

CUMHAL called out, bending his head,
Till Dathi came and stood,
With a blink in his eyes, at the cave-mouth,
Between the wind and the wood.

And Cumhal said, bending his knees,
'I have come by the windy way
To gather the half of your blessedness
And learn to pray when you pray.

I can bring you salmon out of the streams
And heron out of the skies.'
But Dathi folded his hands and smiled
With the secrets of God in his eyes.
And Cumhal saw like a drifting smoke
All manner of blessed souls,

Women and children, young men with books,
And old men with croziers and stoles.

'Praise God and God's Mother, Dathi said,
'For God and God's Mother have sent
The blessedest souls that walk in the world
To fill your heart with content.'

'And which is the blessedest,' Cumhal said,
'Where all are comely and good?
Is it these that with golden thuribles
Are singing about the wood?'

'My eyes are blinking,' Dathi said,
'With the secrets of God half blind,
But I can see where the wind goes
And follow the way of the wind;

'And blessedness goes where the wind goes,
And when it is gone we are dead;
I see the blessedest soul in the world
And he nods a drunken head.

'O blessedness comes in the night and the day
And whither the wise heart knows;
And one has seen in the redness of wine
The Incorruptible Rose,

'That drowsily drops faint leaves on him
And the sweetness of desire,
While time and the world are ebbing away
In twilights of dew and of fire.'

THE CAP AND BELLS

THE jester walked in the garden:
The garden had fallen still;
He bade his soul rise upward
And stand on her window-sill.

It rose in a straight blue garment,
When owls began to call:
It had grown wise-tongued by thinking
Of a quiet and light footfall;

But the young queen would not listen;
She rose in her pale night-gown;
She drew in the heavy casement
And pushed the latches down.

He bade his heart go to her,
When the owls called out no more;
In a red and quivering garment
It sang to her through the door.

It had grown sweet-tongued by dreaming
Of a flutter of flower-like hair;
But she took up her fan from the table
And waved it off on the air.

'I have cap and bells,' he pondered,
'I will send them to her and die';
And when the morning whitened
He left them where she went by.

She laid them upon her bosom,
Under a cloud of her hair,
And her red lips sang them a love-song
Till stars grew out of the air.

She opened her door and her window,
And the heart and the soul came through,
To her right hand came the red one,
To her left hand came the blue.

They set up a noise like crickets,
A chattering wise and sweet,
And her hair was a folded flower
And the quiet of love in her feet.

DOWN BY THE SALLEY GARDENS

DOWN by the salley gardens my love and I did meet;
She passed the salley gardens with little snow-white feet.
She bid me take love easy, as the leaves grow on the tree;
But I, being young and foolish, with her would not agree.

In a field by the river my love and I did stand,
And on my leaning shoulder she laid her snow-white hand.
She bid me take life easy, as the grass grows on the weirs;
But I was young and foolish, and now am full of tears.

DREAM OF A BLESSED SPIRIT

ALL the heavy days are over;
Leave the body's coloured pride
Underneath the grass and clover,
With the feet laid side by side.

One with her are mirth and duty;
Bear the gold-embroidered dress,
For she needs not her sad beauty,
To the scented oaken press.

Hers the kiss of Mother Mary,
The long hair is on her face;
Still she goes with footsteps wary
Full of earth's old timid grace.

With white feet of angels seven
Her white feet go glimmering;
And above the deep of heaven,
Flame on flame, and wing on wing

HE BIDS HIS BELOVED BE AT PEACE

IHEAR the Shadowy Horses, their long manes a-shake,
Their hoofs heavy with tumult, their eyes glimmering white;
The North unfolds above them clinging, creeping night,
The East her hidden joy before the morning break,
The West weeps in pale dew and sighs passing away,
The South is pouring down roses of crimson fire:
O vanity of Sleep, Hope, Dream, endless Desire,
The Horses of Disaster plunge in the heavy clay:
Beloved, let your eyes half close, and your heart beat
Over my heart, and your hair fall over my breast,
Drowning love's lonely hour in deep twilight of rest,
And hiding their tossing manes and their tumultuous feet.

HE REMEMBERS FORGOTTEN BEAUTY

WHEN my arms wrap you round I press
My heart upon the loveliness
That has long faded from the world;
The jewelled crowns that kings have hurled
In shadowy pools, when armies fled;
The love-tales wrought with silken thread
By dreaming ladies upon cloth
That has made fat the murderous moth;
The roses that of old time were
Woven by ladies in their hair,
The dew-cold lilies ladies bore
Through many a sacred corridor
Where such grey clouds of incense rose
That only God's eyes did not close:
For that pale breast and lingering hand
Come from a more dream-heavy land,
A more dream-heavy hour than this;
And when you sigh from kiss to kiss
I hear white Beauty sighing, too,
For hours when all must fade like dew,
But flame on flame, and deep on deep,
Throne over throne where in half sleep,
Their swords upon their iron knees,
Brood her high lonely mysteries.

HIS DREAM

ISWAYED upon the gaudy stern
The butt-end of a steering-oar,
And saw wherever I could turn
A crown upon the shore.

And though I would have hushed the crowd,
There was no mother's son but said,
'What is the figure in a shroud
Upon a gaudy bed?'

And after running at the brim
Cried out upon that thing beneath

—It had such dignity of limb—
By the sweet name of Death.

Though I'd my finger on my lip,
What could I but take up the song?
And running crowd and gaudy ship
Cried out the whole night long,

Crying amid the glittering sea,
Naming it with ecstatic breath,
Because it had such dignity,
By the sweet name of Death.

THE HOSTING OF THE SIDHE

THE host is riding from Knocknarea
And over the grave of Clooth-na-Bare;
Caoilte tossing his burning hair,
And Niamh calling Away, come away:
Empty your heart of its mortal dream.
The winds awaken, the leaves whirl round,
Our cheeks are pale, our hair is unbound,
Our breasts are heaving, our eyes are agleam,
Our arms are waving, our lips are apart;
And if any gaze on our rushing band,
We come between him and the deed of his hand,
We come between him and the hope of his heart.
The host is rushing 'twixt night and day,
And where is there hope or deed as fair?
Caoilte tossing his burning hair,
And Niamh calling Away, come away.

THE INDIAN TO HIS LOVE

THE island dreams under the dawn
And great boughs drop tranquillity;
The peahens dance on a smooth lawn,
A parrot sways upon a tree,
Raging at his own image in the enamelled sea.

Here we will moor our lonely ship
And wander ever with woven hands,

Murmuring softly lip to lip,
Along the grass, along the sands,
Murmuring how far away are the unquiet lands:

How we alone of mortals are
Hid under quiet boughs apart,
While our love grows an Indian star,
A meteor of the burning heart,
One with the tide that gleams, the wings that gleam and dart,

The heavy boughs, the burnished dove
That moans and sighs a hundred days:
How when we die our shades will rove,
When eve has hushed the feathered ways,
With vapoury footsole by the water's drowsy blaze.

IN THE SEVEN WOODS

IHAVE heard the pigeons of the Seven Woods
Make their faint thunder, and the garden bees
Hum in the lime-tree flowers; and put away
The unavailing outcries and the old bitterness
That empty the heart. I have forgot awhile
Tara uprooted, and new commonness
Upon the throne and crying about the streets
And hanging its paper flowers from post to post,
Because it is alone of all things happy.
I am contented, for I know that Quiet
Wanders laughing and eating her wild heart
Among pigeons and bees, while that Great Archer,
Who but awaits His hour to shoot, still hangs
A cloudy quiver over Pairc-na-lee.

THE LAMENTATION OF THE OLD PENSIONER

ALTHOUGH I shelter from the rain
Under a broken tree
My chair was nearest to the fire
In every company
That talked of love or politics,
Ere Time transfigured me.

Though lads are making pikes again
For some conspiracy,
And crazy rascals rage their fill
At human tyranny,
My contemplations are of Time
That has transfigured me.

There's not a woman turns her face
Upon a broken tree,
And yet the beauties that I loved
Are in my memory;
I spit into the face of Time
That has transfigured me.

THE MAGI

NOW as at all times I can see in the mind's eye,
In their stiff, painted clothes, the pale unsatisfied ones
Appear and disappear in the blue depth of the sky
With all their ancient faces like rain-beaten stones,
And all their helms of silver hovering side by side,
And all their eyes still fixed, hoping to find once more,
Being by Calvary's turbulence unsatisfied,
The uncontrollable mystery on the bestial floor.

THE MOODS

TIME drops in decay,
Like a candle burnt out,
And the mountains and the woods
Have their day, have their day;
What one in the rout
Of the fire-born moods
Has fallen away?

O DO NOT LOVE TOO LONG

SWEETHEART, do not love too long:
I loved long and long,
And grew to be out of fashion
Like an old song.

All through the years of our youth
Neither could have known
Their own thought from the other's,
We were so much at one.

But O, in a minute she changed—
O do not love too long,
Or you will grow out of fashion
Like an old song.

ON A POLITICAL PRISONER

by: W. B. Yeats (1865-1939)

SHE that but little patience knew,
From childhood on, had now so much
A grey gull lost its fear and flew
Down to her cell and there alit,
And there endured her fingers' touch
And from her fingers ate its bit.

Did she in touching that lone wing
Recall the years before her mind
Became a bitter, an abstract thing,
Her thought some popular enmity:
Blind and leader of the blind
Drinking the foul ditch where they lie?

When long ago I saw her ride
Under Ben Bulben to the meet,
The beauty of her country-side
With all youth's lonely wildness stirred,
She seemed to have grown clean and sweet
Like any rock-bred, sea-borne bird:

Sea-borne, or balanced in the air
When first it sprang out of the nest
Upon some lofty rock to stare
Upon the cloudy canopy,
While under its storm-beaten breast
Cried out the hollows of the sea.

PEACE

AH, that Time could touch a form
That could show what Homer's age
Bred to be a hero's wage.
'Were not all her life but storm,
Would not painters paint a form
Of such noble lines,' I said,
'Such a delicate high head,
All that sternness amid charm,
All that sweetness amid strength?'
Ah, but peace that comes at length,
Came when Time had touched her form.

PRESENCES

THIS night has been so strange that it seemed
As if the hair stood up on my head.
From going-down of the sun I have dreamed
That women laughing, or timid or wild,
In rustle of lace or silken stuff,
Climbed up my creaking stair. They had read
All I had rhymed of that monstrous thing
Returned and yet unrequited love.
They stood in the door and stood between
My great wood lectern and the fire
Till I could hear their hearts beating:
One is a harlot, and one a child
That never looked upon man with desire,
And one, it may be, a queen

RECONCILIATION

SOME may have blamed you that you took away
The verses that could move them on the day
When, the ears being deafened, the sight of the eyes blind
With lightning, you went from me, and I could find
Nothing to make a song about but kings,
Helmets, and swords, and half-forgotten things
That were like memories of you—but now

We'll out, for the world lives as long ago;
And while we're in our laughing, weeping fit,
Hurl helmets, crowns, and swords into the pit.
But, dear, cling close to me; since you were gone,
My barren thoughts have chilled me to the bone

THE ROSE OF THE WORLD

WHO dreamed that beauty passes like a dream?
For these red lips, with all their mournful pride,
Mournful that no new wonder may betide,
Troy passed away in one high funeral gleam,
And Usna's children died.

We and the labouring world are passing by:
Amid men's souls, that waver and give place
Like the pale waters in their wintry race,
Under the passing stars, foam of the sky,
Lives on this lonely face.

Bow down, archangels, in your dim abode:
Before you were, or any hearts to beat,
Weary and kind one lingered by His seat;
He made the world to be a grassy road
Before her wandering feet.

THE SONG OF WANDERING AENGUS

IWENT out to the hazel wood,
Because a fire was in my head,
And cut and peeled a hazel wand,
And hooked a berry to a thread;

And when white moths were on the wing,
And moth-like stars were flickering out,
I dropped the berry in a stream
And caught a little silver trout.

When I had laid it on the floor
I went to blow the fire a-flame,
But something rustled on the floor,
And some one called me by my name:
It had become a glimmering girl

With apple blossom in her hair
Who called me by my name and ran
And faded through the brightening air.

Though I am old with wandering
Through hollow lands and hilly lands,
I will find out where she has gone,
And kiss her lips and take her hands;
And walk among long dappled grass,
And pluck till time and times are done
The silver apples of the moon,
The golden apples of the sun.

THESE ARE THE CLOUDS

THESE are the clouds about the fallen sun,
The majesty that shuts his burning eye:
The weak lay hand on what the strong has done,
Till that be tumbled that was lifted high
And discord follow upon unison,
And all things at one common level lie.
And therefore, friend, if your great race were run
And these things came, so much the more thereby
Have you made greatness your companion,
Although it be for children that you sigh:
These are the clouds about the fallen sun,
The majesty that shuts his burning eye.

TO A CHILD DANCING IN THE WIND

DANCE there upon the shore;
What need have you to care
For wind or water's roar?
And tumble out your hair
That the salt drops have wet;
Being young you have not known
The fool's triumph, nor yet
Love lost as soon as won,
Nor the best labourer dead
And all the sheaves to bind.
What need have you to dread
The monstrous crying of wind?

TO A SHADE

IF you have revisited the town, thin Shade,
Whether to look upon your monument
(I wonder if the builder has been paid)
Or happier-thoughted when the day is spent
To drink of that salt breath out of the sea
When grey gulls flit about instead of men,
And the gaunt houses put on majesty:
Let these content you and be gone again;
For they are at their old tricks yet.

A man
Of your own passionate serving kind who had brought
In his full hands what, had they only known,
Had given their children's children loftier thought,
Sweeter emotion, working in their veins
Like gentle blood, has been driven from the place,
And insult heaped upon him for his pains,
And for his open-handedness, disgrace;
Your enemy, an old foul mouth, had set
The pack upon him.

Go, unquiet wanderer,
And gather the Glasnevin coverlet
About your head till the dust stops your ear,
The time for you to taste of that salt breath
And listen at the corners has not come;
You had enough of sorrow before death—
Away, away! You are safer in the tomb

TO A YOUNG GIRL

MY dear, my dear, I know
More than another
What makes your heart beat so;
Not even your own mother
Can know it as I know,
Who broke my heart for her
When the wild thought,
That she denies

And has forgot,
Set all her blood astir
And glittered in her eyes.

TO SOME I HAVE TALKED WITH BY THE FIRE

WHILE I wrought out these fitful Danaan rhymes,
My heart would brim with dreams about the times
When we bent down above the fading coals
And talked of the dark folk who live in souls
Of passionate men, like bats in the dead trees;
And of the wayward twilight companies
Who sigh with mingled sorrow and content,
Because their blossoming dreams have never bent
Under the fruit of evil and of good:
And of the embattled flaming multitude
Who rise, wing above wing, flame above flame,
And, like a storm, cry the Ineffable Name,
And with the clashing of their sword-blades make
A rapturous music, till the morning break
And the white hush end all but the loud beat
Of their long wings, the flash of their white feet

TO THE ROSE UPON THE ROOD OF TIME

RED Rose, proud Rose, sad Rose of all my days!
Come near me, while I sing the ancient ways:
Cuchulain battling with the bitter tide;
The Druid, grey, wood-nurtured, quiet eyed,
Who cast round Fergus dreams, and ruin untold;
And thine own sadness, whereof stars, grown old
In dancing silver-sandalled on the sea,
Sing in their high and lonely melody.
Come near, that no more blinded by man's fate,
I find under the boughs of love and hate,
In all poor foolish things that live a day,
Eternal beauty wandering on her way.

Come near, come near, come near — Ah, leave me still
A little space for the rose-breath to fill!
Lest I no more hear common things that crave;

The weak worm hiding down in its small cave,
The field-mouse running by me in the grass,
And heavy mortal hopes that toil and pass;
But seek alone to hear the strange things said
By God to the bright hearts of those long dead,
And learn to chaunt a tongue men do not know
Come near; I would, before my time to go,
Sing of old Eire and the ancient ways:
Red Rose, proud Rose, sad Rose of all my days.

THE TWO TREES

BELOVED, gaze in thine own heart,
The holy tree is growing there;
From joy the holy branches start,
And all the trembling flowers they bear.
The changing colours of its fruit
Have dowered the stars with merry light;
The surety of its hidden root
Has planted quiet in the night;
The shaking of its leafy head
Has given the waves their melody,
And made my lips and music wed,
Murmuring a wizard song for thee.
There the Loves a circle go,
The flaming circle of our days,
Gyring, spiring to and fro
In those great ignorant leafy ways;
Remembering all that shaken hair
And how the wingèd sandals dart,
Thine eyes grow full of tender care:
Beloved, gaze in thine own heart.

Gaze no more in the bitter glass
The demons, with their subtle guile,
Lift up before us when they pass,
Or only gaze a little while;
For there a fatal image grows
That the stormy night receives,
Roots half hidden under snows,

Broken boughs and blackened leaves.
For all things turn to barrenness
In the dim glass the demons hold,
The glass of outer weariness,
Made when God slept in times of old.
There, through the broken branches, go
The ravens of unresting thought;
Flying, crying, to and fro,
Cruel claw and hungry throat,
Or else they stand and sniff the wind,
And shake their ragged wings; alas!
Thy tender eyes grow all unkind:
Gaze no more in the bitter glass.

WHEN HELEN LIVED

WE have cried in our despair
That men desert,
For some trivial affair
Or noisy, insolent sport,
Beauty that we have won
From bitterest hours;
Yet we, had we walked within
Those topless towers
Where Helen walked with her boy,
Had given but as the rest
Of the men and women of Troy,
A word and a jest.

WHEN YOU ARE OLD

WHEN you are old and grey and full of sleep,
And nodding by the fire, take down this book,
And slowly read, and dream of the soft look
Your eyes had once, and of their shadows deep;

How many loved your moments of glad grace,
And loved your beauty with love false or true,
But one man loved the pilgrim soul in you,
And loved the sorrows of your changing face;

And bending down beside the glowing bars,
Murmur, a little sadly, how Love fled
And paced upon the mountains overhead
And hid his face amid a crowd of stars

THE SORROW OF LOVE

THE quarrel of the sparrows in the eaves,
The full round moon and the star-laden sky,
And the loud song of the ever-singing leaves,
Had hid away earth's old and weary cry.

And then you came with those red mournful lips,
And with you came the whole of the world's tears,
And all the sorrows of her labouring ships,
And all the burden of her myriad years.

And now the sparrows warring in the eaves,
The curd-pale moon, the white stars in the sky,
And the loud chaunting of the unquiet leaves
Are shaken with earth's old and weary cry.

TO AN ISLE IN THE WATER

SHY one, shy one,
Shy one of my heart,
She moves in the firelight
Pensively apart.

She carries in the dishes,
And lays them in a row.
To an isle in the water
With her would I go.

She carries in the candles,
And lights the curtained room,
Shy in the doorway
And shy in the gloom;

And shy as a rabbit,
Helpful and shy.
To an isle in the water
With her would I fly.

THE HOST OF THE AIR

O 'DRISCOLL drove with a song
The wild duck and the drake
From the tall and the tufted reeds
Of the drear Hart Lake.

And he saw how the reeds grew dark
At the coming of night-tide,
And dreamed of the long dim hair
Of Bridget his bride.

He heard while he sang and dreamed
A piper piping away,
And never was piping so sad,
And never was piping so gay.

And he saw young men and young girls
Who danced on a level place,
And Bridget his bride among them,
With a sad and a gay face.

The dancers crowded about him
And many a sweet thing said,
And a young man brought him red wine
And a young girl white bread.

But Bridget drew him by the sleeve
Away from the merry bands,
To old men playing at cards
With a twinkling of ancient hands.

The bread and the wine had a doom,
For these were the host of the air;
He sat and played in a dream
Of her long dim hair.

He played with the merry old men
And thought not of evil chance,
Until one bore Bridget his bride
Away from the merry dance.

He bore her away in his arms,
The handsomest young man there,

And his neck and his breast and his arms
Were drowned in her long dim hair.

O'Driscoll scattered the cards
And out of his dream awoke:
Old men and young men and young girls
Were gone like a drifting smoke;

But he heard high up in the air
A piper piping away,
And never was piping so sad,
And never was piping so gay.

TO IRELAND IN THE COMING TIMES

KNOW, that I would accounted be
True brother of a company
That sang, to sweeten Ireland's wrong,
Ballad and story, rann and song;
Nor be I any less of them,
Because the red-rose-bordered hem
Of her, whose history began
Before God made the angelic clan,
Trails all about the written page.
When Time began to rant and rage
The measure of her flying feet
Made Ireland's heart begin to beat;
And Time bade all his candles flare
To light a measure here and there;
And may the thoughts of Ireland brood
Upon a measured quietude.

Nor may I less be counted one
With Davis, Mangan, Ferguson,
Because, to him who ponders well,
My rhymes more than their rhyming tell
Of things discovered in the deep,
Where only body's laid asleep.
For the elemental creatures go
About my table to and fro,
That hurry from unmeasured mind

To rant and rage in flood and wind;
Yet he who treads in measured ways
May surely barter gaze for gaze.
Man ever journeys on with them
After the red-rose-bordered hem.
Ah, faeries, dancing under the moon,
A Druid land, a Druid tune!

While still I may, I write for you
The love I lived, the dream I knew.
From our birthday, until we die,
Is but the winking of an eye;
And we, our singing and our love,
What measurer Time has lit above,
And all benighted things that go
About my table to and fro,
Are passing on to where may be,
In truth's consuming ecstasy,
No place for love and dream at all;
For God goes by with white footfall.
I cast my heart into my rhymes,
That you, in the dim coming times,
May know how my heart went with them
After the red-rose-bordered hem.

THE CAT AND THE MOON

THE cat went here and there
And the moon spun round like a top,
And the nearest kin of the moon,
The creeping cat, looked up.
Black Minnaloushe stared at the moon,
For, wander and wail as he would,
The pure cold light in the sky
Troubled his animal blood.
Minnaloushe runs in the grass
Lifting his delicate feet.
Do you dance, Minnaloushe, do you dance?
When two close kindred meet,
What better than call a dance?

Maybe the moon may learn,
Tired of that courtly fashion,
A new dance turn.
Minnaloushe creeps through the grass
From moonlit place to place,
The sacred moon overhead
Has taken a new phase.
Does Minnaloushe know that his pupils
Will pass from change to change,
And that from round to crescent,
From crescent to round they range?
Minnaloushe creeps through the grass
Alone, important and wise,
And lifts to the changing moon
His changing eyes.

THE WHITE BIRDS

I WOULD that we were, my beloved, white birds on the foam of the sea!
We tire of the flame of the meteor, before it can fade and flee;
And the flame of the blue star of twilight, hung low on the rim of the sky,
Has awakened in our hearts, my beloved, a sadness that may not die.

A weariness comes from those dreamers, dew-dabbled, the lily and rose;
Ah, dream not of them, my beloved, the flame of the meteor that goes,
Or the flame of the blue star that lingers hung low in the fall of the dew:
For I would we were changed to white birds on the wandering foam: I and you!

I am haunted by numberless islands, and many a Danaan shore,
Where Time would surely forget us, and Sorrow come near us no more;
Soon far from the rose and the lily, and fret of the flames would we be,

Were we only white birds, my beloved, buoyed out on the foam of the sea!

LINES WRITTEN IN DEJECTION

WHEN have I last looked on
The round green eyes and the long wavering bodies
Of the dark leopards of the moon?
All the wild witches, those most notable ladies,
For all their broom-sticks and their tears,
Their angry tears, are gone.
The holy centaurs of the hills are vanished;
I have nothing but the embittered sun;
Banished heroic mother moon and vanished,
And now that I have come to fifty years
I must endure the timid sun.

THE VALLEY OF THE BLACK PIG

THE dews drop slowly and dreams gather; unknown spears
Suddenly hurtle before my dream-awakened eyes,
And then the clash of fallen horsemen and the cries
Of unknown perishing armies beat about my ears.
We who still labour by the cromlech on the shore,
The grey cairn on the hill, when day sinks drowned in dew,
Being weary of the world's empires, bow down to you,
Master of the still stars and of the flaming door

He Mourns for the Change that has come upon him and his beloved, and longs for the end of the World

DO you not hear me calling, white deer with no horns?
I have been changed to a hound with one red ear;
I have been in the Path of Stones and the Wood of Thorns,
For somebody hid hatred and hope and desire and fear
Under my feet that they follow you night and day.
A man with a hazel wand came without sound;
He changed me suddenly; I was looking another way;
And now my calling is but the calling of a hound;
And Time and Birth and Change are hurrying by.
I would that the Boar without bristles had come from the West

And had rooted the sun and moon and stars out of the sky
And lay in the darkness, grunting, and turning to his rest.

A POET TO HIS BELOVED

I BRING you with reverent hands
The books of my numberless dreams,
White woman that passion has worn
As the tide wears the dove-grey sands,
And with heart more old than the horn
That is brimmed from the pale fire of time:
White woman with numberless dreams,
I bring you my passionate rhyme.

HE WISHES HIS BELOVED WERE DEAD

WERE you but lying cold and dead,
And lights were paling out of the West,
You would come hither, and bend your head,
And I would lay my head on your breast;
And you would murmur tender words,
Forgiving me, because you were dead:
Nor would you rise and hasten away,
Though you have the will of wild birds,
But know your hair was bound and wound
About the stars and moon and sun:
O would, beloved, that you lay
Under the dock-leaves in the ground,
While lights were paling one by one.

MEN IMPROVE WITH THE YEARS

I AM worn out with dreams;
A weather-worn, marble triton
Among the streams;
And all day long I look
Upon this lady's beauty
As though I had found in a book
A pictured beauty,
Pleased to have filled the eyes
Or the discerning ears,

Delighted to be but wise,
For men improve with the years;
And yet, and yet,
Is this my dream, or the truth?
O would that we had met
When I had my burning youth!
But I grow old among dreams,
A weather-worn, marble triton
Among the streams.

RED HANRAHAN'S SONG ABOUT IRELAND

THE old brown thorn-trees break in two high over Cummen Strand,
Under a bitter black wind that blows from the left hand;
Our courage breaks like an old tree in a black wind and dies,
But we have hidden in our hearts the flame out of the eyes
Of Cathleen, the daughter of Houlihan.

The wind has bundled up the clouds high over Knocknarea,
And thrown the thunder on the stones for all that Maeve can say.
Angers that are like noisy clouds have set our hearts abeat;
But we have all bent low and low and kissed the quiet feet
Of Cathleen, the daughter of Houlihan.

The yellow pool has overflowed high up on Clooth-na-Bare,
For the wet winds are blowing out of the clinging air;
Like heavy flooded waters our bodies and our blood;
But purer than a tall candle before the Holy Rood
Is Cathleen, the daughter of Houlihan.

THE UNAPPEASABLE HOST

THE Danaan children laugh, in cradles of wrought gold,
And clap their hands together, and half close their eyes,
For they will ride the North when the ger-eagle flies,
With heavy whitening wings, and a heart fallen cold:
I kiss my wailing child and press it to my breast,
And hear the narrow graves calling my child and me.
Desolate winds that cry over the wandering sea;

Desolate winds that hover in the flaming West;
Desolate winds that beat the doors of Heaven, and beat
The doors of Hell and blow there many a whimpering ghost;
O heart the winds have shaken, the unappeasable host
Is comelier than candles at Mother Mary's feet

Chapter 11

Summary and Analysis

The Lake Isle of Innisfree"

Summary

The poet declares that he will arise and go to Innisfree, where he will build a small cabin "of clay and wattles made." There, he will have nine bean-rows and a beehive, and live alone in the glade loud with the sound of bees ("the bee-loud glade"). He says that he will have peace there, for peace drops from "the veils of morning to where the cricket sings." Midnight there is a glimmer, and noon is a purple glow, and evening is full of linnet's wings. He declares again that he will arise and go, for always, night and day, he hears the lake water lapping "with low sounds by the shore." While he stands in the city, "on the roadway, or on the pavements grey," he hears the sound within himself, "in the deep heart's core."

Form

"The Lake Isle of Innisfree" is written mostly in hexameter, with six stresses in each line, in a loosely iambic pattern. The last line of each four-line stanza shortens the line to tetrameter, with only four stresses: "And *live alone* in the *bee*-loud *glade.*" Each of the three stanzas has the same ABAB rhyme scheme. Formally, this poem is somewhat unusual for Yeats: he rarely worked with hexameter, and every rhyme in the poem is a full rhyme; there is no sign of the half-rhymes Yeats often prefers in his later work.

Commentary

"The Lake Isle of Innisfree," published in Yeats's second book of poems, 1893's *The Rose,* is one of his first great poems, and one of his most enduring. The tranquil, hypnotic hexameters recreate the rhythmic pulse of the tide. The simple imagery of the quiet life the speaker longs to lead, as he enumerates each of its qualities, lulls the reader into his idyllic fantasy, until the penultimate line jolts the speaker—and the reader—back into the reality of his drab urban existence: "While I stand on the roadway, or on the pavements grey." The final line—"I hear it in the deep heart's core"—is a crucial statement for Yeats, not only in this poem but also in his career as a whole. The implication that the truths of the "deep heart's core" are essential to life is one that would preoccupy Yeats for the rest of his career as a poet; the struggle to remain true to the deep heart's core may be thought of as Yeats's primary undertaking as a poet.

"Adam's Curse"

Summary

Addressing his beloved, the speaker remembers sitting with her and "that beautiful mild woman, your close friend" at the end of summer, discussing poetry. He remarked then that a line of poetry may take hours to write, but if it does not seem the thought of a single moment, the poet's work has been useless. The poet said that it would be better to "scrub a kitchen pavement, or break stones / Like an old pauper, in all kinds of weather," for to write poetry is a task harder than these, yet less appreciated by the "bankers, schoolmasters, and clergymen" of the world.

The "beautiful mild woman"—whose voice, the speaker notes, is so sweet and low it will cause many men heartache—replied that to be born a woman is to know that one must work at being beautiful, even though that kind of work is not discussed at school. The speaker answered by saying that since the fall of Adam, every fine thing has required "labouring." He said that there have been lovers who spent time learning "precedents out of beautiful old books," but now such study seems "an idle trade enough."

At the mention of love, the speaker recalls, the group grew quiet, watching "the last embers of daylight die." In the blue-green sky the moon rose, looking worn as a shell "washed by time's waters as they rose and fell / About the stars and broke in days and years." The speaker says that he spoke only for the ears of his beloved, that she was beautiful, and that he strove to love her "in the old high way of love." It had all seemed happy, he says, "and yet we'd grown / As weary-hearted as that hollow moon."

Form

"Adam's Curse" is written in heroic couplets, which is a name used to describe rhyming couplets in iambic pentameter. Some of the rhymes are full (years/ears) and some are only partial (clergymen/thereupon).

Commentary

"Adam's Curse" is an extraordinary poem; though it was written early in Yeats's career (appearing in his 1904 collection *In the Seven Woods*), and though its stylistic simplicity is somewhat atypical for Yeats, it easily ranks among his best and most moving work. Within an emotional recollection of an evening spent with his beloved and her friend, Yeats frames a philosophical argument: that because of the curse of labour that God placed upon Adam when He expelled him from the Garden of Eden, every worthwhile human achievement (particularly those aimed at achieving beauty, whether in poetry, physical appearance, or love) requires hard work. The simple, speech-like rhythms of the iambic pentameter fulfill the poet's dictate that a poetic line should seem "but a moment's thought," and the bittersweet emotional tone appears wholly organic, a natural result of the recollection. The speaker loves the woman to whom the poem is addressed, and speaks "only for [her] ears"; but though the scene seems happy, their hearts are as weary as shells worn by the waters of time.

Behind the natural, unsophisticated feel of the poem, of course, lies a great deal of hard work and structure—just as the poem's speaker says must be true of poetry generally. (One of the most charming aspects of this poem is its mirroring of the aesthetic principles laid out by the speaker in the first stanza.) The discussion of work and beauty is divided into three progressive parts: the speaker's claims about poetry, the friend's claims about physical beauty, and the speaker's claims about love. This last claim affords Yeats the chance both to hush the trio and to soften the mood of the poem, and the speaker looks outward to the rising moon, which becomes a metaphor for the effects of time on the human heart, a weariness presumably compounded by the labour of living "since Adam's fall."

"The Wild Swans at Coole"

Summary

With the trees "in their autumn beauty," the speaker walks down the dry woodland paths to the water, which mirrors the still October twilight of the sky. Upon the water float "nine-and-fifty swans." The speaker says that nineteen years have passed since he first came to the water and counted the swans; that first time, before he had "well finished," he saw the swans mount up into the sky and scatter, "whelling in great broken rings / Upon their clamorous wings." The speaker says that his heart is sore, for after nineteen autumns of watching and being cheered by the swans, he finds that everything in his life has changed. The swans, though, are still unwearied, and they paddle by in the water or fly by in the air in pairs, "lover by lover." Their hearts, the speaker says, "have not grown cold," and wherever they go they are attended by "passion or conquest." But now, as they drift over the still water, they are "Mysterious, beautiful," and the speaker wonders where they will build their nests, and by what lake's edge or pool they will "delight men's eyes," when he awakes one morning to find that they have flown away.

Form

"The Wild Swans at Coole" is written in a very regular stanza form: five six-line stanzas, each written in a roughly iambic meter, with the first and third lines in tetrameter, the second, fourth, and sixth lines in trimeter, and the fifth line in pentameter, so that the pattern of stressed syllables in each stanza is 434353. The rhyme scheme in each stanza is ABCBDD.

Commentary

One of the most unusual features of Yeats's poetic career is the fact that the poet came into his greatest powers only as he neared old age; whereas many poets fade after the first burst of youth, Yeats continued to grow more confident and more innovative with his writing until almost the day he died. Though he was a famous and successful writer in his youth, his poetic reputation today is founded almost solely on poems written after he was fifty. He is thus the great poet of old age, writing honestly and with astonishing force about the pain of time's passage and feeling that the ageless heart was "fastened to a dying animal," as he wrote in "Sailing to Byzantium." The great struggle that enlivens many of Yeats's best poems is the struggle to uphold the integrity of the soul, and to preserve the mind's connection to the "deep heart's core," despite physical decay and the pain of memory.

"The Wild Swans at Coole," part of the 1919 collection of the same name, is one of Yeats's earliest and most moving testaments to the heart-ache of living in a time when "all's changed." (And when Yeats says "All's changed, changed utterly" in the fifteen years since he first saw the swans, he means it—the First World War and the Irish civil war both occurred during these years.) The simple narrative of the poem, recounting the poet's trips to the lake at Augusta Gregory's Coole Park residence to count the swans on the water, is given its solemn serenity by the beautiful nature imagery of the early stanzas, the plaintive tone of the poet, and the carefully constructed poetic stanza—the two trimeter lines, which give the poet an opportunity to utter short, heartfelt statements before a long silence ensured by the short line ("Their hearts have not grown old..."). The speaker, caught up in the gentle pain of personal memory, contrasts sharply with the swans, which are treated as symbols of the essential: their hearts have not grown old; they are still attended by passion and conquest.

"An Irish Airman foresees his Death"

Summary

The speaker, an Irish airman fighting in World War I, declares that he knows he will die fighting among the clouds. He says that he does not hate those he fights, nor love those he guards. His country is "Kiltartan's Cross," his countrymen "Kiltartan's poor." He says that no outcome in the war will make their lives worse or better than before the war began. He says that he did not decide to fight because of a law or a sense of duty, nor because of "public men" or "cheering crowds." Rather, "a lonely impulse of delight" drove him to "this tumult in the clouds." He says that he weighed his life in his mind, and found that "The years to come seemed waste of breath, / A waste of breath the years behind."

Form

This short sixteen-line poem has a very simple structure: lines metered in iambic tetrameter, and four grouped "quatrains" of alternating rhymes: ABABCDCDEFEFGHGH, or four repetitions of the basic ABAB scheme utilizing different rhymes.

Commentary

This simple poem is one of Yeats's most explicit statements about the First World War, and illustrates both his active political consciousness ("Those I fight I do not hate, / Those I guard I do not love") and his increasing propensity for a kind of hard-edged mystical rapture (the airman was driven to the clouds by "A lonely impulse of delight"). The poem, which, like flying, emphasizes balance, essentially enacts a kind of accounting, whereby the airman lists every factor weighing upon his situation and his vision of death, and rejects every possible factor he believes to be false: he does not hate or love his enemies or his allies, his country will neither be benefited nor hurt by any outcome of the war, he does not fight for political or moral motives but because of his "impulse of delight"; his past life seems a waste, his future life seems that it would be a waste, and his death will balance his life. Complementing this kind of tragic arithmetic is the neatly balanced structure of the poem, with its cycles of alternating rhymes and its clipped, stoical meter.

"The Second Coming"

Summary

The speaker describes a nightmarish scene: the falcon, turning in a widening "gyre" (spiral), cannot hear the falconer; "Things fall apart; the center cannot hold"; anarchy is loosed upon the world; "The blood-dimmed tide is loosed, and everywhere / The ceremony of innocence is drowned." The best people, the speaker says, lack all conviction, but the worst "are full of passionate intensity."

Surely, the speaker asserts, the world is near a revelation; "Surely the Second Coming is at hand." No sooner does he think of "the Second Coming," then he is troubled by "a vast image of the *Spiritus Mundi,* or the collective spirit of mankind: somewhere in the desert, a giant sphinx ("A shape with lion body and the head of a man, / A gaze as blank and pitiless as the sun") is moving, while the shadows of desert birds reel about it. The darkness drops again over the speaker's sight, but he knows that the sphinx's twenty centuries of "stony sleep" have been made a nightmare by the motions of "a rocking cradle." And what "rough beast," he wonders, "its hour come round at last, / Slouches towards Bethlehem to be born?"

Form

"The Second Coming" is written in a very rough iambic pentameter, but the meter is so loose, and the exceptions so frequent, that it actually seems closer to free verse with frequent heavy stresses. The rhymes are likewise haphazard; apart from the two couplets with which the poem opens, there are only coincidental rhymes in the poem, such as "man" and "sun."

Commentary

Because of its stunning, violent imagery and terrifying ritualistic language, "The Second Coming" is one of Yeats's most famous and most anthologized poems; it is also one of the most thematically obscure and difficult to understand. (It is safe to say that very few people who love this poem could paraphrase its meaning to satisfaction.) Structurally, the poem is quite simple—the first stanza describes the conditions present in the world (things falling apart, anarchy, etc.), and the second surmises from those conditions that a monstrous Second Coming is about to take place, not of the Jesus we first knew, but of a new messiah, a "rough beast," the slouching sphinx rousing itself in the desert and lumbering toward Bethlehem. This brief exposition, though intriguingly blasphemous, is not terribly complicated; but the question of what it should signify to a reader is another story entirely.

Yeats spent years crafting an elaborate, mystical theory of the universe that he described in his book *A Vision*. This theory issued in part from Yeats's lifelong fascination with the occult and mystical, and in part from the sense of responsibility Yeats felt to order his experience within a structured belief system. The system is extremely complicated and not of any lasting importance—except for the effect that it had on his poetry, which is of extraordinary lasting importance. The theory of history Yeats articulated in *A Vision* centers on a diagram made of two conical spirals, one inside the other, so that the widest part of one of the spirals rings around the narrowest part of the other spiral, and vice versa. Yeats believed that this image (he called the spirals "gyres") captured the contrary motions inherent within the historical process, and he divided each gyre into specific regions that represented particular kinds of historical periods (and could also represent the psychological phases of an individual's development).

"The Second Coming" was intended by Yeats to describe the current historical moment (the poem appeared in 1921) in terms of these gyres. Yeats believed that the world was on the threshold of an apocalyptic revelation, as history reached the end of the outer gyre (to speak roughly) and began moving along the inner gyre. In his definitive edition of Yeats's poems, Richard J. Finneran quotes Yeats's own notes:

The end of an age, which always receives the revelation of the character of the next age, is represented by the coming of one gyre to its place of greatest expansion and of the other to its place of greatest contraction... The revelation [that] approaches will... take its character from the contrary movement of the interior gyre...

In other words, the world's trajectory along the gyre of science, democracy, and heterogeneity is now coming apart, like the frantically widening flight-path of the falcon that has lost contact with the falconer; the next age will take its character not from the gyre of science, democracy, and speed, but from the contrary inner gyre—which, presumably, opposes mysticism, primal power, and slowness to the science and democracy of the outer gyre. The "rough beast" slouching toward Bethlehem is the symbol of this new age; the speaker's vision of the rising sphinx is his vision of the character of the new world.

This seems quite silly as philosophy or prophecy (particularly in light of the fact that it has not come true as yet). But as poetry, and understood more broadly than as a simple reiteration of the mystic theory of *A Vision*, "The Second Coming" is a magnificent statement about the contrary forces at work in history, and about the conflict between the modern world and the ancient world. The poem may not have the thematic relevance of Yeats's best work, and may not be a poem with which many people can personally identify; but the aesthetic experience of its passionate language is powerful enough to ensure its value and its importance in Yeats's work as a whole.

'The Second Coming' was written in January 1919, according to what George Yeats told Richard Ellmann (*The*

Identity of Yeats), and first appeared in *The Dial* and *The Nation* in November 1920 and then in book form in *Michael Robartes and the Dancer* (1922). Jon Stallworthy has analysed the drafting process of the poem in *Between the Lines* (and the drafts also appear in the Cornell series, *Michael Robartes and the Dancer*), showing how Yeats originally referred to Burke, Pitt and the Germans on the Russian border, but these details were removed and much of the poem's power derives from its prophetic generalisation and vagueness. In this it has Biblical resonances from the Prophets of the Old Testament, with its dismayed view of the current state of the world and its foreboding about what will come.

The opening image derives from the System and the widening gyre, an historical movement or trend that started at the birth of Christ, is figured as a falcon's towering. In the System, this gyre is accompanied by a diminishing gyre which reaches its minimum at the same time as the first reaches its widest extent, which may therefore be linked to the 'twenty centuries of stony sleep'; these gyres have the inevitability of the tides, and like them are connected to the Moon and its phases. In the symbol of the falcon, the falconer represents control but stands at the lowest point of the gyre's apex, so that, as the falcon towers higher, it can no longer hear the controlling centre.

This leads to the stark, simple statements 'Things fall apart; the centre cannot hold'. Indeed, much of the power of the opening section derives from the simplicity of its language, as well as the accumulation of symbols and images, which proceed with an oneiric logic through a single sentence: falcon's gyre widening, disintegration, anarchy, tide of blood, drowning of ceremony of innocence, weakness and passion. The word 'Mere' means both pure and only, and the first section further emphasises the generality and absoluteness of the situation with words such as 'everywhere' and 'all'. The 'Mere anarchy' which is loosed (by whom?) like a plague or scourge then becomes a tide dimmed by blood, recalling the bloody seas of the Revelation of St John, the flood from the mouth of the serpent and the vials of wrath. The phrase 'The ceremony of innocence' is linked to a poem from later in 1919, 'A Prayer for my Daughter', where the poet asks 'How but in custom and ceremony / Are innocence and beauty born?'; here the phrase suggests a vague image of whatever the reader's imagination summons (perhaps white cloth or candles?), which is then engulfed in the crimson of the multitudinous seas.

The view then moves to society and the abstract groupings of its best and worst: the best are paralysed by lack of conviction, while the worst are fired with 'passionate intensity', possibly linked to the red tide of anarchy. Yeats is constantly wary of the intoxicating or brutalising effect of fanaticism and hatred, both in himself and others, and especially in the context of the struggle for Irish independence, the Easter Rising and the Civil War: see, for example, "Easter 1916" (September 1916); "On a Political Prisoner" (January 1919); "A Prayer for My Daughter" (June 1919); "Meditations in Time of Civil War" (1921-23), especially the last two parts, VI and VII; "Remorse for Intemperate Speech" (August 1931).

The repetitions and echoes of the first section ('Turning and turning', 'loosed . . . loosed', 'falcon . . . falconer. . . fall') are emphasised at the beginning of the second section: 'Surely some revelation is at hand; /Surely the Second Coming is at hand. / The Second Coming!' The phrase used in the drafts was 'the second birth', but in the final version the idea is linked far more clearly to the Second Coming of Christ, and this is reinforced by the mention of Bethlehem in the last line. Yet if this is a second coming, it is not the second coming of Christ envisaged in Revelation or the Gospels.

The poem moves from generality to a vision experienced in the first person, which Stallworthy characterises as 'that most common Yeatsian pattern of an objective first movement passing into a more subjective second movement' (*Between the Lines*, 24). An image emerges from '*Spiritus Mundi*', the world's creative and active mind (cf. *Anima Mundi*, the world-soul), which recalls a vision that Yeats himself experienced when the

Tattwic symbol of Fire was pressed to his forehead by Mathers. Here, however, the figure is not a Titan emerging from ruins, but a figure in 'sands of the desert' like the Sphinx at Giza, which is itself probably an image of solar deity, 'A shape with lion body and the head of a man'. (It is worth noting that the sphinx was regarded in the Golden Dawn as a combination of elemental forces, particularly the 'Sphynx' of their Enochian magic, and with this appearance represents the combination of Fire and Air, or Leo [lion] and Aquarius [human] possibly therefore linked with the coming age of Aquarius.

But Yeats deliberately does not call it a sphinx, describing rather than naming it, and another source of the symbol's inspiration was slightly different: in the Introduction to *The Resurrection* he notes how, at around the time of writing *On Baile's Strand* (1904), 'I began to imagine, as always at my left side just out of the range of sight, a brazen winged beast which I associated with laughing, ecstatic destruction', noting that the beast was 'Afterwards described in my poem "The Second Coming."'. The Sphinx also appears, named in another poem from 1919, 'The Double Vision of Michael Robartes', where it takes on the Greek female form, 'A Sphinx with woman breast and lion paw', and it is possible that Yeats associated the term more fully with the murderous inquisitor of the Oedipus myth, since the name literally means strangler. In 'The Double Vision' the Sphinx is one of the 'heraldic supporters guarding the mystery of the fifteenth phase', at which a new religious dispensation starts, and symbolises the conjunction of Jupiter and Saturn which presides over the start of an *antithetical* dispensation

The image of 'The Second Coming' is no heraldic emblem but moves, its pitiless inhumanity reflected from its human head, and the reeling of the desert birds echoes the falcon's towering at the opening of the poem. The 'slow thighs' emphasise its physicality and almost sexual aura. At this stage the vision ends, but the poem's speaker then moves on to a conclusion: 'now I know'. What he knows, however, is couched in the most gnomic terms: 'That twenty centuries of stony sleep / Were vexed to nightmare by a rocking cradle'. Given Yeats's idea of the two-thousand-year cycles, one of which started at Christ's birth, we have an appropriate period (though the first printing in *The Dial* had 'thirty centuries', the drafts and all later versions have 'twenty'); but who is the sleeper? is it the stony sphinx or the world? Elsewhere, Yeats refers to the representative of the *antithetical tincture* as 'Old Rocky Face' and it is possible that he saw the ancient polytheistic past associated with the *antithetical* as having lain in stasis during the cycle of monotheism, associated with its opposite, the *primary*.

The *antithetical*awaits revivification, like 'mummy-wheat' which will sprout when it is sown again, and its dormancy has been a kind of stony sleep which might well regard the ascendancy of its opposite as a nightmare. The rocking cradle appears to allude to the baby Jesus, yet Christ is almost never pictured as lying in a cradle, rather the beasts' manger, so that in some respects Yeats divorces the nightmare's stimulus from Jesus and it may be linked to the 'Babe' of 'The Mental Traveller', who is reborn in a reversing cycle of victimage, which Yeats links to the reversing cycles of *A Vision* and the birth of a 'child or era'. The final question mark makes the last clause ambiguous, since the phrase can be read in two ways: 'now I know. . . what rough beast' and 'what rough beast?'. The question, though, predominates, since even within the framework of Yeats's System the future is uncertain: the broad outline is inevitable, but the 'particulars are the work of the *Thirteenth Cone* or cycle', which represents the divine, so that *A Vision* itself ends in a series of questions. Yeats therefore knows that this coming is of a 'rough beast',that the beast's hour has 'come round at last', the phrasing indicating the cyclical nature of this hour, and that it slouches towards Bethlehem, but still questions its nature. The word 'Slouches' adds to the sinister aura, with its precise, feline blend of casualness and stalking, but despite the sensuousness of this verb and of the 'slow thighs', the beast has not yet been born into the physical world.

The beast's birth at Bethlehem links it to the birth of Jesus, but Bethlehem is more a symbolic state than a geographical place (like Blake's Jerusalem, for instance). In the System of *A Vision*, Yeats indicates that the coming Avatar, or divine incarnation, because it is *antithetical* will be multiple rather than single, and he represents the classical predecessor of Christ in a variety of ways. In one guise, the counterpart is Oedipus, who 'lay upon the eath at the middle point between four sacred objects. . . and he sank down soul and body into the earth. I would have him balance Christ who, crucified standing up, went into the abstract sky soul and body. . . .'. In the poem 'Leda and the Swan' (also titled just 'Leda'), however, he sees the rape of Leda by Zeus in the form of a swan as the heroic age's key moment: 'I imagine the annunciation that founded Greece as made to Leda. . . .'. It is the counterpart to the annunciation to Mary by the Holy Ghost, represented by a dove, and he titles the section of *A Vision* on historical cycles 'Dove or Swan'. Leda's daughter, Helen, precipitates the Trojan War and her other daughter, Clytemnestra, kills her husband, Agamemnon: 'A shudder in the loins engenders there / The broken wall, the burning roof and tower / And Agamemnon dead'. It is a form of this classical *antithetical* annunciation, similar to that of the Swan but different, which will be repeated.

Who Goes with Fergus?

Summary

The poet asks who will follow King Fergus' example and leave the cares of the world to know the wisdom of nature. He exhorts young men and women alike to leave off brooding over "love's bitter mystery" and to turn instead to the mysterious order of nature, over which Fergus rules.

Analysis

This short poem is full of mystery and complexity. It was James Joyce's favourite poem, and figures in his famous novel *Ulysses,* where Stephen Daedalus sings it to his dying mother.

On one level, the poem represents Yeats' exhortation to the young men and women of his day to give over their political and emotional struggles in exchange for a struggle with the lasting mysteries of nature. He suggests that Fergus was both brave and wise to give up his political ambition in exchange for the wisdom of the Druids, as depicted in the poem "Fergus and the Druid." Of course, from that poem we know that Fergus' sacrifice was complicated. He did not find a life of frolic and happiness with the Druids. But he did find knowledge, wisdom and perspective - perhaps, indeed, too much.

On a second level, the poem captures Yeats' frustration at his own failed love affair. He seems desperate to turn from the contemplation of love's mysteries that have preoccupied him for so many of the poems in *The Rose*, convinced that this meditation has only increased his sorrow without providing any means of improving his situation. The exhortation, on this level, is directed inward, to his own heart. He challenges himself to take Fergus' direction and leave love behind him.

Moreover, the fact that Yeats draws upon the imagery of Fergus to make his point suggests his inclination to reference the mythic and legendary heritage of his country rather than the present political struggles that engaged Ireland. In this light, the question, "Who goes with Fergus?" seems to ask Ireland to join him in contemplating the mythic past rather than the sticky present. A return to Fergus entails a move away from the reference points of contemporary politics, toward the mythology of the Irish people.

Finally, the poem suggests the journey toward death. A return to nature, as also seen in the previous poem, "The Countess Cathleen in Paradise," expresses a movement away from worldly cares and possessions analogous to death. Yeats summons the courage that one requires to look beyond the mysteries one knows and suffers under - those of love, of politics - to deeper and weirder mysteries - the wood, the sea, the wandering stars.

In all, the poem has a beauty, especially when spoken aloud, that evades simple readings and analyses. It captures the political, social, emotional and national ambiguity at the heart of Yeats' collection, as well as his reverence for the imagination.

Cuchulain's Fight with the Sea

Summary

A swineherd comes to Emer, his mother, who is making clothing, and says that he does not need to watch the road anymore. Emer throws down her web, and raises her hands reddened with dye and cries out loud.

She asks him what if his master comes home triumphant, why would he be afraid? He is too strong to idle away his life as a swineherd.

He asks where he can find his father, and she says in the Red Branch camp. Cuchulain lives among these men, and even King Conchubar sings his praise. Cuchulain notices that the swineherd has invaded their camp, and fights the young man - his son, though he does not know that - remarking that the stranger looks like a woman he once loved.

As Cuchulain kills the swineherd, the youth reveals that he is Cuchulain's son. Cuchulain is so full of grief and rage that King Conchubar is afraid that he will slaughter them all. He asks the druids to chant ancient spells into Cuchulain's ears, so that when he arises, enraged, he will fight the sea rather than humans.

Analysis

Although Yeats writes poetry that is lyric in form, the subject matter of this piece is epic, in the style of Homer or the ancient Irish bards. It has a clear narrative with a beginning, middle and end. The poem enacts a familiar Oedipal struggle. Instead of the son slaying his father, as is the case in the Oedipus myth, the father, Cuchulain, slays his son. Madness ensues.

Cuchulain's fight with the sea is based on a tale from the ancient Irish sagas, in which the hero loses touch with his wife, Emer. Emer urges her son to find his father and wreak revenge on him, but Cuchulain is so powerful that he slaughters him.

Fergus and the Druid

Summary

This poem is expressed in a conversation between Fergus and a druid. The druid, at first only asks him what he would like to do.

Fergus says that he has followed the druid for the whole day as he changed shapes, and that now he finally holds a human form. He recounts how young Conchubar sat at his side, and seemed so wise that he gave his crown to him, to ease his own sorrows. He tried to become one of the people, but failed, still feeling like a king. Fergus then expresses a desire to be as wise as a druid, despite the druid's warnings that such wisdom severs one from humanity.

The druid gives him a bag of dreams to open. Fergus sees what he has been in his life, but sees it all as a web of sorrow. Knowing all, he is filled with sadness.

Analysis

This poem primarily treats the isolation of a king who is weary of his rule and his social role. King Fergus is an Irish historical figure who figures in the Tain. Fergus fell in love with Ness, and gave up his throne to Conchubar, who was the son of Ness by another marriage. Myths look on this variously as an usurption and as a source of great happiness for Fergus, who did not enjoy being king.

Yeats's version of the myth is somewhat consistent with both interpretations. Fergus is ambivalent about whether he did the right thing in surrendering his throne. He has not assimilated into non-royal society. He seeks the help of a druid, an ancient healing or religious figure in Celtic societies, to clarify whether he has made the right choice.

The druid's help, which comes in the form of a "slate-coloured thing" which refers both to the bag of dreams and, perhaps, to the grave. With the help of this bag of dreams, Fergus "know[s] all" at the poem's end. But this knowledge does not quell his anxiety; rather, it sinks him into depression.

By knowing all, he has robbed himself of the hope that comes with uncertainty. He is as sure as death, and as futureless

The Lake Isle of Innisfree

Summary

Yeats expresses his desire to build a small cabin at Innisfree, out of natural materials, and live alone.

He will find peace on the lake, where it drops from the morning, and the beautiful midnight.

He determines to leave immediately, because even when he stands in a road or on a city pavement, he hears the lapping of the lake waters in his heart.

Analysis

Yeats's profession of love for nature is one of his most famous and beautiful poems. It is unusual in this collection as it contains no references to the Irish nationalist movement, to Maude Gonne, or to ancient Irish mythology. Yeats first wrote the poem in London, in 1890, where he was feeling intensely homesick.

Innisfree, whose name means "heather island" in Gaelic, is an island off the coast of Ireland of intense natural beauty. It is located in County Sligo, which is where Yeats's mother's family came from, and which he identified as the part of Ireland and the world closest to his heart. In the idea of building a home there and living as a hermit, Yeats was influenced by American transcendentalists such as Thoreau. He wrote in a letter: "My father read to me some passage out of *Walden,* and I planned to live some day in a cottage on a little island called Innisfree

The Sorrow of Love

Summary

The poem follows a loose narrative. In the first stanza, natural images overshadow the sorrow of humankind. In the second, a figure with "red mournful lips" arises, seeming to carry with her the weight of epic tragedy. She moves into the natural world, and the images that seemed sufficient in themselves - the sparrow, the moon - now express the infinite sadness of human misery.

Analysis

This poem was written in 1891, only two years after Yeats met and fell in love with Maud Gonne. Yeats uses two classical allusions in the highly structured poem, one comparing the woman's doom to Odysseus, who helped in the expedition to recover Helen when Paris took her from Sparta. He only returned after ten years. "Proud as Priam" refers to Paris's father, who was killed by Achilles's son, Neoptolemus, after the fall of Troy.

Before the woman's presence in this poem, the world exists apart from humankind. It's natural beauty and struggle "blot out" the more complicated struggles of humankind. The influence of the mournful woman, though, invites human meaning into the poem. First, the woman inspires the poet with epic comparisons; then, when she moves out into nature, she recasts the moon, sparrow and leaves in terms of human sorrow.

Yeats thus suggests the inspiring, albeit sorrowful, nature of love - both in terms of a particular beloved and in terms of the feminine in general. The beautiful woman does not "compose" the natural elements around her, but her influence renders them incapable of expressing any meaning other than that of humankind. Whether the woman stands for Ireland, for Maud Gonne, or for the spirit of the feminine, she redefines the force of the world, focusing it into an expression of human sorrow.

The White Birds

Summary

The poet wishes that he and his beloved could escape from their circumstances and be together. This wish is captured in the image of the two of them transformed into white birds floating on the sea-foam. He asks his beloved not to concentrate on temporal and sorrowful images - the fading meteor, the rose and lily - and reiterates his desire to be apart from the world with her, as white birds together.

Analysis

Yeats composed this poem for Maud Gonne's in 1892 when the pair went for a walk along the cliffs of Howth, a seaside village just south of Dublin. The poem was written the day after Yeats had unsuccessfully proposed to her for the first time. Gonne reecalls that she said that she would rather be a seagull than any other bird. Yeats sent her this poem three days later.

The "Danaan Shore" refers to Tier-nan-Oge (or Tir na nOg in Gaelic), an imaginary land where mortals live as long as fairies. Yeats interpreted Gonne's wish to become a seagull as a wish for freedom from sorrow and time. He wishes, in vain, that they could escape the political and social circumstances that keep them apart, whether on an isolated island, in a mythic environment, or by becoming white birds.

A Dream of Death

Summary

The poet dreams that his loved one had died in a foreign place among strangers. The peasants nail her coffin shut, raise a rude cross above her coffin, and plant cypress trees around the grave. They leave her to the "indifferent stars" until the finds her and writes her epitaph: "She was more beautiful than thy first love / But now lies under boards."

Analysis

The poem is based on Maude Gonne's journey to France to recover from fatigue. She had a predisposition to tuberculosis, so Yeats was worried that she would die in France, among strangers. He sent her this poem while she was there.

Perhaps more than any other, the poem expresses a conventionally Romantic disposition in Yeats. The setting - a foreign land - the subject - lonely death - and the upshot - that the poet can play a role in immortalizing the death of a beauty - are common themes in Romantic poetry. For instance, Wordsworth's famous poem "She Walked in Beauty" touches upon the same themes

The Man who Dreamed of Faeryland

Summary

This poem uses surreal imagery to describe visions of an imaginary world from the point of view of a man before and after his burial. In the first stanza, the man is in a crowd, thinking about his beloved, but he is shaken out of his ease when a pile of fish sing about a forgotten isle where people love eternally. The man next wanders on the beach of Lisadell, and the worms too sing about the isle, though he doesn't understand them. Again, at Scanavin, the grass sings to him.

In the final stanza, we find the man buried under the hill of Lugnagall where he hopes to know eternal peace. But the worms proclaim that God has made a beautiful pattern in the sky. The man does not rest in peace.

Analysis

The title of this poem is somewhat misleading. The man in the poem is invited to contemplate Faeryland, but he repeatedly fails to do so. He cannot "listen" to the songs of the fish, the worms, the grass, who could tell him of Faeryland. Faeryland, in this poem, might be thought of as a place of universals and absolutes, where truths are unqualified by human context. The man never gives up his petty loves and hates, and so cannot attain eternity even in his death.

The naturalistic imagery in the poem, as well as the specific place names that Yeats assigns to where the man wanders, stems from his experience as a youth in Sligo. Sligo is a county in westernmost Ireland, a place that Yeats said affected his poetry more than anywhere else in the world. The images of fish, worms and other natural creatures also resonate with Yeats' expressed aim in "The Rose upon the Rood of Time" that he wishes to notice the lowly things in the world, not just the searing bright things. Indeed, in this poem, it is the lowly, overlooked creatures who contain a spark of divinity. They are the key to eternal contemplation. The man, like many of us, remains deaf to them.

"The Man Who dreamed of Faeryland" is similar to "Who goes with Fergus?" in that the poet implicitly urges Irish men and women to return to nature. Indeed, "Faeryland" evokes very strongly the spirit of the druids, who felt that all natural things contain the divine. Yeats asks that his countrymen reflect upon the land that they purport to love and defend in their political battles. He also suggests that the ultimate value in life is to be found in such contemplation, not in the temporary concerns of politics.

The Dedication to a Book of Stories selected from the Irish Novelists

Summary

Yeats imagines a time when the Irish ruled Eire (Ireland). He envisions a green branch hung with bells. These bells sang in the weather - sometimes happy, sometimes sad - and charmed the people of Ireland away from their daily tasks to think upon them. Yeats suggests that however hard times may be in Ireland - where times can be very bad indeed - the bells and the memories they summon make one forget the petty injustice and bitterness of daily life.

Analysis

Yeats touches upon a theme familiar in from the two preceding poems. Those poems suggested that it is worthwhile for the Irish to return to the eternities that follow from contemplating nature. This poem illustrates, in the image of the bell tree, how such contemplation can carry one away from the bitter cares of being Irish and reunite one with Ireland's mythic, peaceful past.

This poem is nostalgic for the old Eire (Gaelic for Ireland). Yeats imagines that peace existed in ancient Ireland, which is hard or even impossible to recapture after the arrival of the English. "A Book of Stories Selected from the Irish Novelists" thus describes a pre-colonized country, even before the invaders have withdrawn.

Munster and Connemara refer to two provinces which were designated before the English arrival. Munster is the southern province, while Connemara is an area in County Galway, facing the Atlantic Ocean.

The Rose

The Rose is a collection of twenty-two poems that W.B. Yeats published in 1893. It was only his second lyrical collection, but contains many of his famous mythological poems. At this point in his life, Yeats was steeped deeply into the world of ancient Ireland, characterized in popular imagination as the "isle of saints and scholars." He evoked his legendary home country and its fantastical creatures with a poetic vocabulary at once lush and precise.

Yeats wrote these poems under the influence of Maude Gonne, his great unrequited love. Though Gonne resisted his wooing at the time of *The Rose,* her rejection of him was not yet definitive. Thus the poems in this collection lack the pensive sadness that typifies his later style, instead tending toward whimsy and wonder at the beauty of his beloved. Yeats' approach to Ireland in *The Rose* likewise reflects the influence of Gonne, whose dark beauty came to embody Ireland in his imagination; though Gonne was a fierce nationalist, however, Yeats treats his home country with a more mythic than nationalistic style. Ireland in the 1890s was a political place, but few at this time suspected the impending nationalist fervor that would sweep through Ireland in the twentieth century. Yeats was a politically involved individual at the time of composition of *The Rose* - for instance, he was a member of the Gaelic League - but he was not a radical by any means.

Thus his celebration of Ireland, as recorded in this collection, is largely symbolic and apolitical. The unifying symbol of this collection of poetry is found in its title: *The Rose*. Yeats uses the rose to mean a variety of things, but it always stands for untamed Irish beauty in one way or another. Ireland is called "Roisin Dubh" in Irish mythology, which translates from the Irish language as "the dark rose." His transfiguration of the rich natural and narrative history of his homeland into poetry is the unifying force behind the poems in the collection. Like its namesake flower, Yeats' collection is at once beautiful, sensual and thorny. Taken as a whole, these poems comprise the young Yeats' homage to his homeland.

The Countess Cathleen in Paradise

Summary

The poem describes the Countess Cathleen after her death. She has left behind the raiment and pride of her worldly existence and walks with mournful beauty. She dances among the angels and all the universe in in accord with Heaven.

Analysis

The Countess Cathleen is a figure out of Irish legend. Yeats later wrote a play about her, in fact. According to her legend, a famine strikes Ireland and Satan sends demons to buy the souls of the starving Irish. The Countess sells her vast estates and possessions in order to purchase the people food and to keep them from selling their souls. She is thwarted by Satan, however, and eventually sacrifices her own life for the Irish poor.

The Countess' legendary donation of her worldly possessions takes on an otherworldly aspect in this poem. It suggests that Cathleen, in giving over her body, lets go of her heavy burden. She dances lightly and wisely in the heavens, celebrating her sacrifice and her role in the grand order of the universe.

The Pity of Love

Summary

An inexpressible pity hides within love. The people who are engaged in trade, the cold wind, and the hazel grove all threaten the poet's beloved.

Analysis

The object of Yeats's affection in this poem, as in all poems of this period, is Maud Gonne. Yeats takes a self-pitying note, arguing that he is wretched due to his experience of unrequited love. He cannot even experience the innocuous pleasures of nature - "the shadowy hazel grove" - without feeling his love for Gonne to be threatened.

Yeats is quite right in worrying that any number of natural or social phenonomena might take his love away from him. Maud Gonne was deeply involved in Irish nationalism, a movement for which Yeats had complicated feelings. The "folk who are buying and selling" could represent those who were negotiating Ireland's future - in Ireland of the 1890s, that was the Home Rule party, led by John Redmond. The result of these negotiations could and did affect Yeats's relationship with Gonne. Because they were unsuccessful, Gonne radicalized further, moving away from Yeats' politics.

The Lamentation of the Old Pensioner

Summary

The poem is spoken from the point of view of an old man who looks upon the political and romantic obsessions of the young Irish. He suggests that once upon a time he too "talked of love and politics" but that now, with his age and perspective, his thoughts rest on Time and eternal questions. In the final stanza we learn that these meditations are not pleasant, as he suggests that no woman pay him attention due to his age, though he still recalls the women he once loved. The poem ends as he curses Time, which has changed him from young to old.

Analysis

This poem is based on a conversation that Yeats had with an elderly poet. He wrote in a letter that the peom was "little more than a translation into verse of the very words of an old Wicklow peasant." Wicklow, by the way, is a green, rural county south of Dublin. This precise technique of observation of peasants is what Yeats later recommended to J.M. Synge upon meeting him in Paris, and which led to successful works like *The Playboy of the Western World*.

The elderly peasant's lamentation is that time has transformed him into someone that is no longer important or viable. This is in contrast to Yeats's other, more wistful and gentle portrayal of age in the rest of the collection. The pikes to which the "old pensioner" refers are the weapons traditionally used in nationalist uprisings against the British, which the man is too old for, so regards as futile.

This poem complicates Yeats' earlier poems, many of which exhort the Irish to contemplate eternal questions like Time rather than take up their pikes, so to speak, for a passing political issue. This old man, who is forced away from politics and love, shows the downside of such contemplative non-participation in life. Of course, he is still tormented by the passions of his youth for women and conversation, and so his meditations aren't exactly what Yeats has in mind in poems like "Who Goes with Fergus?" and "The Man Who Dreamed of Faeryland."

To Ireland in the Coming Times

Summary

The poet declares that he would like to be considered among the poets who have sweetened Ireland's miserable history with songs and rhymes. He asks that he be judged this way despite the presence of a woman throughout the poems.

He wishes to be considered alongside Davis, Mangan, and Ferguson, because his rhymes like their tales tell of death, and of fairies and druids. The poet further suggests that these tales are not the simple legends and entertainments they may seem at first reading, but that he has captured dark and elusive human truths in his poems if one cares to delve for them.

The poet says, indeed, that his poems are a document of his complex human heart, which we should look into because life is very short and we should make room for such abstract meditations as those on God, time, love and dream, lest they pass us by altogether.

Analysis

This poem was first published under the title "Apologia addressed to Ireland in the coming days." It is a defensive action on the part of Yeats, who wishes to explain that his love for Maud Gonne, which is so foregrounded in the collection, is an important part of the struggle for Irish independence. He thinks that his nationalism is not to be considered less than older patriots.

Those whom he mentions specifically are Thomas Osborne Davis (1814-45) who was the leader of the Young Ireland party and wrote poetry; James Clarence Mangan (1803-49) who was a translator and Irish romantic poet; and Sir Samuel Ferguson (1810-86), a poet who translated Gaelic legends into English.

Moreover, Yeats invites us to consider the role of poetic contemplation in a world torn by political strife. He argues that it is very easy to get caught up in the day to day, to forget the eternal realm of dreams that poetry has access to. Indeed, Yeats offers his poet's heart - the various dimensions of which he has expressed in the ensuing poems - as his contribution to Irish independence.

He is a warrior of the imagination, a present-day druid, offering respite and wisdom to a present-day Fergus or Cuchulain. And this contribution, he suggests throughout his poems, is as vital as any party affiliation could possibly be.

To Some I have Talked with by the Fire

Summary

The poet writes that while composing poetry he thinks back on times he talked at the fireside of "the dark men" - i.e. the dark urges and warlike deeds - within passionate people. They also discuss the mix of sorrow and content that comes with a passionless life, and of the music of swords on the battlefield.

Analysis

This poem anticipates some of Yeats's later work (especially after he began to be influenced by Ezra Pound) in its spareness and its lack of specifically Irish allusions. The poem is bleak and full of ambiguous images, spilling from descriptions of the ways men engage battle to a weird bat-like image at the poem's end.

The poem can be read as a reflection on Yeats' own writing. It begins, "When I wrought out these fitful Danaan rhymes," inviting us to consider the poem as a document of Yeats' imaginative process. Indeed the poem touches upon several of the identities captured in the preceding poems - the passionate dark individualist, the sorrowful resigned soul, the multitudes at battle. And through it all, Yeats spins eerie images of bats and animals, which seem both to refer to his poems about communion with nature, but which also seem like expressions of pure, inexplicable imaginative fire. He is capturing for us - performing for us - the free-associative brilliance that makes his poetry so challenging and rewarding.

On a more concrete level, the "blossoming dream" is possibly an allusion to Irish Republicanism. The 'Republic of Eire' was a name that could not be spoken in Ireland, as it had dangerous nationalist connotations. Hence the description of the multitudes rising up in battle with the 'Ineffable Name' on their lips, which might well represent the Republicans striving against England for liberty.

A Faery Song

Summary

Fairies sing a song over the burial monument of Diarmuid and Grania. They sing that the pair is "old and gay," and ask for them to be given rest away from human life.

The fairies say that they are also old and gay, maybe thousands of years old.

Analysis

Yeats begins the poem with a play on the cliche "old and gray," describing the mythical pair as "old and gay." This demonstrates a nostalgia for the ancient Irish period of heroes and scholars, and, importantly, the lack of a British presence in Ireland.

Diarmuid and Grania belong to an ancient Irish tale. Diarmuid was an infantryman in the army called the Fianna, which fought for the ancient hero Finn MacCumhall. Finn wanted to marry Grania, but she ran away with Diarmuid. Finn eventually killed Diarmuid, and thus regained Grania's attentions for himself.

A Cradle Song

Summary

Yeats stands over the cradle of an infant, noting that the angels, sick of the dead, are also there. God is pleased in heaven, as are the "Sailing Seven" to see such a well-behaved infant. Yeats kisses the infant, sad because he knows that he will miss the baby as it grows up.

Analysis

This sweet, simple poem takes a much more traditional, rhyming form than most of Yeats's work. Rather than being a free-form lyrical poem, it is three stanzas of four lines each, rhyming in the pattern ABAB CDCD EFEF. Each line is two iambs.

The "sailing seven" refers to either the planets, or the seven stars of the Pleiades. They link the child to a cosmic order, suggesting that an infants pleasure not only affects human beings, but resonates with the order of the universe as a whole.

The Ballad of Father Gilligan

Summary

Yeats tells a story in verse. An old priest was weary and sad because most of his flock had died. He was sent for by a sick man, but fell asleep in his chair before answering the call. The stars multiplied and God talked to mankind.

In the morning, Father Gilligan awoke with a start, realizing that he had not done his duty. He rides to the sick man's house where his wife answers the door and says that the man has died. Father Gilligan is horrified and cries "mavrone!" until the woman thanks him for coming the previous night. He falls to his knees and thanks God for sending an angel down to do his work when he was too tired to do so.

Analysis

This poem takes a ballad form - a traditional form, usually sung, with regular, short stanzas that tell a story. It has a more overtly religious content than most of Yeats's poems. As a protestant who turned to theosophy and mysticism, Yeats usually stays away from Catholic themes. Yeats also usually stays away from the Irish language, which he uses in this poem when he writes, "mavrone!" which is the Irish, "mo bhron," a cry of grief.

The poem not only speaks to the poverty of rural Ireland, but also to their extreme religiosity. The priest is horrified by the fact that he did not make it to the bedside of the sick man before he died because no one performed the rites of extreme unction, meaning in the Catholic tradition that the man did not die in a state of grace, and therefore cannot go to heaven. The divine intervention which caused this not to be the case is an affirmation of a loving, kind God.

Yeats intends this ballad as an homage to the traditional poetry and legend of his country. He was a collector of similar Irish stories and songs and appreciated their immediate, naive beauty. Certainly this tale draws upon the character as well as the form of the traditional Irish ballad.

The Two Trees

Summary

The poet invites his beloved to look inside her heart, where a holy tree grows. Joy shakes its leaves. The shaking of the tree has made him murmur a wizard song for you.

The poet continues, telling his beloved not to look into the mirror, or only for a little while, because a dangerous image grows there. All things turn to barrenness and mirrors hold the image of out tiredness. In those frightening places the ravens of unresting thought fly, and make one's eyes unkind.

Analysis

This poem, like many that are addressed to Maud Gonne, contrasts her inward with her outward beauty. On a simple level, the poem suggests that the beloved look within herself to the spirit of her nature (the tree), which he himself loves. Further, she should shun the mirror, which captures her external appearance. Her appearance, though beautiful now, will fade with age. Her inner tree, though, will never grow any less beautiful.

On a more arcane level, the holy tree could refer either to the tree of knowledge or to the Sephirotic tree of the Kabbalah. The Sephirotic tree resonates with both good and evil. This poem would fit with the Kabbalic notion of man, which is divided between good and evil. Looking in a glass makes the tree into its reverse image, barren and threatening. Yeats was certainly familiar with the Kabbalah from his theosophic practices.

When You Are Old

Summary

Yeats exhorts his beloved: when you are old and falling asleep by your fire, take down this book, and dream of how you used to be as you read it.

Dream of how many people loved you when you were younger. Only one man loved you as you grew older.

Murmur to yourself sadly about how Love paced on the mountains and hid his face in stars as you grew old.

Analysis

Like so many of the poems in this collection, "When You Are Old" was written for Maud Gonne. It is based on Ronsard's "Quand Vous Serez Bien Vieille," *Sonnets Pour Helene* (1578), which maintains the Maud Gonne/Helen of Troy parallel that Yeats so often draws. The idea of love in age is an ancient one, meant to express the fact that love inheres not merely in youth, but in something deeper and more lasting.

Yeats capitalizes "Love," thus personifying the concept, which is is a nod to the poem's 16th century roots. Although monotheism had taken over Europe, Greek and Roman gods were very much a part of 16th century consciousness. Yeats's "Love" is a modernization of the ancient figure, Eros

"Lapis Lazuli,"

The speaker begins by telling us that "the hysterical women" are disgusted with artists who are always detached, because the times demand some serious action or else they will all be obliterated.

Yeats wrote this poem in 1938 just as WWII was beginning in Europe. So those women are fearing they will be become victims of the airplane and Zeppelins that were used to bomb

London during WWI. The allusion to "King Billy bomb-balls in" is a pun on William III at the Battle of the Boyne and Kaiser Wilhelm.

First Stanza

Yeats takes his line from an anonymous ballad that appeared in the Irish Ministry: "King James pitched his tents between / The lines for to retire; / but King William threw his bomb-balls in, / And set them all on fire." *Yeats fashions his pun this way: "... Aeroplane and Zeppelin will come out, / Pitch like King Billy bomb-balls in / Until the town lie beaten flat." So the first stanza sets the stage for Yeats' commentary on remaining tranquil under stressful events, but unlike the "hysterical women," the speaker of the poem feels that art is the way to transcending the chaos.

Second Stanza

The second stanza begins, "All perform their tragic play, / There struts Hamlet, there is Lear, / That's Ophelia, that Cordelia...." These lines liken "real life" to the stage. The actors portray their roles without "break[ing] up their lines to weep." The actors do not stop to cry over the tragedy that befalls their characters, because they know "that Hamlet and Lear are gay; / Gaiety transforming all that dread."

The term "gay" for Yeats' era had a different set of connotations from those we 21st century Americans attach to it. It did not refer to homosexuality, nor did it refer to lighthearted fun. The term's meaning was closer to impetuous or possessing a lack of seriousness, not given to deep depression about one's lot in life. Actors, even while portraying a grieving character like a Hamlet or a Lear, remain detached. And even if all the curtains on all stages drop at once, "It cannot grow by an inch or an ounce." "It" refers to tragedy— "Tragedy wrought to its uttermost." The art of the theatre provides the actors a way of transcending the tragedy, even as they perform it.

Third Stanza

The third stanza reminds us that "Old civilisations [have been] put to the sword." Civilizations have risen and fallen, like great waves of the sea. It is a gloomy thought, but "they (the civilizations) and their wisdom went to rack." Then the speaker reminds us that the art of Callimachus, "who handled marble as if it were bronze" is now gone. But then "All things fall"—then we have a glimmer of optimism, because even though they fall, they "are built again."

Yeats was given a lapis lazuli carving in 1935 by Harry Clifton (Henry Talbot de Vere Clifton), the poet to whom Yeats dedicates this poem. Now we come to the last two stanzas for which the poem is titled. The carving on lapis lazuli features a scene wherein three Chinese men are climbing up a mountain. A long-legged bird flies overhead, and Yeats tells us that bird is "A symbol of longevity." Also, one of the Chinese men, Yeats assumes, is a servant, because he carries a musical instrument.

The three men are trekking up the mountain toward what Yeats calls a "little half-way house." But I imagine that little house to be a temple. Yeats interprets the edifice as something resembling an Irish pub, where the men will stop for a drink, listen to some mournful melodies and then trek on. I think the men are Buddhist monks who will stop at the temple to worship; the musical instrument will be used in chanting.

Individual Interpretation

I would like to add that this is a place where interpretation can be free for the individual. There is nothing in the poem that determines the little edifice is either a pub or a temple. Because I have not seen the craving which Yeats is describing, I base my interpretation on the paintings of the artist Sesshu, who traveled widely in China, painting scenes very much like the one Yeats describes.

But the final point may be made, whether we take the little half-way house as pub or temple. Yeats writes: "I / Delight to imagine them seated there; / There, on the mountain and the sky, / On all the tragic scene they stare." So Yeats has taken us from Western civilization that rises and falls with tragedy to the East where tragedy still exists.

Art and Religion

"One asks for mournful melodies; / Accomplished fingers begin to play": The Chinese men's listening to mournful melodies parallels the Western theatre audience watching Hamlet or King Lear, and as they watch, "Their eyes mid many wrinkles, their eyes, / Their ancient, glittering eyes, are gay," that is, they are detached, whether listening to the mournful melody or chanting in worship.

Art, similar to religion, from theatre to poetry to music has the power to help the human mind and heart transcend the pain of tragedy for the ancients as well as for the contemporaries in both Western and Eastern culture.

"Sailing to Byzantium"

Summary

The speaker, referring to the country that he has left, says that it is "no country for old men": it is full of youth and life, with the young lying in one another's arms, birds singing in the trees, and fish swimming in the waters. There, "all summer long" the world rings with the "sensual music" that makes the young neglect the old, whom the speaker describes as "Monuments of unageing intellect."

An old man, the speaker says, is a "paltry thing," merely a tattered coat upon a stick, unless his soul can clap its hands and sing; and the only way for the soul to learn how to sing is to study "monuments of its own magnificence." Therefore, the speaker has "sailed the seas and come / To the holy city of Byzantium." The speaker addresses the sages "standing in God's holy fire / As in the gold mosaic of a wall," and asks them to be his soul's "singing-masters." He hopes they will consume his heart away, for his heart "knows not what it is"—it is "sick with desire / And fastened to a dying animal," and the speaker wishes to be gathered "Into the artifice of eternity."

The speaker says that once he has been taken out of the natural world, he will no longer take his "bodily form" from any "natural thing," but rather will fashion himself as a singing bird made of hammered gold, such as Grecian goldsmiths make "To keep a drowsy Emperor awake," or set upon a tree of gold "to sing / To lords and ladies of Byzantium / Or what is past, or passing, or to come."

Form

The four eight-line stanzas of "Sailing to Byzantium" take a very old verse form: they are metered in iambic pentameter, and rhymed ABABABCC, two trios of alternating rhyme followed by a couplet.

Commentary

"Sailing to Byzantium" is one of Yeats's most inspired works, and one of the greatest poems of the twentieth century. Written in 1926 and included in Yeats's greatest single collection, 1928's *The Tower*, "Sailing to Byzantium" is Yeats's definitive statement about the agony of old age and the imaginative and spiritual work required to remain a vital individual even when the heart is "fastened to a dying animal" (the body). Yeats's solution is to leave the country of the young and travel to Byzantium, where the sages in the city's famous gold mosaics (completed mainly during the sixth and seventh centuries) could become the "singing-masters" of his soul. He hopes the sages will appear in fire and take him away from his body into an existence outside time, where, like a great work of art, he could exist in "the artifice of eternity." In the astonishing final stanza of the poem, he declares that once he is out of his body he will never again appear in the form of a natural thing; rather, he will become a golden bird, sitting on a golden tree, singing of the past ("what is past"), the present (that which is "passing"), and the future (that which is " to come").

A fascination with the artificial as superior to the natural is one of Yeats's most prevalent themes. In a much earlier poem, 1899's "The Lover Tells of the Rose in His Heart," the speaker expresses a longing to re-make the world "in a casket of gold" and thereby eliminate its ugliness and imperfection. Later, in 1914's "The Dolls," the speaker writes of a group of dolls on a shelf, disgusted by the sight of a human baby. In each case, the artificial (the golden casket, the beautiful doll, the golden bird) is seen as perfect and unchanging, while the natural (the world, the human baby, the speaker's body) is prone to ugliness and decay.

What is more, the speaker sees deep spiritual truth (rather than simply aesthetic escape) in his assumption of artificiality; he wishes his soul to learn to sing, and transforming into a golden bird is the way to make it capable of doing so.

"Sailing to Byzantium" is an endlessly interpretable poem, and suggests endlessly fascinating comparisons with other important poems—poems of travel, poems of age, poems of nature, poems featuring birds as symbols. (One of the most interesting is surely Keats's "Ode to a Nightingale," to which this poem is in many ways a rebuttal: Keats writes of his nightingale, "Thou wast not born for death, immortal Bird! / No hungry generations tread thee down"; Yeats, in the first stanza of "Sailing to Byzantium," refers to "birds in the trees" as "those dying generations.") It is important to note that the poem is not autobiographical; Yeats did not travel to Byzantium (which was renamed Constantinople in the fourth century A.D., and later renamed Istanbul), but he did argue that, in the sixth century, it offered the ideal environment for the artist. The poem is about an imaginative journey, not an actual one.

And in the frosty season

About the poem

An extract from *The Prelude* by William Wordsworth (1770-1850). *The Prelude* is a very long autobiographical poem, with the alternative title *Growth of a Poet's Mind*. The passage here comes from the first book of twelve. The whole poem is several hundred pages long in standard print size.

What is the Poem about?

Wordsworth describes skating on a frozen lake just as night is falling. Comment on the information about time; what the poet could see, in different directions; the various sounds made by him and his friends and the way these echoed off the surrounding features of the landscape; the games he and his friends were playing; what is the poet describing at the end of the second section?

Word Study

This poem was first published in 1805. It contains many words not used nowadays, and many other words which are used differently today from the way Wordsworth uses them.For each one, write an explanation of how it is used in the poem, whether it is still used today, and whether it has changed meaning.

The Host of the Air

About the poem

This poem is an English version of an old Gaelic (Irish) ballad which the poet heard sung and translated in Ballisodare, County Sligo. In the original poem, the husband (O'Driscoll) finds mourners weeping for his wife when he comes home.

What is the poem about?

Yeats tells a story about a man who works apparently as a kind of game-keeper driving water-fowl from reed beds (perhaps for wildfowlers to shoot). He falls asleep and has a strange dream about his newly-wed wife. First he sees a group of dancers, then he is invited to eat bread and drink wine, which have magical qualities. Next he is invited to play cards with a band of old men, while his bride is stolen from him by a handsome young man. At this, he scatters the cards away and wakes, only to hear, still playing the strange piping music he heard in his dream.

*"The host of the air" refers to the bread and wine. In the Roman Catholic church service of mass, the bread and wine represent Jesus, who is the "Host" of the meal which the worshippers share.

The Cap and Bells

About the poem

This ballad comes from the same collection of poems (*The Wind Among the Reeds*, 1899) as *The Host of the Air*. Both poems relate events which are dreamed. *The Host of the Air* is an anonymous ballad, originally sung in Irish, and translated by Yeats; the story in it may be believed by the singer's audience. *The Cap and Bells* is Yeats's memory of a dream of his own.

What is the poem about?

Yeats tells a story about a jester who tries to impress a young queen. He sends her his soul and his heart, but she ignores him. Finally, he sends his jester's cap and bells, and she is happy to accept the gift. Like The Host of the Air, this poem has an ambiguous (unclear) ending: we do not know if the queen and the jester have anything more to do with each other.

Night Mail

About the poem

This poem was written by W.H. Auden (1907-1973) to be a commentary for a documentary film made in 1936, and also called *Night Mail*. Near the end of the 24-minute film this poem is read by Auden to the accompaniment of music composed by Benjamin Britten.

"Leda and the Swan"

Summary

The speaker retells a story from Greek mythology, the rape of the girl Leda by the god Zeus, who had assumed the form of a swan. Leda felt a sudden blow, with the "great wings" of the swan still beating above her. Her thighs were caressed by "the dark webs," and the nape of her neck was caught in his bill; he held "her helpless breast upon his breast." How, the speaker asks, could Leda's "terrified vague fingers" push the feathered glory of the swan from between her thighs? And how could her body help but feel "the strange heart beating where it lies"? A shudder in the loins engenders "The broken wall, the burning roof and tower, and Agamemnon dead." The speaker wonders whether Leda, caught up by the swan and "mastered by the brute blood of the air," assumed his knowledge as well as his power "Before the indifferent beak could let her drop."

Form

"Leda and the Swan" is a sonnet, a traditional fourteen-line poem in iambic pentameter. The structure of this sonnet is Petrarchan with a clear separation between the first eight lines (the "octave") and the final six (the "sestet"), the dividing line being the moment of ejaculation—the "shudder in the loins." The rhyme scheme of the sonnet is ABAB CDCD EFGEFG.

Commentary

Like "The Second Coming," "Leda and the Swan" describes a moment that represented a change of era in Yeats's historical model of gyres, which he offers in *A Vision*, his mystical theory of the universe. But where "The Second Coming" represents (in Yeats's conception) the end of modern history, "Leda and the Swan" represents something like its beginning; as Yeats understands it, the "history" of Leda is that, raped by the god Zeus in the form of a swan, she laid eggs, which hatched into Clytemnestra and Helen and the war-gods Castor and Polydeuces—and thereby brought about the Trojan War ("The broken wall, the burning roof and tower, / And Agamemnon dead"). The details of the story of the Trojan War are quite elaborate: briefly, the Greek Helen, the most beautiful woman in the world, was kidnapped by the Trojans, so the Greeks besieged the city of Troy; after the war, Clytemnestra, the wife of the Greek leader Agamemnon, had her husband murdered. Here, however, it is important to know only the war's lasting impact: it brought about the end of the ancient mythological era and the birth of modern history.

Also like "The Second Coming," "Leda and the Swan" is valuable more for its powerful and evocative language—which manages to imagine vividly such a bizarre phenomenon as a girl's rape by a massive swan—than for its place in Yeats's occult history of the world. As an aesthetic experience, the sonnet is remarkable; Yeats combines words indicating powerful action (sudden blow, beating, staggering, beating, shudder, mastered, burning, mastered) with adjectives and descriptive words that indicate Leda's weakness and helplessness (caressed, helpless, terrified, vague, loosening), thus increasing the sensory impact of the poem.

The poem's power of image and language is to some extent independent of Yeats's own ideas, and by using Biblical echoes, both in style and reference, Yeats gives the poem an immediacy, which some of the others that derive from the System of *A Vision* lack. It draws on the cultural context or schema in which we tend read it, giving expression to millennial dread and the feeling that we live in times of unprecedented upheaval, whether or not we actually do. 'The Second Coming' also has a intrinsic linguistic vividness that is witnessed by the frequency with which is quoted. From Chinua Achebe's novel, *Things Fall Apart,* to Joan Didion's *Slouching Towards Bethlehem,* almost every phrase in the poem has been used, usually more than once, to entitle a book or an article of greater or lesser impact (there is a collage version of the poem at deuceofclubs.com that uses some of these to build the poem from book-covers; some bits work better than others). Even relatively small modifications of language weaken it considerably, as is evidenced by Joni Mitchell's generally respectful reworking, 'Slouching Toward Bethlehem'.

Yeats had written in 1900 that: 'It is only by ancient symbols, by symbols that have numberless meanings besides the one or two the writer lays an emphasis upon, or the half-score he knows of, than any highly subjective art can escape from the barrenness and shallowness of a too conscious arrangement, into the abundance and depth of Nature. The poet of essences and pure ideas must seek in the half-lights that glimmer from symbol to symbol as if to the ends of the earth, all that the epic and dramatic poet finds of mystery and shadow in the accidental circumstances of life'. The symbols that he uses here similarly partake of a wider symbolism of 'numberless meanings' rather than just the ones which are linked to his System and the poem's immediate inspiration, so that although a knowledge of Yeats's ideas certainly clarifies elements in the poem, 'The Second Coming' has no single explanation.

Byzantium"

Summary

At night in the city of Byzantium, "The unpurged images of day recede." The drunken soldiers of the Emperor are asleep, and the song of night-walkers fades after the great cathedral gong. The "starlit" or "moonlit dome," the speaker says, disdains all that is human—"All mere complexities, / The fury and the mire of human veins." The speaker says that before him floats an image—a man or a shade, but more a shade than a man, and still more simply "an image." The speaker hails this "superhuman" image, calling it "death-in-life and life-in-death." A golden bird sits on a golden tree, which the speaker says is a "miracle"; it sings aloud, and scorns the "common bird or petal / And all complexities of mire or blood."

At midnight, the speaker says, the images of flames flit across the Emperor's pavement, though they are not fed by wood or steel, nor disturbed by storms. Here, "blood-begotten spirits come," and die "into a dance, / An agony of trance, / An agony of flame that cannot singe a sleeve," leaving behind all the complexities and furies of life. Riding the backs of dolphins, spirit after spirit arrives, the flood broken on "the golden smithies of the Emperor." The marbles of the dancing floor break the "bitter furies of complexity," the storms of images that beget more images, "That dolphin-torn, that gong-tormented sea."

Form

The pronounced differences in "Byzantium"'s line lengths make its stanzas appear very haphazard; however, they are actually quite regular: each stanza constitutes eight lines, and each rhymes AABBCDDC. Metrically, each is quite complicated; the lines are loosely iambic, with the first, second, third, fifth, and eighth lines in pentameter, the fourth line in tetrameter, and the sixth and seventh line in trimeter, so that the pattern of line-stresses in each stanza is 55545335.

Commentary

We have read Yeats's account of "Sailing to Byzantium"; now he has arrived at the city itself, and is able to describe it. In "Sailing to Byzantium" the speaker stated his desire to be "out of nature" and to assume the form of a golden bird; in "Byzantium," the bird appears, and scores of dead spirits arrive on the backs of dolphins, to be forged into "the artifice of eternity"—ghostlike images with no physical presence ("a flame that cannot singe a sleeve"). The narrative and imagistic arrangement of this poem is highly ambiguous and complicated; it is unclear whether Yeats intends the poem to be a register of symbols or an actual mythological statement. (In classical mythology, dolphins often carry the dead to their final resting-place.)

In any event, we see here the same preference for the artificial above the actual that appeared in "Sailing to Byzantium"; only now the speaker has encountered actual creatures that exist "in the artifice of eternity"—most notably the golden bird of stanza three. But the preference is now tinged with ambiguity: the bird looks down upon "common bird or petal," but it does so not out of existential necessity, but rather because it has been coerced into doing so, as it were—"by the moon embittered." The speaker's demonstrated preoccupation with "fresh images" has led some critics to conclude that the poem is really an allegory of the process by which fantasies are rendered into art, images arriving from the "dolphin-torn, the gong-tormented sea," then being made into permanent artifacts by "the golden smithies of the Emperor."

It is impossible to say whether this is all or part of Yeats's intention, and it is difficult to see how the prevalent symbols of the afterlife connect thematically to the topic of images (how could images be dead?). For all its difficulty and almost unfixed quality of meaning—the poem is difficult to place even within the context of *A Vision*—the intriguing imagery and sensual language of the poem are tokens of its power; simply as the evocation of a fascinating imaginary scene, "Byzantium" is unmatched in all of Yeats.

"The Circus Animals' Desertion"

Summary

The speaker describes searching in vain for a poetic theme: he says that he had tried to find one for "six weeks or so," but had been unable to do so. He thinks that perhaps, now that he is "but a broken man," he will have to be satisfied with writing about his heart, although for his entire life ("Winter and summer till old age began") he had played with elaborate, showy poetic themes that paraded like "circus animals": "Those stilted boys, that burnished chariot, / Lion and woman and the Lord knows what."

What can he do, he wonders, but list his old themes in the absence of a new one? He remembers writing of a "sea-rider" named Oisin, who traveled through "three enchanted islands"; but the speaker says that as he wrote about Oisin, he was secretly "starved for the bosom of his fairy bride." He remembers writing a play called "The Countess Cathleen," about a "pity-crazed" woman who gave her soul away; but the speaker says that the dream inspired by a woman who was forced to destroy her own soul "had all my thought and love." He remembers writing of the hero Cuchulain's battle with the sea while the Fool and the Blind Man "stole the bread"; but even then, he was enchanted by the dream—the idea of "Character isolated by a deed / To engross the present and dominate memory." He says that he loved the "players and painted stage," and not the things they symbolized.

The speaker says that those images were masterful because they were complete. He says that they grew in pure mind, and asks out of what they began. He answers his own question: they issued from "Old kettles, old bottles, and a broken can, / Old iron, old bones, old rags, that raving slut / Who keeps the till." Now that his "ladder" is gone, the speaker says, he must lie down "where all the ladders start / In the foul rag and bone shop of the heart."

Form

The five stanzas of "The Circus Animals' Desertion" are written in the same form as the stanzas of "Sailing to Byzantium": in lines in iambic pentameter, rhymed ABABABCC. The poem is subdivided into three numerical sections (I, II, and III), with the three middle stanzas falling in section II; section I contains only the first stanza, and section III contains only the last.

Commentary

"The Circus Animals' Desertion," one of the last poems Yeats completed before his death in 1939, finds him looking back over his poetic career, reinterpreting his past work and his motivations for writing it, and searching for the truths that remain when all the vanities and illusions of life have been stripped away by the decay of age and the corruptions of time. "At last," the speaker writes, he is "but a broken man," and his poetic faculties have abandoned him. Sickened by what he perceives to be the gaudiness and illusion of his past work, he thinks of his former poetic creations as "circus animals" that have been "on show" his entire life, and which have now deserted him.

In the three stanzas of the second section, Yeats looks back at three specific works from earlier in his life, and questions their honesty and his commitment to them. In the first stanza of section II, he looks back at *The Wanderings of Oisin,* a long narrative poem from 1889 in which the hero Oisin follows his beloved Niamh across a trio of magical islands; Yeats claims that his real motive for writing the poem was not a noble one—that he was simply, pathetically "starved" for "the bosom of his fairy bride." In the second stanza of the section, he looks at a play entitled *The Countess Cathleen,* which was first performed (with Maude Gonne in the starring role) in 1899; in the play, the countess sells her soul to the devil to feed her starving subjects; Yeats says that his real motive for writing the play was the "dream" inspired by his belief that his "dear" "must her own soul destroy." In the third stanza, Yeats looks back at another play, this one entitled *On Bailee's Strand,* and featuring a scene in which the mythological Irish hero Cuchulain, having unknowingly killed his son in battle, commits suicide by attempting to battle the ocean; at the same time, two characters called the Fool and the Blind Man rob the ovens. Yeats says that in writing this play he was preoccupied with the theater and with the idea that character could be "isolated" by a single deed— but not with the actual symbols of the play itself.

In the final stanza of the poem, Yeats takes a hard look at his "masterful" imagery, and realises that though it seemed to grow in "pure mind," it actually began in the ugly, common experiences of everyday life, which work upon the mind. So in a sense, Cuchulain stemmed from "a mound of refuse or the sweepings of a street." Wearily but with resolve, Yeats states that he must lie down in the place where poetry and imagery begin: "In the foul rag and bone shop of the heart." The stark physicality of the final line of Yeats's last great formulation of a poetic credo contrasts shockingly with his first one, in "The Lake Isle of Innisfree," in which he declared his fidelity to "the deep heart's core." Throughout his fifty-year literary career, he has delved so deep into the heart's core that he has discovered, not the lapping waters of Innisfree, but the foul rag and bone shop in which he now lies down. As Yeats wrote in an earlier poem, "The Coming of Wisdom with Time,"

Chapter 12

Study Questions

Q.1. Discuss Psycho-Sexual Therapy in Action in Yeats's 'Leda and the Swan'

Or

Q. Analyze the ambiguities in Leda and the Swan

W.B. Yeats's heavily anthologized poem, "Leda and the Swan," can be read in endless ways: as a political poem, a poem influenced by Nietzsche's idea of "Will to Power," a poem of knowledge ultimately achieved through violence. Is the poem simply referring to a myth? Is it addressing historical determinism? Critical methodologies attempt to address these issues and more in their treatments of "Leda and the Swan."

However, to understand fully the poem and its implications, a formal close reading of the text must be combined with supplementary biographical information to inform a final psychoanalytic reading of the poem. An understanding of the events surrounding Yeats's life, then, will contribute to a textual analysis to show that the poem can be re ad as Yeats's own particular rape fantasy, in which Maud Gonne is Leda and Yeats himself the swan; and in displacing his frustrations into the poem, Yeats turns destructive impulses into a constructive thing of beauty.

"Leda and the Swan" is a sonnet, one of the most precise forms of literature known. An interesting paradox emerges, however, at first glance. The poem is written in a traditional form (sonnet), using a traditional rhyme scheme, yet the subject matter is extremely non-traditional (violent rape as opposed to the usual love sonnets). This paradox is representative of the many oppositional elements which abound in the text and which help form the basis for understanding the oppositions which influence bot h Yeats and the poem.

The rhyme scheme is traditional (ABAB CDCD EFG EFG) yet interestingly imperfect in that four of the rhymes are not perfect: "push" and "rush," "up" and "drop". This again is another oppositional element, typical of Yeats, and could be seen to symbolize the opposition between Yeats, the last Romantic, and Yeats, the Modernist.

A transition exists in the poem's language, from an aggressive intensity to a vague passive distance. The language in the beginning of the poem sets the tone of an aggressive sense of urgency. Priscilla Washburn Shaw makes an excellent point when she states.

The action interrupts upon the scene at the beginning with 'a sudden blow,' and again, in the third stanza, with 'a shudder in the loins.' It may seem inaccurate to say that a poem begins by an interruption when nothing precedes, but the effect of t he opening is just that.

The effect of this device is that it draws the spectator/ narrator, and subsequently the reader, into the action and into the poem.

The action continues for the first three lines of the first quatrain. Yeats doesn't bother with a full syntax until the final line of the quatrain, at which point, the urgency relaxes. The language in the first full quatrain is represent ative of the opposition inherent in the poem; in this case, between intensity and distance.

The imagery, and wording in general, in "Leda" is also representative, in an initial reading, of oppositional elements within the text. A first reading shows Leda described in concrete terms and the swan in abstract terms. Leda is "the staggering girl" and the poem refers to "Her thighs," "her nape," "her helpless breast," and "her loosening thighs." The swan is never actually called Zeus or even the Swan (in fact, Agamemnon is the only name mentioned in the body of the poem). The swan is described as "great wings," "dark webs," "that white rush," "blood," "indifferent beak," and "feathered glory."

A second reading of the poem, however, shows that ambiguities do exist. The concrete and abstract merge. Generalized terms are used for Leda ("terrified vague fingers") and concrete terms for the swan (wings, bill, beak). The purpose of this ambiguity could be, as Nancy Hargrove explains, "to stress that the god is, after all, a real, physical swan engaged in a physical act". Regardless, this ambiguity is, again, representative of the conflict within the poem.

Verbs play a major role in understanding "Leda and the Swan." They are present tense through the octave and the first part of the sestet ("holds," "push," "feel," "engenders"). They then shift to past tense in the last part of the sestet ("caught," "ma stered," "Did"). The verbs in the present tense imply an intense immediacy while those in the past tense distance the reader (and perhaps the aggressor as well) from what has just occurred. Additionally, as Nancy Hargrove points out, there is a juxtaposition between active and passive verbs so that the active verb forms ("holds," "engenders") belong to the swan while passive verb forms ("caressed," "caught," "mastered") belong to Leda. The verb forms, then, play an active role in contributing to a close textual reading.

Yeats continuously makes use of various devices to further heighten ambiguous, oppositional, and dramatic elements within his poetry. "In his minimal use of the possessive adjective, and the consequently greater use of somewhat unusual alternative for ms, Yeats achieves effects which are curiously suspended between the concrete and the general", thus highlighting the ambiguities in the text. Further still, "the linguistic suggestiveness of the absence of any qualifiers for 'body' is considerable". It is considerable in that it makes us even more aware of the ambiguities (whose body?). It linguistically suggests the lack of an identity; it is essentially a dehumanizing element.

While the subject matter of the poem is violent and disturbing, the structure of "Leda" conveys feelings of safety and beauty. Hargrove submits that the intensity of the rape is controlled by the narrow confines of the sonnet, an aesthetically pleasing and heavily structured art form. Douglas Archibald asserts, "The sonnet form achieves for 'Leda'" this: "violence and historical sweep held in one of the most tightly controlled of poetic forms". The violence of the rape is then controlled within the constraints of the sonnet. Additionally, the sonnet itself is brief, thus ensuring the rape will be brief as well.

While the rape is controlled through the structure of the poem, the organization of the poem "reflects in an orderly manner the progress of the rape".

The first quatrain presents the assault. The second quatrain reflects Leda's emotions. The first half of the sestet presents the ejaculation scene. The cut line represents a dramatic moment in time: a death-like silence. The final part of the sestet shows the act receding into memory while posing the question of meaning.

Yeats makes use of several technical devices to convey the intensity of what is being portrayed in the poem. Among these devices are alliteration ("brute blood"), iambic pentameter, and the meter in general. Bernard Levine notes that "no regular metric al pattern" exists but "there is a pervading rhythmic base in which verbal stress displaces the accent-guided line". Nancy Hargrove elaborates by showing that the meter imitates the gasping and throbbing pulsations of the rape by its irregularity, its sudden sharp caesuras, its sentences spilling over from line to line, its dramatic broken lines in the sestet, its piling of stressed syllables.

The ambiguities in "Leda" imply a confrontation both real and imagined, physical and intellectual. Bernard Levine addresses the ambiguity surrounding "the staggering girl" in line three. "Staggering" as intransitive participle means that the girl is literally physically staggering, but the transitive verb form shows that she "staggers" the mind (of the swan), so to speak. Levine addresses another ambiguity in the connotation of the word "still" in line one. The bird is described (we assume) as having just dropped down on Leda, yet the word "still" implies a timeless continuity.

The text, then, presents the rape scene, painting a vivid and terrifying picture of its aggressive violence and its subsequent transition to passivity. The text also shows a pattern of oppositions and ambiguities which are manifestations of a series of conflicts between the material world and the spiritual world: the physical and the intellectual. Nancy Hargrove remarks that the apparent opposition between abstract and concrete is representative of that between "human and divine". Shaw views it in a more personal light: as the opposition "between self and world".

The oppositions inherent within the text, and the subsequent series of conflicts which they represent, are important in that they are manifestations of and parallels to oppositional conflicts occurring in Yeats's own life. The violent textual rape is the result of his inability to reconcile these personal conflicts and the poem, then, is an example of Yeats displacing his frustration, and doing so in a positive and safe manner.

If this assertion is indeed accurate, "Leda and the Swan" would be consiste nt with Yeats's later poems. Edmund Wilson writes, "The development of Yeats's later style seems to coincide with a disillusionment". Cleanth Brooks argues that Yeats "proposed to substitute a concrete, meaningful system, substituting symbol" as a way of combating harsh, technical reality."Leda" is consistent with the assertions.

And, the key to the reality Yeats is attempting to address is Maud Gonne.

Maud Gonne was a militant Irish nationalist with whom Yeats was very much in love, and who appeared as a tortured image in much of his poetry. She gave herself completely to her country and expected the same type of nationalistic dedication from Yeats. They loved one another deeply but were never able to reconcile the differences in their feelings. Maud Gonne loved Yeats in a platonic sense; Yeats desired a more all-encompassing love.

Both Yeats and Maud Gonne considered themselves mystics. They belonged to the Heretic Order of the Golden Dawn, a society in which they attended seances. Maud desired a "pure" spiritual life and felt that type of life precluded physical contact (sex) w ith Yeats. Yeats aspired to a like belief system, but was unable to live up to these idealized standards. Under these conditions, Yeats and Maud Gonne entered into a "spiritual" marriage. Bernard Levine explains that "The marriage was based on a communication through dream correspondence and astral vision (controlled release of spiritual tension)". Levine suggests this spiritual marriage was "the background and psychological excuse for the writing of 'Leda and the Swan'". Well before the poem was written, Maud Gonne had become an identifiable entity in Yeats's poetry. Infact, Geoffrey Thurley refers to the poem as another "Maud/ Helen" poem.

Levine also states that Maud had become identified with Helen (the mythological daughter of Leda) as early as 1908 and goes on to identify Maud with Leda as well.

Consistent with his penchant for myth-as-metaphor, and mythology in general, Yeats declared sexual desire to be a myth. Yet, at the same time, he wrote that he "used to puzzle Maud Gonne by always avowing ultimate defeat as a test" and he believed that his "spiritual love for Maud could never be consummated except through sexual union," supporting the idea that the "'mystic way and sexual love' are inextricably related". This conflict serves as an example of the type of opposition Yea ts could never reconcile and which would later manifest itself in "Leda and the Swan."

Yeats viewed Maud Gonne as having achieved purity and felt as though he too should be above sexual longing. Levine argues that, unable to overcome his sexual needs, Yeats had little alternative but to interpret his continual sexual longing as a betrayal of Maud. Interestingly enough, Yeats "kept" a woman in London for a time. Perhaps Yeats provides a good example for us of a man suffering from the Virgin/Whore syndrome. The "pure" women in his life are untouchable and are romanticized in his po etry while those who succumb to his needs are referred to as "harlots" ("Presences").

Yeats's sense of betrayal, coupled with his failed attempts to suppress unacceptable desires, conceivably led to an enormous amount of guilt. In reference to sexuality and guilt, Francis Oppel suggests that Yeats understood the psychology of tragedy, in that orgasm (which engenders life and also equals death of sexual desire) enables one to overcome pain and, by extension, guilt and death. This overwhelming sense of guilt resulted in a disillusioned and angst-ridden Yeats, and the resultant frust ration led to, as Joseph Hassett terms it, an "overwhelming preoccupation with hate" (Introduction viii) and a sense of self hatred. This (self) hatred led a despondent Yeats to contemplate suicide. Levine quotes Virginia Moore as stating, "Yeats dreame d that, walking along a path by a broken wall a precipice, he felt dizzy and longed to throw himself over".

By "Leda and the Swan," Yeats was preoccupied with death, both consciously and unconsciously. Bernard Levine states simply that "Because his relationship with Maud Gonne remained unconsummated," Yeats's "imagination fastened quite decidedly in his later years on the themes of sex and death". A bridge that Levine doesn't seem to wish to cross, however, is the idea that Yeats's later themes do focus on sex and death out of this sense of self hatred engendered by the guilt over his inability to live up to Maud's standards and, initially, by the frustration he felt over Maud's unwillingness to comply with his desires.

Some critics even contend that hate is Yeats's generative principle. Joseph M. Hassett contends that Yeats "used his hate to penetrate the uncharted depths of his own mind" (Introduction viii). Ashok Bhargava reaffirms this love-hate antithesis found in later Yeats. Quite simply, Yeats consciously attempted to suppress his physical desire and failed. This failure led to an unconscious resentment of the figure (Maud) perceived as responsible for this resulting guilt/self hatred. This (repressed) resentment resulted in violent tendencies and the rape scene in "Leda" is, finally, the sublimation of sexual impulse.

Several instances exist to support the correlation between aspects of the spiritual marriage and elements within the poem. Levine, again, cites Moore in noting these instances. During the summer of 1908, Yeats saw a vision of Maud and himself "joined b y a 'sort of phantom ecstasy,'" which was accompanied by an impression of a swan floating in water. This was followed by a dream in which "Maud reproached Yeats because she could not break down some barrier". Another time Maud wrote that she and Y eats had "become one with ecstasy" and Yeats had appeared to her triumphantly in a dream, after which she woke to a gust of wind blowing in her room and a voice of "an archangel who announced that from her union a 'great beauty may be born,' once she had been 'purified by suffering'". There is evidence of other such examples.

Yeats, the idealistic Romantic, could not let go of the hope that Maud would one day become a willing participant, physically. Yeats must have hoped that his persistent passion and intensity would eventually persuade her to give in. Elements from the just-noted example would support this hope and are found in the text of the poem: the swan image, barrier image, the idea of unity through sexual union. At this point, could Yeats's unconscious have been softening the tone (and implications) of the rape in the poem? These examples suggest that is indeed the case. Additionally, as previously mentioned, the tone of the poem moves from aggressive to passive. Furthermore, a clue which supports the idea of a hope Yeats harbored lies in the revision process.

Richard Ellman informs us that the poem went through several stages of revision. In earlier versions, Yeats portrayed the scene as an inarguable rape in which Leda is mounted. In the later, anthologized version of 1928, Leda has been given "loo sening thighs," suggesting a type of acquiescence on Leda's part. The implication for this shift, then, in language and tone in the final version of "Leda and the Swan" is that the change is an example of Yeats displacing his fantasy that Maud Gonne woul deventually be swayed to engage him sexually and would become a willing, if passive, participant. In the earlier versions, Yeats was displacing his aggression. In the final revised version, Maud Gonne as Leda takes an active response role.

Finally, "Leda and the Swan" is a violent poem and can be seen as Yeats's own particular rape fantasy; however, it remains an object of beauty. A close reading of the text focusing on the oppositions inherent within the poem, combined with an understand ing of the circumstances surrounding Yeats's spiritual marriage to Maud Gonne shows the poem to be a manifestation of the conflict between reality and ideal, human and divine that Yeats spent years trying to reconcile. The poem allows Yeats to displace h is violent fantasies concerning Maud, yet it does so in a structured, controlled manner (ensuring safety), and it allows Yeats to, finally, retain a certain amount of romantic hope. "Leda and the Swan" was Yeats's only realistic alternative to the conflict in his life, and as a form of self therapy, it remains a nearly perfect work of art.

Q.2. Compare and contrast William Butler Yeats poem, Leda and the Swan and Fred Chappel's Narcissus and Echo

Or

Q. Discuss Yeats poem Leda and the Swan with reference to Greek mythology

Poets use many different stylistic devices to capture the attention of the reader. After all, who wants to read a boring poem? Many times, it is the opening line that acts as the "hook." What better way to capture someone's attention than to incite emotion with the first word. Some poets use form to their advantage. Perhaps by writing the words out in different shapes, they will create a broader readership. Some poets use symbolism, or structure to benefit their artistic license. I prefer the subtler and less common stylistic devices. Fred Chappel, in "Narcissus and Echo," and William Butler Yeats poem, "Leda and the Swan." use different, yet effective stylistic devices to capture the attention of the reader and hold on to them throughout the entire poem.

By echoing the last sound of each line in his poem, Chappel is able to create two separate poetic rhythms. The first is the fundamental poem written about two mythological characters. Narcissus, the first character, was so enthralled with his own beauty that he fell in love with his own reflection in a pond. He, being so brokenhearted that he could never be with his true love (himself), wasted away until all that was left was a beautiful flower. Hence that flower called Narcissus. Echo is the other character in this "tragic" love story. She fell in love with Narcissus. This was before he turned into a flower, of course. She followed him, trying to speak to him but in his vanity he did not notice her. She was heartbroken and withered away until all that was left was her voice to follow him. Hence the echo. It was her voice combined with his reflection that Narcissus fell in love with. After all, who wouldn't want to hear their words echoed back to them by their lover?

Chappel uses this story as the base for his poem, which seems to be of Narcissus' love. The difference is that the words that are echoed back are not quite the same as the original. They seem to be almost an ironic look into the shallow nature of this character. In the seventh line, Chappel brings this irony to light when he writes, "teasing playfully the one being. Unbeing" (181), almost as if he is trying to tell Narcissus that his love is a pretense. This poem turns to portray the tragic loneliness that Echo must have felt as she echoes back, "Is your heart not stone?" (181 lines 8-11). The purpose behind this particular stylistic device is to give the reader the feeling that she is seeing this moment directly from the eyes of each character without the poem being a narrative. This is extremely effective.

In contrast to the soft language and delicately chosen word use of Chappel, William Butler Yeats uses slant rime and forceful language to bring life to another Greek myth. "Leda and the Swan," opens with the image of a swan flying above a young woman. By opening it with direct language, "A sudden blow: the great wings beating still/ above the staggering girl" (179 lines 1-2), Yeats creates an image of the power that this immaculate swan must have had. He also uses vivid imagery of an intimate moment between the swan (Zeus), and Leda (a Spartan queen). He uses such strong words as "beating" to describe with force both the rhythm of the bird's wings, and that of this woman's heart.

Yeats also uses rhyme as an advantageous stylistic device. By using quatrains in an "abab" rhyme scheme for the first half of the poem, he effectively holds the interest of the reader. What is unique, hovever, is that toward the end of this poem, he switches to off rime at the ends of each line. The reason that this is advantageous is that it does not leave the reader feeling that she has been reading a song. It adds to the power behind the poem without taking away from it.

Chappel's method of echo verse creates a more subtle effect that carefully guides the reader through this delicate poem. In contrast, Yeats' sharp, forceful language and slant rime push the reader to the point. Both are extremely effective methods of stylistic device that create different, yet equally effective poems

Q.3. Discuss Celtic Mythology in The Rose

Or

Q. Discuss the Irish "cycles"

The most difficult allusions in Yeats are not to Roman or Greek history, but rather to Celtic mythology. The Celts were a group who inhabited Ireland long before the Norman or British invasions. Druids, which Yeats mentions often, were the healers and priests of these ancient societies.

There are four great cycles that make up extant Irish mythology. The first is the Mythological Cycle, which describes the origins of Irish deities. Yeats draws especially on the second cycle, the Ulster Cycle (sometimes called the Red Branch Cycle). The main character of this group of myths is Conchubar, who succeeded the previous king of Ulster, Fergus. Conchubar ruled around the time of Christ, in conflict with Queen Medh of Connacht. The most famous story in the Ulster cycle is the Tain bo Cuailnge, or "The Cattle Raid of Cooley." Cattle were the primary resource of ancient Ireland, so a raid on an enemy's cattle can be seen as symbolic as an attack on his wealth and prosperity in general.

Cuchulainn is another major figure in the Ulster cycle. He is the most famous hero of Irish myth. At seventeen years old, Cuchulainn is deemed the only warrior fit to protect Ulster against the machinations of Queen Medh. He defeats all of her combatants in one-on-one fighting, and engages in a grueling fight against his foster brother. Cuchulainn asked to be tied upright on a post so that he could continue fighting, which he did until he died. This death became a powerful symbol for 20th century Irish nationalists.

The third cycle, called the Fenian Cycle, is so called after the hero, Finn MacCumhall. Finn MacCumhall is most famous for building an army called the Fianna. Famously, a member of the Fianna, Diarmuid, ran away with Grania, whom the aged Finn had fallen in love with. This story is the basis for Yeats' "A Faery Song."

The last myth cycle, the Historical Cycle, is generally considered drier than the other cycles, and contains many accounts of kings and their politics. Yeats draws often on the middle two, less on the first cycle, and not at all on the last

Q.4. Discuss the Human Image in Yeats

Or

Q. Analyze the irreconcilable claims of body and soul in yeats

In Yeats, a poet intensely and often painfully preoccupied with the irreconcilable claims of Soul and Body: 'body and soul/Estranged amid the strangeness of themselves'. Intensely and painfully, because being a poet he was driven toward images of 'wholeness', unity, and 'perfection'. There seemed no possibility of realizing 'Unity of Being'; the poetic metaphor was frustrate at every point. In 'King and No King' he had written:

And I that have not your faith, how shall I know
That in the blinding light beyond the grave,
We'll find so good a thing as that we have lost?
The hourly kindness, the day's common speech,
The habitual content of each with each
When neither soul nor body has been crossed.

There were many moments in which Yeats thought – or hoped against hope – that everything would be fulfilled in the accords of a distinguished human body; that the body, in splendid animation, would certify an undissociated unity of being, like the transfiguration which Ribh conjured at the tomb of Baile and Aillinn. But again he would find the body a dissociated and dying animal.

This is Yeats as patient. As agent he sought to heal himself: first, by lamenting the lost harmony, invoking a great-rooted chestnut tree that suffered from none of man's dissociations. And again: with a dramatist's instinct he broke down the crux into its two great conflicting parts; thereafter interpreting experience, as his 'condition' prodded, now in terms of Soul (or Spirit), now in terms of Body (or Nature). The crux was a complex and unmanageable simultaneity: Yeats replaced it, imperatively, by a more tolerable scheme of successiveness. He resolved a contradictory 'yes-no' situation by setting up a plot that developed from 'yes' to 'no' and *vice versa*. (1)

In *The Wanderings of Oisin, Crossways, The Rose* and *The Wind among the Reeds,* Yeats located the Spirit in a realm of picturesque sorrow with 'numberless islands', 'many a Danaan shore', and a 'woven world-forgotten isle'. In those books whatever mode of existence is identified with the Spirit is protected, in tenderness, from the critique of Body or Nature. Those early poems are a long and intermittently beautiful 'yes' to the Spirit; but the Spirit is abused, maimed, because torn from the Body. In later years and with different materials Yeats often said 'yes' to the Spirit; under the guise of Mind, for instance, as in 'All Souls' Night':

Such thought — such thought have I that hold it tight
Till meditation master all its parts,
Nothing can stay my glance
Until that glance run in the world's despite
To where the damned have howled away their hearts,
And where the blessed dance:
Such thought, that in it bound
I need no other thing,
Wound in mind's wandering
As mummies in the mummy-cloth are wound.

In this poem Yeats praises those adepts who, like Florence Emery, meditate upon unknown thought and repudiate the Body:

What matter who it be,
So that his elements have grown so fine
The fume of muscatel
Can give his sharpened palate ecstasy
No living man can drink from the whole wine.
Ours are 'gross palates'.

This is one situation, one act in the plot. Its counterpart is the Crazy Jane series in *Words for Music Perhaps*.

The year is 1929. Yeats is recovering from an attack of Maltese fever. Behind him, or so he fancies, are the world of politics, the Irish Senate, and 'a sixty-year-old smiling public man'. He writes to Olivia Shakespear from Rapallo: 'No more opinions, no more politics, no more practical tasks.' Joyful riddance: it is a prosperous moment. Sixty-four years old, Yeats feels new strength and sexual energy returning to his body. He is impelled to have recourse to that 'nature' (in bodily terms) from which he had withdrawn, estranged, to a more gracious world of pure Mind. Now he withdraws again, provisionally, not only from pure Mind but from a 'practical' scene of disillusion. Ridding himself of a 'practical' world he reduces his scene accordingly: he identifies his will, provisionally, with the urges of the body in revolt, giving it — for protection and definition — the name 'Crazy Jane'.

It is a simplification on Yeats's part, and therefore an evasion. Indeed, each of Yeats's books of poems is a strategic simplification, a trial account of his universe devoted not to the entire complex truth but to a particular bias which is dominant for the time being. Some are phoenix books; others turtle books; what one longs for is the mutual flame:

Hearts remote, yet not asunder;
Distance, and no space was seen.

In the Crazy Jane poems Yeats for the time being places as much trust in the bodily (a turtle, surely) as Racine in the greatly passionate, or Wordsworth in the greatly sensitive. The bodily imperative is the 'myth' of the Crazy Jane poems, corresponding to the anthropological myth of 'The Waste Land'.

Words for Music Perhaps: the words are for music, not because they are to be sung, but because their burden, like that of the ballad, belongs to the folk. The context of the book is that quantity of folk-experience which has 'the body's potencies' — Lawrence's phrase — as its prime motive.

The connotations are important. It is 'that foul body' in 'Those Dancing Days are Gone', but this does not mean — as a recent critic maintains — that Yeats 'identifies the physical, corporeal aspects of love with that which is *foul*', or that in his later poems, going one better, he 'regards the sexual act as mostly beastly'. Quite the opposite. There is a curious tonality in those Crazy Jane poems:

Come, let me sing into your ear;
Those dancing days are gone,
All that silk and satin gear;
Crouch upon a stone,
Wrapping that foul body up
In as foul a rag:

The body is not foul. What is foul — here — is its decay, its loss of power, mainly sexual ('the vigour of its blood'). Six days before writing this poem Yeats had rendered that bodily power in 'Crazy Jane Grown Old Looks at the Dancers':

God be with the times when I
Cared not a thraneen for what chanced
So that I had the limbs to try
Such a dance as there was danced —
Love is like the lion's tooth.

Again in 'Mad as the Mist and Snow' the winds are foul because they testify to decay. In 'All Souls' Night' the years are foul because they wear away Florence Emery's beauty. Indeed, Yeats uses the word when he has in mind sheer mutability. The trickiest case is 'Crazy Jane Talks with the Bishop':

I met the Bishop on the road
And much said he and I.
'Those breasts are flat and fallen now,
Those veins must soon be dry;
Live in a heavenly mansion,
Not in some foul stye.'

The choice is offered as if it were unanswerable; the Bishop, as rhetorician, has no time for the Gidean problematic. Here, of course, 'foul' is censorial, and we expect the Bishop to be whipped for his cliché. Crazy Jane accepts the word and its challenge:

'Fair and foul are near of kin,
And fair needs foul,' I cried.

There is also, she claims, the God of Love; and He has rights, a trim decorum, and His own special mansion. And the term He proffers — since two can play the rhetorical game — have a sanction prior to that of the Bishop's God, because they are certified by the axioms of the body and by 'the heart's pride':

A woman can be proud and stiff
When on love intent;

But Love has pitched his mansion in
The place of excrement;
For nothing can be sole or whole
That has not been rent.
A devotee of Blake, she has the last word.

She has the first word in 'Crazy Jane on the Day of Judgement', and here her interpretation of love has a wider circumference than usual. Indeed the Crazy Jane of this poem encompasses the three great dramatic roles through which, as Richard Ellmann has observed, Yeats voiced his conceptions. First, she is the Seer:

'Love is all
Unsatisfied
That cannot take the whole
Body and soul';
The Victim:
'Naked I lay,
The grass my bed;
Naked and hidden away,
That black day';
Finally, the Assessor:
'What can be shown?
What true love be?
All could be known or shown
If Time were but gone.'

The poem is intensely moving because it is willing to test the possibilities of growth and extension in a conception of love based on the bodily imperative. Crazy Jane's speculations do not go very far, and anything like an Incarnational view of the body is as far removed from her as from Yeats himself at any point; but in this poem there is an urge to face radical questions which are often evaded in *Words for Music Perhaps.* This book is devoted to a partial view of things: Crazy Jane has a deeper idea of love than Jack the Journeyman, but she is less urgently engaged in refining this idea than In knocking down Aunt Sally's like the Bishop. In the later 'Supernatural Songs' Ribh plays a similar rôle; not so much enacting the whole as insisting upon the part which, he asserts, the Christian view discards; 'the phallic consciousness', again Lawrence's phrase:

Natural and supernatural with the sell-same ring are wed.
As man, as beast, as an ephemeral fly begets, Godhead begets Godhead,
For things below are copies, the Great Smaragdine Tablet said.

Crazy Jane and Ribh are propagandists, speaking hall-truths by vocation. They may be more humanely 'right' than the Bishop, but they are just as severely dissociated as he, and the poetic metaphor is just as far beyond their grasp. If the speaker in 'All Souls' Night' is a Paleface, Crazy Jane and Ribh are Redskins — to use Philip Rahv's famous terms; countering the 'sensibility' of *The Tower* with their own 'experience'. But the experience is raw, and therefore equally vulnerable to irony.

Yeats wanted his 'Poems for Music' to be 'all emotion and all impersonal'. On March 2, 1929 — the day on which he wrote 'Crazy Jane and the Bishop' and 'Crazy Jane Grown Old Looks at the Dancers' — he referred to the poems: 'They are the opposite of my recent work and all praise of joyous life, though in the best of them it is a dry bone on the shore that sings the praise.' Joyous life in this book is life in which the prime commitment is to the body. Everything else may change or be dissolved, but not that.

Reading Yeats we find a poet who 'believed in' none of the public, institutional faiths. But he needed their authority, their momentum, or at least authority and momentum from similar sources. And he was a spectacular opportunist. So he used each of the public faiths whenever he felt that one of its patterns of insight was specially relevant to the feeling in hand. He may have been drawn to these local 'allegiances' by sensing a purely formal congruity between the pattern in the 'public' structure and the pattern implicit in the private feeling. This would account for the Way of the Cross in 'The Travail of Passion', to certify feeling akin to its own; or the figure of the Guardian Angel in 'A Prayer for My Son'. Similarly in the

Crazy Jane poems the bodily imperative is a 'public' pattern of experience, with the force of public authority, complete with dogmas, rites, mysteries—and these by universal assent. The great advantage of the bodily imperative as a source of verbal communication is that it is prior to all conflicts of thought or belief; it undercuts the contentious levels of experience. In lofty moments Yeats would invoke the Great Memory as the source and means of communication, and he would speak beautifully under its sign, but there would always be something problematic in its operation. The human body was more reliable; indeed, the body was the only universal church to which Yeats would belong.

We have described a strategic simplification and called it — harshly — evasion. And we would suggest that a great mind which has recourse to such a strategy must harbour severe misgivings, knowing that it omits so much, condones so much distortion. That is why one has the feeling, reading through the later books, that very often Yeats is adopting certain roles not to protect himsell from tourists but because he rather fancies himself in the parts; like the 'character part' of the lusty old man. A new and distressing kind of picturesque, this leads to a certain hardening of the arteries in such a poem as 'News for the Delphic Oracle'. Here is part of the first stanza:

Man-picker Niamh leant and sighed
By Oisin on the grass;
There sighed amid his choir of love
Tall Pythagoras.

Porphyry's Elysian Fields are very like Yeats's Islands of Forgetfulness, and Yeats — sly old virtuoso — can now jeer at both. With the same virtuosity he can laugh at the equestrian Innocents:

Straddling each a dolphin's back
And steadied by a fin,
Those Innocents re-live their death,
Their wounds open again.
The last word is Yeats's: he offers it, surely, as critique:
Foul goat-head, brutal arm appear,

Belly, shoulder, bum,
Flash fishlike, nymphs and satyrs
Copulate in the foam.

Touché. Yes, but isn't it, itself, in a weak position, despite the bodily imperative and the sophisticated accent? The poem has ended, but one could envisage a fourth stanza in which the Old-Yeatsian heaven of the third would be shown for the vulnerable thing it is. The critique is valid enough as far as it goes, but not valid enough to justify the tone, the shrill exhibitionist mockery. The Yeats of the *Last Poems* did not often laugh in the tragic joy of Lear and Hamlet; his laughter is too shrill for that.

This shrillness in Yeats's late work issues, I think, from those misgivings which I have mentioned. In *Words for Music Perhaps, A Full Moon in March,* and many of the *Last Poems* Yeats's strategic simplifications placed him in a false position; hence the strident tone.

He soon got tired of Crazy Jane, though, perhaps acknowledging the limited range of her insight. He used her once again, innocuously, cursing puny times and a world bereft of Cuchulains.

Words for Music Perhaps — a final comment before we look at other human images in Yeats — is a valuable book because it enables us to re-enact a movement of feeling downward into the limited, finite *thing*. The movement is touching in itself, in its compulsions and embarrassments; only the most sullen reader could fail to be moved and disturbed by this partial image of the human condition. The pathos of the book is that when Yeats had reached down into the finite Body there was little he could do with it; he saw no means of penetrating the finite without transcending it and thereby destroying it, as Roderick destroyed Madeline, in a rage for essence. The trouble was that he could not value the human body in itself; only when it agreed to wear a bright halo of animation.

It is a painful dialectic. The poet for whom plenitude of being is everything finds himself kicking several of man's faculties out of the way in his rage for essence. The devotee of 'perfection' bows before fragments. In his most perceptive moments he knows that it is a desperate expedient, that even his Byzantine eternity is artifice.

It seems that I must bid the Muse go pack,
Choose Plato and Plotinus for a friend
Until imagination, ear and eye,
Can be content with argument and deal
In abstract things; or be derided by
A sort of battered kettle at the heel.

If you reduce a human being to his consciousness, and then provide a diet of unknown thought, argument, and abstraction, you must face the risks involved; attrition, emaciation, a desert of mummies. Time and again in *The Tower* Yeats prays for a kinder unity: 'O may the moon and sunlight seem/One inextricable beam/For if I triumph I must make men mad.' But that book is a little too engrossed with its own exposure to allow much consideration for other people; apart from a few chosen friends, the rest are given as hot-faced bargainers and money-changers. And what can we say of the monstrous crudity, the sheer vulgarity, of 'Mrs French,/Gifted with so fine an ear'? Grant that Yeats's position was difficult, perhaps impossible. 'All Souls' Night' was written under the sign of body-wearied Plotinus; as in the fourth *Ennead*, the dying animal of 'Sailing to Byzantium' is here dead, a mummy, and the 'soul' moves from its prison of diminished being. But in Yeats it has nowhere to go; the poet could not make anything of Plotinus's belief in the later stages of emanation toward the One. Hence the desperate stratagem, six years later, of Byzantium.

'All Souls' Night' is almost a test case for the hazard of the human image. It is a thrilling poem; we are at once thrilled and shocked to find Yeats driving himself into such a terrifying corner. The position itself — we feel at once — is untenable. It is unnecessarily dissociative. Mind — as the gentle philosopher Philip Wheelwright puts it — 'does not stand alone: it exists intentively in relation to objects and it exists dialogically in relation to other selves'. So the intensity of 'All Souls' Night' amounts to this; a stern mind denying the most serviceable relations in a humane life, and holding this denial 'to the end of the line.

Does this matter? Or is it the fury in the words that matters, and not the words?

The received opinion among readers of Yeats is that the classic poems are in *The Tower* and *The Winding Stair*. And yet by comparison with *The Wild Swans at Coole* the human image in those spectacular books is curiously incomplete; remarkably intense, but marginal; a little off-centre. Does this matter? Yes, it does; intensity is not enough. It matters greatly that *The Wild Swans at Coole* is at the very heart of the human predicament, groping for values through which man may define himself without frenzy or servility.

This book is concerned with the behaviour of man in the cold light of age and approaching death. The ideal stance involves passion, self-conquest, courtesy, and moral responsibility. Yeats pays the tribute of wild tears to many personages and to the moral beauty which they embody; the entire book is rammed with moral life. Most of the poems were written between 1915 and 1919, and it is significant that those were the years in which Yeats was perfecting his dance-drama; because the dancer was the culmination of the efforts which Yeats made in *The Wild Swans at Coole* to represent the fullness of being as a dynamic action. In 'The Double Vision of Michael Robartes' the girl who dances between the Sphinx and the Buddha dreams of dancing and has outdanced thought; which I take to mean that in her Action is not distinct from Vision but is Vision itself formulated. The moral equivalent of this is a certain nonchalance or recklessness, Castiglione's *sprezzatura*, a certain high daring; mastery, rather than singularity, to cite Valéry's distinction. As we gloss we may quote a few sentences from Buber's meditations upon Nijinsky:

'The decisive power in the development of the dance was neither play nor expression, but what bound them both and gave them law: magic. That is the response to the chaotic and furiously inrushing happening through the bound, lawful movement, through movement as form. The bound binds.'

Above all, it must be dynamic, this ideal behaviour; it must not be complacently picturesque. In T. S. Eliot's later poems this ideal condition appears a little static; the poet may say, 'at the still point, there the dance is', but there is very little energy in that dance, and we have to exert some goodwill before we can register it at all. In some of Wallace Stevens's poems the ideal condition is given as a still life – a blue woman, in August, registering grape leaves and clouds – someone sitting in a park watching the archaic form of a woman with a cloud on her shoulder. These are handsome moments, and we are free to relish them. But Yeats knew that they are at best provisional, at worst evasive; in his greatest poems static effects denote a failure of being.

The Wild Swans at Coole is committed to action; not to thought or concept or feeling, except that these are essential to the full definition of action. We are to register action as the most scrupulous notation of human existence, far more accurate, more 'creatural', than thought or concept – which are simplifications; far more comprehensive, too. Action is silent articulation of experience. Yeats's dancer has outdanced thought, summarized thought in a pattern of gestures. Her dance is an act of desire toward the God-state, or God-term; the dancer strives toward an 'essential' human image, an image of dynamic perfection freely formulated – fulfilled – at the end of the body-line. This is probably what Yeats meant in that great letter which he wrote a few weeks before his death; in which he said, 'It seems to me that I have found what I wanted. When I try to put all into a phrase, I say, "Man can embody truth but he cannot know it."' Truth is embodied in the figure of action, the dancer for whom meaning is embodied in gesture and gesture the only expression there is. Thought is not enough; even the 'thinking of the body': the most accurate annotation is that act which outdances thought and sums up human potentiality in gesture.

In *The Wild Swans at Coole* the dance which engrosses Yeats is the dance of the sell and the anti-self. In 'Ego Dominus Tuus' the Yeatsian speaker says:

I *call to the mysterious one who yet*
Shall walk the wet sands by the edge of the stream
And look most like me, being indeed my double,
And prove of all imaginable things
The most unlike, being my anti-self,
And, standing by these characters, disclose
All that I seek...

The appropriate gloss is from 'Anima Hominis': 'Unlike the rhetoricians, who get a confident voice from remembering the crowd they have won or may win, we sing amid our uncertainty; and, smitten even in the presence of the most high beauty by the knowledge of our solitude, our rhythm shudders.' Add to this that Art is a vision of reality: in the artist this vision is animated by his own passion, and in the passion his rhythm shudders.

It is also dialogue, the fruitful grappling of self and anti-self. Hence the number of poems in *The Wild Swans at Coole* in which the structure is 'dialogical' and the animation is the rhythm of speech. One of the finest examples is 'The People':

'What have I earned for all that work,' I said
'For all that I have done at my own charge?
The daily spite of this unmannerly town,
Where who has served the most is most defamed,
The reputation of his lifetime lost
Between the night and morning. I might have lived,
And you know well how great the longing has been,
Where every day my footfall should have lit
In the green shadow of Ferrara wall;

This is the mutual flame. A poet, in weariness and sell-pity, claims the reward of the rhetorician; quarrelling with others, he makes a sullen rhetoric. He is in the condition of earth, 'the place of heterogeneous things', and he is admonished by his phoenix, the spirit of fire 'that makes all simple'. The common ground between them is the human world, Castiglione's aristocrats and 'the people'. The poet prolongs the dispute by setting up a rivalry between the purity of a natural force and the definitions of the analytic mind; but the dispute is helpless. The real dialogue, the dance, is under the words, in the meeting of selves, the leaping of his heart at her phoenix-words, the sinking of his head abashed. This is the poet's quarrel with himself.

If we feel that the only appropriate response to this poem is intimacy and assent, this is — because it commits itself to the human situation, to the specific occasion of dialogue; it commits itself to time, place, and circumstance, to history, to beginning, middle, and end, to authentic syntax, to action; and — as the animation of all these — to the behaviour of speech, certified idiom. Wallace Stevens in his great essay 'The Noble Rider and the Sounds of Words' persuades us to acknowledge the genial interdependence of reality and the imagination, that when Horatio says, 'Now cracks a noble heart. Good night, sweet prince,/ And flights of angels sing thee to thy rest!' — here reality and the imagination are equal and inseparable. In Yeats's poem reality — the violence without, the pressure of external events upon the poet's consciousness — is answered, at once caught, sustained, and 'formed', by his great imagination, the violence within.

Yeats's spokesman in 'Ego Dominus Tuus' justifies his tracing characters upon the sands instead of imitating the great masters: 'Because I seek an image, not a book'. Thought is not enough, though the poet will sometimes fancy otherwise in *The Tower*. The image he seeks is described by Robartes in 'The Phases of the Moon'; at the fourteenth phase 'the soul begins to tremble into stillness, to die into the labyrinth of itself':

All thought becomes an image and the soul
Becomes a body.

The body and the image, I assume, are the dancer and the dance, dynamic, indistinguishable, the final gesture in the dialogue of sell and anti-self.

The argument, to bring these matters to a conclusion, is that in *The Wild Swans at Coole* the balloon of speculation is brought into the shed of common experience: in this book more radically than elsewhere Yeats takes 'the living world for text'.

We have to realise this before we can register the impassioned gravity of its later pages.

Perhaps this explains why the poems in *The Wild Swans at Coole* seem peculiarly 'central' to our experience. The burden of meaning has been placed firmly where it belongs, in action, and in the Value embodied in action. The book is an anthology of represented lives in which private vision becomes incarnate in public action; Lionel Johnson, John Synge, George Pollexfen, Robert Gregory, Solomon and Sheba, Iseult Gonne, the anonymous and classic fisherman — and many more. The poems speak to us directly, to our sense of the human predicament; and in the last reckoning this is a more reliable mode of communication than the Great Memory or even the Body.

The human image in this book is at once sweet and serviceable; it hides behind no platitudes that it can see; it does not feel called upon to take possession of the world or to set up as God. It acknowledges human limitation and tries to live as well as possible under that shadow. This image chimes with our own sense of the 'creatural' situation; it is continuous with our own unspectacular experience in its assent to common occasion. Here is one such occasion, in the poem 'Her Praise':

She is foremost of those that I would hear praised,
I have gone about the house, gone up and down
As a man does who has published a new book,
Or a young girl dressed out in her new gown,
And though I have turned the talk by hook or crook
Until her praise should be the uppermost theme,
A woman spoke of some new tale she had read,
A man confusedly in a half dream
As though some other name ran in his head.
She is foremost of those that I would hear praised.
I will talk no more of books or the long war
But walk by the dry thorn until I have found
Some beggar sheltering from the wind, and there
Manage the talk until her name come round.
If there be rags enough he will know her name

And be well pleased remembering it, for in the old days,
Though she had young men's praise and old men's blame,
Among the poor both old and young gave her praise.

Yeats wrote that poem in 1915, the year in which T. S. Eliot wrote Prufrock's more famous love song. Mr Eliot's poem is very rich, but perhaps a little insecure, like the newly rich in any age; it is aware of its affluence, and wears it a little ostentatiously. Yeats's poem seems more comfortable in its older weeds.

In placing these two poems together we move toward a question which can hardly be evaded: was Symbolism necessary?; or was it perhaps an aberration, a retreat? In this case it is impossible to be wise after the event, because the event is still with us: 'modern poetry' still means, for most people, symbolist or post-symbolist poetry, poems like 'The Waste Land' and 'Mauberly'. But in the light of Yeats's great central poems Symbolism seems at best a strategic retreat. Unable to compete with the new, virile sciences, poets conceded to the scientists not only the materials of speech and idea, but — alas! — many of the resources of commonsense. Poetry did not become nonsense, but sense so 'special' and uncommon that it could no longer accommodate the roughage or the rationale of daily experience. Poetry took refuge in an inscrutable 'manner', in an air of large-scale profundity without the restrictions of local meaning; it absolved itself from the rhetoric of argument and proof. This partly accounts for the tendency to assimilate poems to solid objects in space; since statues or apples or urns cannot be required to yield any 'meaning' other than their being. Hence — to cite one example — Mallarmé's poems offer themselves as, in the first instance, visual events, sophisticated and inscrutable arrangements of black marks on a white page. Poetry became sculpture; speech became music.

This is gross oversimplification but justifiable. Perhaps the most incorrigible defect of symbolist poetry is that it is arbitrary; not safely referable to the common life of feeling or to a human situation acknowledged as real. This is where Yeats's solid commonsense imposes itself. He was as 'modern' as any of his contemporaries: he took even greater risks of fancy and magic; but his roots were in common experience, he spoke a common idiom, harboured a tenacious commonsense. He knew that he was human.

There are three letters which must be mentioned even in a brisk account of the question. Yeats wrote them in 1937. To Mrs Moya Davies he said:... 'like Balzac I know no one who shares the premises from which I work. What can I do but cry out, lately in simple peasant songs that hide me from the curious'. Then to Dorothy Wellesley: 'I am reading Roger Fry's translation of Mallarmé. He gives the originals and a commentary by a French critic. I find it exciting, as it shows me the road I and others of my time went for certain furlongs. It is not the way I go now, but one of the legitimate roads. He escapes from history; you and I are in history, the history of the mind. Your "Fire" has a date or dates, so has my "Wild Old Wicked Man".' And finally to Edmund Dulac: 'All my life I have tried to get rid of modern subjectivity by insisting on construction and contemporary words and syntax.'

It was 'Prufrock', though, which brought in the new age and defined the new tone. In recent years many of the younger poets have been labouring to avoid the melody which Mr Eliot and his colleagues established; often picking up snatches of an older tune and rehearsing them again. John Crowe Ransom some time ago discussed the magnificent confusion which obtained in the years after 'Prufrock', and he remarked that present signs suggest that there is still going to be a continuity between the old poetry and the poetry of the 'sixties. I think he hopes that the new poetry will be written under the sign of that sturdy old eagle Thomas Hardy. My own guess is that it will be under the sign of Yeats. Hardy would serve many an occasion, but his human image is a little too long-suffering, hardly strenuous enough, to serve our new needs. The Yeats of *The Wild Swans at Coole* and the Stevens of *The Rock*; these rather than Mr Eliot or Mr Pound would point the new poet toward a properly 'public' poetry, a poetry which would uphold man's intelligence, his reverence for life, and his assent to the common life of feeling.

Those who know about such matters tell us that the young poet writing today wants above all to evade the Symbolist cul-de-sac, that of the poet admiring the image in his own mirror. The new direction is outward; and this is healthy, provided we do not rush to the naturalistic extreme and drown the individual in the destructive element. Yeats would sponsor this new direction, if we think of him now as the poet of *The Wild Swans at Coole*; many of the noblest poems in that book charted it, convinced that human life is substantial, that a moral lexicon should include Alfred Pollexfen if it includes Tamburlane, that a great — literally, great — part of life consists of other people and the values they help us to realise in action. Action may often seem merely the struggle of the fly in marmalade, but the speaker who so describes it in 'Ego Dominus Tuus' also says: 'I seek an image...,' and the seeking is itself action, discipline, and vision. *The Wild Swans at Coole* is a human-sized book, a book of acts, hence of morals. A grammatical analysis would disclose its commitment to 'will' and 'shall' and 'ought', the ground of our own beseeching.

Q.5. Discuss the gothic element in Yeats's

Or

Q. Do you think Yeats textual work is impressive

On June 11, 1925, in the course of a debate in the Seanead Eireann (the Senate of the Irish Free State) on the first reading of Bills of Divorce in both Houses of the Irish Parliament, one Senator strayed a little from the matter in hand. On that occasion, Dr W. B. Yeats's mind turned back to the marital irregularities of Daniel O'Connell (about whom "It was said,... in his own day, that you could not throw a stick over a workhouse wall without hitting one of his children"), and then the decidedly nobler figure cut by Charles Stuart Parnell. "We had a good deal of trouble", the Senator reminded his audience, "about Parnell when he married a woman who became thereby Mrs Parnell." Lord Glenavy, in the Chair, felt at this point obliged to ask the question, "Do you not think we might leave the dead alone?", but this barely interrupted

Yeats's oratorical flow: "I am passing on," he responded. "I would hate to leave the dead alone."

Of course, Yeats was not especially good at leaving things alone: the texts and canon of his poems and other writings, like the recollected details of his own life, were subject to perpetual revision; and the small army of his chosen dead could never escape the poet's earnest and repeated interrogations. By the 1920s, the séances and magical invocations of Yeats's youth and middle age had been replaced, in large part, by the hard work of his wife George's automatic writing. This provided a stream of convoluted communion with those kindred spirits who were no longer alive, but were keen to aid (or sometimes hinder) the development of the ageing Irish writer's philosophy of being and history – a project which reached its first culmination with the appearance of A Vision (1925). Some spirits who were never, strictly speaking, alive in the first place found a voice in the introduction to that book, and they rather resented Yeats's persistent interest in them, as "Owen Aherne" pointed out, recalling a chance meeting with "Michael Robartes" in the National Gallery some eight years before:

> I brought him to a seat in the middle of the room, and I had begun to speak of the changed world we met in when he said: "Where is Yeats? I want his address. I am lost in this town and I don't know where to find anybody or anything". I felt a slight chill, for we had both quarrelled with Mr Yeats on what I considered good grounds. Mr Yeats had given the name of Michael Robartes and that of Owen Aherne to fictitious characters, and made those characters live through events that were a travesty of real events. "Remember", I said, "that he not only described your death but represented it as taking place amid associations which must, I should have thought, have been highly disagreeable to an honourable man."

Robartes, on mature reflection, was content with Yeats's announcement of his death (in the story "Rosa Alchemica" of 1897), judging that "he had done me a service" since "One by one my correspondents ceased to write".

Robartes and Aherne were characters from Yeats's prose fiction of the late 1890s, who underwent resurrection in very much later work. Unable to leave them alone, the poet imagined them failing to leave him alone: in the 1925 introduction, the stalkers reach "the little Bloomsbury court where Mr Yeats had his lodging", but Robartes reasons that "it will be better to write and make an appointment", since "He is almost certain to be out". Years pass, and finally the pair meet Yeats, much against Aherne's wishes ("Mr Yeats has intellectual belief but he is entirely without moral faith", he protests to his companion), to pass over to him the materials to be written up as A Vision. Eight years earlier, in The Wild Swans at Coole, the same characters had shared the poem "The Phases of the Moon", turning up this time at Yeats's tower, Thoor Ballylee, where Aherne asks Robartes, "Why should not you / Who know it all ring at his door?". Here, Robartes gives Yeats and his 1890s fiction some brisk treatment:

He wrote of me in that extravagant style
He had learnt from Pater, and to round his tale
Said I was dead; and dead I choose to be.

Not so much dead as never alive, Robartes still had plenty of business to transact with Yeats; and Yeats, for his part, had no intention of leaving him alone. Ideas of resuscitating prose fiction as one of his genres are aired by the poet in a letter to Ezra Pound of 1918, where "a bundle of stories and dialogues concerning Michael Robartes" is mentioned. (The project is not very promising: "One that I am thinking out at present", Yeats explains, "concerns the Egyptian Sphinx which becomes jealous of Christ and thinks of being born.") By 1922, Yeats reported to his bibliographer, Allan Wade, that "I have brought him [Robartes] back to life", and shared the joke about his character's demise: "My new story is that he is very indignant because I used his real name in describing a number of fictitious adventures, and that because I called my fictitious hero by his name, many people have supposed him to be dead". By 1924, sending Edmund Dulac "my preface, or rather Owen Aherne's" to illustrate for A Vision, Yeats could scribble the postscript, "I am just off to Senate" – there to fail again, presumably, to leave the dead alone.

All through the mid-1920s, Yeats busied himself with the repackaging of his own writings. In the potentially profitable wake of his 1923 Nobel Prize, Yeats's publishers, Macmillan, undertook The Collected Works of W. B. Yeats and shaped these eventually into seven volumes. Early Poems and Stories, which appeared in 1925, brought together Yeats's fiction from The Celtic Twilight (1893) and The Secret Rose (1897), both of which books had been revised and republished by the poet already once or more, with the early (and enduringly popular) poetry alongside which the stories, supernatural anecdotes and ventures into folklore of his short prose had been composed. In this 1925 volume, Robartes and Aherne found themselves back in circulation (just when A Vision, published privately, was allowing them to express satisfaction at having dropped out of sight), in stories first printed near the end of the previous century. The "extravagant style" in which they had come to birth now had its wings clipped, resembling less what Yeats supposed to be the style of Walter Pater; at the same time, more recent Yeatsian idioms and preoccupations were allowed a certain prominence. In his dealings with the writings of his own past self in the mid-1920s, Yeats worked to a strictly contemporary artistic agenda.

Editing and rearranging the large mass of his early prose, Yeats tried to bring into coherence a diffuse body of writing. The pieces which were first collected in The Celtic Twilight were largely concerned with Irish folklore. These detailed, and occasionally meandering, reports from what Yeats considered the front line of racial memory and pagan religious instinct were deliberately distinct both in tone and procedure from the already established methods of the folklorist. The young Yeats's prose is highly wrought, and yet this style is at the service of no real argument.

It is important to the effect of The Celtic Twilight that its first-person voice should be identified as that of a young modern poet, importing much un-Victorian primitivism and mystery into contemporary writing; beyond that, larger patterns of coherence (and even smaller ones) are neglected. Ghosts abound, but not as the agents of philosophical instruction or religious apocalypse. "Drumcliff and Rosses", Yeats writes of his own home ground, "are choke-full of ghosts", adding a catalogue which seems to tire of its own effects: "By bog, road, rath, hillside, sea-border they gather in all shapes: headless women, men in armour, shadow hares, fire-tongued hounds, whistling seals, and so on". Just in case his readers might baulk at the last item (having taken the others in their stride), Yeats tops this off with, "A whistling seal sank a ship the other day". The supernatural is everywhere, but its meaning and intentions (if any) are generally inscrutable. One anecdote tells of how the Devil approaches two women as a lover: he offers a lift to one; she refuses, and he vanishes. The story of the second woman is similarly un-scary:

> The other was out on the road late at night waiting for her young man, when something came flapping and rolling along the road up to her feet. It had the likeness of a newspaper, and presently it flapped up into her face, and she knew by the size of it that it was the Irish Times. All of a sudden it changed into a young man, who asked her to go walking with him. She would not, and he vanished.

Although this dates in fact from 1902, Yeats was able to place it in The Celtic Twilight with artistic propriety; the idiosyncratically worldly grasp of the supernatural was essential to the collection of ten years before, even if the idea of the Devil taking the physical shape of a copy of a Unionist newspaper tickled the sense of humour of a slightly older and more experienced man. Later still, Senator Yeats was content to put back into print a joke which he might no longer, perhaps, be altogether inclined to make.

The younger self who wrote The Celtic Twilight was, for Yeats, indistinguishable from the author of the verse which had eventually delivered him a measure of celebrity, but which his own later poetry had – artistically and intellectually – far outstripped. For this reason, Early Poems and Stories made a useful conjunction. Yeats's work begins in an apprehension of the supernatural, but the core of his achievement is in the lifelong labour of understanding that initial – uncertain, conflicted and self-doubting – series of encounters. In the early prose, Yeats wrote as a bystander of his own poetic inspiration – with results that were occasionally more fully achieved, in their way, than the early poems themselves. The narrative voice of this prose is observant and sometimes ironic: it is liable to exchange a scientifically tinged tone of objectivity for the rapt over-expressiveness of abandoned credulousness; yet it is a fresh voice, and one capable both of economy and arresting directness.

Of the many figures who make up The Celtic Twilight's cast, the most important is that cut by Yeats himself as narrator. It is perhaps unsurprising that this figure should have haunted an older Yeats in a troubling way; for taking care of the business of a literary career, as well as the compulsions of an autobiographical artistic temperament, meant that hc could not leave this particular spirit alone. In "The Old Town", a memory of incidents in 1887, first published in 1902, Yeats told the story of a walk with his two Middleton cousins through the ruins of Sligo's "Old Town", burned to the ground in the Cromwellian wars. In his account, all three are poised "on the threshold, between sleeping and waking, where Sphinxes and Chimeras sit open-eyed and where there are always murmurings and whisperings".

At first, it is only Lucy Middleton who is seeing something strange, but soon the two men also witness the appearance of a "small bright light on the horizon, as it seemed, mounting up slowly towards the sky". A dance of strange lights follows, and Yeats then allows himself some apparently candid reflections on the experience:

We saw it all in such a dream, and it seems all so unreal, that I have never written of it until now, and hardly ever spoken of it, and even when thinking, because of some unreasonable impulse, I have avoided giving it weight in the argument. Perhaps I have felt that my recollections of things seen when the sense of reality was weakened must be untrustworthy.

Characteristically, Yeats qualifies his scruples with a supplementary anecdote of the inexplicable and the uncanny (where a mirror emits tapping sounds as if struck by "a shower of peas"). The rationalizing voice of controlled recollection, as often in The Celtic Twilight, finds itself unable to keep up with the pace and sheer oddity of its material, and the narrative presence of Yeats is constantly being surprised by what lies outside its power to explain.

For the young Yeats (as for his older self, in a different way), experience was a story, to which all manner of other stories – from myth, history, religion and folklore – were subservient, and for which they were readily serviceable. Keen to convey a sense of his own visionary capacities, Yeats's need to emphasize his rational (and literary) abilities meant that other, more self-abandoned, visionary figures had to be created to fill out the Irish autobiographical fiction that was being created. Country people of all kinds were dragooned to this purpose (notably Mary Battell, housekeeper to Yeats's uncle), but so was the poet's friend and contemporary, George Russell, who in his youth was given to taking long walks in the Dublin hills, "talking to half-mad and visionary peasants", as Yeats puts it in The Celtic Twilight. In a chapter which he entitles simply "A Visionary" (and where Russell is "X"), Yeats puts some distance between himself and his companion in the matter of supernatural apprehension:

"Is it the influence of some living person who thinks of us, and whose thoughts appear to us in that symbolic form?" I said; for I am well instructed in the ways of the visionaries and in the fashion of their speech. "No," he replied; for if it were the thoughts of a person who is alive I should feel the living influence in my living body, and my heart would beat and my breath would fail. It is a spirit. It is someone who is dead or who has never lived."

The George Russell who had lived (and was indeed still living) to be a contemporary of Yeats in the 1920s found himself recollected in The Trembling of the Veil (1922) as someone who "saw visions continually, perhaps more continually than any modern man since Swedenborg". This older Yeats insisted that "I wanted him to examine and question his visions.... I thought symbolic what he thought real", and reached the conclusion that "The wholeness of the supernatural world can only express itself in personal form, because it has no epitome but man". If there was no such confidence in "A Visionary", haunted as the piece is by the possibility of meeting as "a spirit" "someone who is dead or has never lived", there is an altogether more literary emphasis both on Russell's having given up the career of a poet, and (implicitly, at least) the narrator's own poetic achievements. "X" meets on his walks "an old peasant who, dumb to most men, poured out his cares for him", these cares culminating in the lament "The fret [Irish for doom] is over me". The refrain was taken up in Yeats's poem "The Old Pensioner", a slight two-stanza affair of 1890: "And therefore do I wander on / And the fret is on me.... The well-known faces are all gone, / And the fret is on me".

In its earliest printings, "A Visionary" both quoted Russell's own poetry at length, with faint emanations of praise, and gave broad hints at the superior Yeatsian handling of the material to be found in The Countess Kathleen and Various Legends and Lyrics, published the year before The Celtic Twilight.

But Russell was not quite "X" in reality, and was himself perfectly capable of criticizing his old friend's poems. It was a recurring irritation to Yeats that Russell persisted in remembering (and quoting) the earlier versions of these poems, giving to them a protracted, ghostly existence. So, when Yeats came to absorb The Celtic Twilight within Early Poems and Stories, "The Old Pensioner" was treated (pointedly) to a supercharged rewrite, becoming "The Lamentation of the Old Pensioner" and losing its original, Russell-supplied refrain; now, the wandering old man would announce that "I spit into the face of Time / That has transfigured me." To all intents and purposes, the new version is a 1920s Yeats poem, its rhetoric and certainty obliterating the spirit of its nineteenth-century source. Nevertheless, the bothersome figure of "X", like someone dead or perhaps never (quite) alive, lingered in the print of the 1925 collection.

Yeats's gift for fiction was profitable enough to be developed by the poet in the course of the 1890s, and the stories which were to form The Secret Rose show a more ambitious artist at work, shaping folkloric materials into very carefully crafted form. It was this writing which Yeats was later to see as blighted stylistically by Pater; but the judgement is in some ways an unfair one, since the prose style puts on display a promisingly developed sense for both the elaborate and the incantatory which, in its way, seldom rings false: the prose is worked, and visibly worked up at times, but it very seldom feels (in the negative sense) artificial: it is undoubtedly true to something at least in Yeats at the time. As originally published, the collection of stories carries a dedication to Russell (now with his pen name "Æ"), and the confession that Yeats believes poetry can only be made "by looking into that little, infinite, faltering, eternal flame that one calls one's self". It is by the weak light of this flame that Yeats recommends an approach to the supernatural. In a concluding flourish, Russell is reminded that in Ireland "no shining candelabra have prevented us from looking into the darkness, and when one looks into the darkness there is always something there". The dedication, in its turn, was dropped, and fell into the darkness of Yeats's publishing history.

The "something there" in the darkness, through all Yeats's revisions and reimaginings of supernatural material, was to remain indefinite. In the fiction, however, "something" can find itself made solid as someone; and here, Yeats created figures that mediated between the mortal world and the world beyond, possessing the comparative solidity of fictional characters. They tended to possess, also, George Russell's red hair. First among these is the poet Red Hanrahan, who appeared in a story of 1892 (as O'Sullivan the Red), and went on to occupy a suite of six stories in The Secret Rose. Yeats's historical model here was a Munster poet of the eighteenth century, Eoghan Rua Ó Súilleabháin, but the figure who emerges in the stories is a peasant alter ego for Yeats himself: tormented by supernatural revelation and unrequited love, the object of popular acclaim at the same time as regular persecution, Hanrahan is a poet doomed by his resistance to "the call of the daughters of the Sidhe" who "will find no comfort in the love of the women of the earth to the end of life and time", since "the cold of the grave is in his heart for ever". The stories follow Hanrahan through both natural and supernatural disappointments to his inevitable death, but Yeats was not by any means finished with the arc of experience thus described. When the poet's next red-headed man, Michael Robartes, appears in the final (heavily and self-consciously fin de siècle) stories of The Secret Rose, it is as Hanrahan's occult successor. Robartes is a magician rather than a folk poet; but he possesses all the elemental abandon of his predecessor, and goes on (at least in The Secret Rose) to share his fate. Yeats gives Hanrahan a mystical-religious straight man, Owen Aherne, who begins "Rosa Alchemica" by talking about Robartes's "tragic end", which took place "more than ten years" ago; and recounts an alarming visit from the magician, heralded by "a loud knocking at the door". "I shuddered", Aherne remembers, "as I drew the bolt": "I found before me Michael Robartes, whom I had not seen for years, and whose wild red hair, fierce eyes, sensitive, tremulous lips and rough clothes, made him look now, just as they used to fifteen years before, something between a debauchee, a saint, and a peasant".

As he and Aherne would do much later, when they come out of the dark and the past to visit Yeats himself, Robartes appears as a not entirely welcome surprise, sending the present back into memories of "years before". In "Rosa Alchemica", Aherne gives his version of a kind of magical orgy hosted by Robartes in the West of Ireland, one which ends in violent revenge taken by the pious (and affronted) locals. This is a very important piece of writing for Yeats, a parable of the necessary end of his own Symbolist poetry, which Robartes's magic partly represents. But any relief at Robartes's presumed end was premature, whether for Yeats (in some moods) or for his readers. Robert Bridges wrote to the poet in 1897, with proper medical regard, that "I hope that you will take care of your body", adding the wish "that the saints or goddesses will preserve you from too much of the Rosa Alchemica"; he let Yeats know, too, that he was "glad that Michael Robartes is dead".

By the 1920s, in the throes of another period of intellectual and stylistic upheaval, Yeats brought Robartes back from the dead by means of the fiction of having the character seek him out, to tantalize him once more with the puzzles and half-cracked codes of occult knowledge. In preparing (yet again) his fictional prose for a new edition, Yeats encountered the vivid ghosts of unfinished business – literary, autobiographical and philosophical – which was coming to seem unfinishable.

At some point, the momentum of Yeats's creativity overwhelmed his ambitions to settle on fixed and final forms of thought. The poetry of The Tower (1928) and The Winding Stair (1933) is ruthlessly committed to pressing everything from the past into service: Yeats's youth and middle age, as much as history and legend, are primarily grist to the poet's artistic mill. In such an unsparing environment, Yeats's past work was just as ripe for plunder as other aspects of his life and thought; and the long-ingrained habits of revision came to be parts of the dynamic process of self-imagining on which all of the poet's later work is founded. But ghosts have a way of upsetting such priorities, since they come back from a past which they – unlike the haunted person – have never outgrown, disowned, or forgotten.

The book called Mythologies was published in 1959, twenty years after Yeats's death, but elements of its arrangement had been settled by the poet in the 1930s, when he was working with Macmillan towards a so-called edition de luxe of his works. Naturally, further changes were made to the arrangement of the early prose in Early Poems and Stories; textual decisions were taken with the impulsiveness of creativity, and the newly imagined edition was no closer than its predecessors to the exact styles and procedures of books like The Celtic Twilight or The Secret Rose. Warwick Gould and Deirdre Toomey have now edited Mythologies in accord with Yeats's latest thoughts. By removing the meditation Per Amica Silentia Lunae (1917), which was never at home in the book of 1959, and which Yeats never intended to appear in that context, Gould and Toomey give us the short prose fiction which the poet wished to preserve, in the form and order that seemed to him acceptable late in life. How far short of the whole story this is may be gauged from the seventy pages of appendices which are necessary to record Yeats's textual changes, and the more than 200 pages devoted to explanatory and textual notes. The critical and textual work here is as impressive as it is copious, and the editors have performed a scholarly service for Yeats far in excess of anything of which he would himself have been capable.There can be no doubt that this edition sheds an extraordinary light on an aspect of Yeats's writing which has generally been left in semi-darkness, and which it is important for critics of the poet to understand. The editorial achievement here is enormous, and it will last.

But now that the textual ghosts of Mythologies are in broad daylight, so to speak, it is also obvious that Yeats was not so much haunted by his past as the haunter of it,subjecting his writings, like his life, to repeated questionings and changes of emphasis. Often, damage is done in the process: there is repeated stylistic damage, for example, in the ways Yeats tended to revise his prose, and wholesale vandalism at times (as in the Lady Gregory-inspired "improvements" to the dialogue of the Red Hanrahan stories, first perpetrated in 1905, and dutifully retained thereafter).The Yeats who published The Secret Rose knew more about the craft of fiction than the old man (and great poet) of the 1930s. To have Mythologies, then, even in an immaculately edited form, is not a substitute for the earlier versions of the material it contains. We can understand that Yeats was unable to leave the dead alone; what is more challenging to appreciate is the fact that Yeats's dead were often never alive, "fictitious characters" who "live through events that were a travesty of real events", as Owen Aherne puts it in A Vision. Was the writer W. B. Yeats one such? As Yeats puts the matter in the first-person voice of "The Circus Animals' Desertion" (1939), he was always engaged in inventing "character isolated by a deed / To engross the present", and it was in fiction, as much as with the dead, that he found the place "where all the ladders start / In the foul rag-and-bone shop of the heart".

At first, it is only Lucy Middleton who is seeing something strange, but soon the two men also witness the appearance of a "small bright light on the horizon, as it seemed, mounting up slowly towards the sky". A dance of strange lights follows, and Yeats then allows himself some apparently candid reflections on the experience:

We saw it all in such a dream, and it seems all so unreal, that I have never written of it until now, and hardly ever spoken of it, and even when thinking, because of some unreasonable impulse, I have avoided giving it weight in the argument. Perhaps I have felt that my recollections of things seen when the sense of reality was weakened must be untrustworthy.

Characteristically, Yeats qualifies his scruples with a supplementary anecdote of the inexplicable and the uncanny (where a mirror emits tapping sounds as if struck by "a shower of peas"). The rationalizing voice of controlled recollection, as often in The Celtic Twilight, finds itself unable to keep up with the pace and sheer oddity of its material, and the narrative presence of Yeats is constantly being surprised by what lies outside its power to explain.

For the young Yeats (as for his older self, in a different way), experience was a story, to which all manner of other stories – from myth, history, religion and folklore – were subservient, and for which they were readily serviceable. Keen to convey a sense of his own visionary capacities, Yeats's need to emphasize his rational (and literary) abilities meant that other, more self-abandoned, visionary figures had to be created to fill out the Irish autobiographical fiction that was being created. Country people of all kinds were dragooned to this purpose (notably Mary Battell, housekeeper to Yeats's uncle), but so was the poet's friend and contemporary, George Russell, who in his youth was given to taking long walks in the Dublin hills, "talking to half-mad and visionary peasants", as Yeats puts it in The Celtic Twilight. In a chapter which he entitles simply "A Visionary" (and where Russell is "X"), Yeats puts some distance between himself and his companion in the matter of supernatural apprehension:

"Is it the influence of some living person who thinks of us, and whose thoughts appear to us in that symbolic form?" I said; for I am well instructed in the ways of the visionaries and in the fashion of their speech. "No," he replied; for if it were the thoughts of a person who is alive I should feel the living influence in my living body, and my heart would beat and my breath would fail. It is a spirit. It is someone who is dead or who has never lived."

The George Russell who had lived (and was indeed still living) to be a contemporary of Yeats in the 1920s found himself recollected in The Trembling of the Veil (1922) as someone who "saw visions continually, perhaps more continually than any modern man since Swedenborg". This older Yeats insisted that "I wanted him to examine and question his visions.... I thought symbolic what he thought real", and reached the conclusion that "The wholeness of the supernatural world can only express itself in personal form, because it has no epitome but man". If there was no such confidence in "A Visionary", haunted as the piece is by the possibility of meeting as "a spirit" "someone who is dead or has never lived", there is an altogether more literary emphasis both on Russell's having given up the career of a poet, and (implicitly, at least) the narrator's own poetic achievements. "X" meets on his walks "an old peasant who, dumb to most men, poured out his cares for him", these cares culminating in the lament "The fret [Irish for doom] is over me".

The refrain was taken up in Yeats's poem "The Old Pensioner", a slight two-stanza affair of 1890: "And therefore do I wander on / And the fret is on me.... The well-known faces are all gone, / And the fret is on me". In its earliest printings, "A Visionary" both quoted Russell's own poetry at length, with faint emanations of praise, and gave broad hints at the superior Yeatsian handling of the material to be found in The Countess Kathleen and Various Legends and Lyrics, published the year before The Celtic Twilight.

But Russell was not quite "X" in reality, and was himself perfectly capable of criticizing his old friend's poems. It was a recurring irritation to Yeats that Russell persisted in remembering (and quoting) the earlier versions of these poems, giving to them a protracted, ghostly existence. So, when Yeats came to absorb The Celtic Twilight within Early Poems and Stories, "The Old Pensioner" was treated (pointedly) to a supercharged rewrite, becoming "The Lamentation of the Old Pensioner" and losing its original, Russell-supplied refrain; now, the wandering old man would announce that "I spit into the face of Time / That has transfigured me." To all intents and purposes, the new version is a 1920s Yeats poem, its rhetoric and certainty obliterating the spirit of its nineteenth-century source. Nevertheless, the bothersome figure of "X", like someone dead or perhaps never (quite) alive, lingered in the print of the 1925 collection.

Yeats's gift for fiction was profitable enough to be developed by the poet in the course of the 1890s, and the stories which were to form The Secret Rose show a more ambitious artist at work, shaping folkloric materials into very carefully crafted form. It was this writing which Yeats was later to see as blighted stylistically by Pater; but the judgement is in some ways an unfair one, since the prose style puts on display a promisingly developed sense for both the elaborate and the incantatory which, in its way, seldom rings false: the prose is worked, and visibly worked up at times, but it very seldom feels (in the negative sense) artificial: it is undoubtedly true to something at least in Yeats at the time. As originally published, the collection of stories carries a dedication to Russell (now with his pen name "Æ"), and the confession that Yeats believes poetry can only be made "by looking into that little, infinite, faltering, eternal flame that one calls one's self". It is by the weak light of this flame that Yeats recommends an approach to the supernatural. In a concluding flourish, Russell is reminded that in Ireland "no shining candelabra have prevented us from looking into the darkness, and when one looks into the darkness there is always something there". The dedication, in its turn, was dropped, and fell into the darkness of Yeats's publishing history.

The "something there" in the darkness, through all Yeats's revisions and reimaginings of supernatural material, was to remain indefinite. In the fiction, however, "something" can find itself made solid as someone; and here, Yeats created figures that mediated between the mortal world and the world beyond, possessing the comparative solidity of fictional characters. They tended to possess, also, George Russell's red hair. First among these is the poet Red Hanrahan, who appeared in a story of 1892 (as O'Sullivan the Red), and went on to occupy a suite of six stories in The Secret Rose. Yeats's historical model here was a Munster poet of the eighteenth century, Eoghan Rua Ó Súilleabháin, but the figure who emerges in the stories is a peasant alter ego for Yeats himself: tormented by supernatural revelation and unrequited love, the object of popular acclaim at the same time as regular persecution, Hanrahan is a poet doomed by his resistance to "the call of the daughters of the Sidhe" who "will find no comfort in the love of the women of the earth to the end of life and time", since "the cold of the grave is in his heart for ever".

The stories follow Hanrahan through both natural and supernatural disappointments to his inevitable death, but Yeats was not by any means finished with the arc of experience thus described. When the poet's next red-headed man, Michael Robartes, appears in the final (heavily and self-consciously fin de siècle) stories of The Secret Rose, it is as Hanrahan's occult successor. Robartes is a magician rather than a folk poet; but he possesses all the elemental abandon of his predecessor, and goes on (at least in The Secret Rose) to share his fate. Yeats gives Hanrahan a mystical-religious straight man, Owen Aherne, who begins "Rosa Alchemica" by talking about Robartes's "tragic end", which took place "more than ten years" ago; and recounts an alarming visit from the magician, heralded by "a loud knocking at the door". "I shuddered", Aherne remembers, "as I drew the bolt": "I found before me Michael Robartes, whom I had not seen for years, and whose wild red hair, fierce eyes, sensitive, tremulous lips and rough clothes, made him look now, just as they used to fifteen years before, something between a debauchee, a saint, and a peasant".

As he and Aherne would do much later, when they come out of the dark and the past to visit Yeats himself, Robartes appears as a not entirely welcome surprise, sending the present back into memories of "years before". In "Rosa Alchemica", Aherne gives his version of a kind of magical orgy hosted by Robartes in the West of Ireland, one which ends in violent revenge taken by the pious (and affronted) locals. This is a very important piece of writing for Yeats, a parable of the necessary end of his own Symbolist poetry, which Robartes's magic partly represents. But any relief at Robartes's presumed end was premature, whether for Yeats (in some moods) or for his readers. Robert Bridges wrote to the poet in 1897, with proper medical regard, that "I hope that you will take care of your body", adding the wish "that the saints or goddesses will preserve you from too much of the Rosa Alchemica"; he let Yeats know, too, that he was "glad that Michael Robartes is dead".

By the 1920s, in the throes of another period of intellectual and stylistic upheaval, Yeats brought Robartes back from the dead by means of the fiction of having the character seek him out, to tantalize him once more with the puzzles and half-cracked codes of occult knowledge. In preparing (yet again) his fictional prose for a new edition, Yeats encountered the vivid ghosts of unfinished business – literary, autobiographical and philosophical – which was coming to seem unfinishable.

At some point, the momentum of Yeats's creativity overwhelmed his ambitions to settle on fixed and final forms of thought. The poetry of The Tower (1928) and The Winding Stair (1933) is ruthlessly committed to pressing everything from the past into service: Yeats's youth and middle age, as much as history and legend, are primarily grist to the poet's artistic mill. In such an unsparing environment, Yeats's past work was just as ripe for plunder as other aspects of his life and thought; and the long-ingrained habits of revision came to be parts of the dynamic process of self-imagining on which all of the poet's later work is founded. But ghosts have a way of upsetting such priorities, since they come back from a past which they – unlike the haunted person – have never outgrown, disowned, or forgotten.

The book called Mythologies was published in 1959, twenty years after Yeats's death, but elements of its arrangement had been settled by the poet in the 1930s, when he was working with Macmillan towards a so-called edition de luxe of his works. Naturally, further changes were made to the arrangement of the early prose in Early Poems and Stories; textual decisions were taken with the impulsiveness of creativity, and the newly imagined edition was no closer than its predecessors to the exact styles and procedures of books like The Celtic Twilight or The Secret Rose. Warwick Gould and Deirdre Toomey have now edited Mythologies in accord with Yeats's latest thoughts. By removing the meditation Per Amica Silentia Lunae (1917), which was never at home in the book of 1959, and which Yeats never intended to appear in that context, Gould and Toomey give us the short prose fiction which the poet wished to preserve, in the form and order that seemed to him acceptable late in life. How far short of the whole story this is may be gauged from the seventy pages of appendices which are necessary to record Yeats's textual changes, and the more than 200 pages devoted to explanatory and textual notes. The critical and textual work here is as impressive as it is copious, and the editors have performed a scholarly service for Yeats far in excess of anything of which he would himself have been capable. There can be no doubt that this edition sheds an extraordinary light on an aspect of Yeats's writing which has generally been left in semi-darkness, and which it is important for critics of the poet to understand. The editorial achievement here is enormous, and it will last.

But now that the textual ghosts of Mythologies are in broad daylight, so to speak, it is also obvious that Yeats was not so much haunted by his past as the haunter of it, subjecting his writings, like his life, to repeated questionings and changes of emphasis. Often, damage is done in the process: there is repeated stylistic damage, for example, in the ways Yeats tended to revise his prose, and wholesale vandalism at times (as in the Lady Gregory-inspired "improvements" to the dialogue of the Red Hanrahan stories, first perpetrated in 1905, and dutifully retained thereafter). The Yeats who published The Secret Rose knew more about the craft of fiction than the old man (and great poet) of the 1930s. To have Mythologies, then, even in an immaculately edited form, is not a substitute for the earlier versions of the material it contains. We can understand that Yeats was unable to leave the dead alone; what is more challenging to appreciate is the fact that Yeats's dead were often never alive, "fictitious characters" who "live through events that were a travesty of real events", as Owen Aherne puts it in A Vision. Was the writer W. B. Yeats one such? As Yeats puts the matter in the first-person voice of "The Circus Animals' Desertion" (1939), he was always engaged in inventing "character isolated by a deed / To engross the present", and it was in fiction, as much as with the dead, that he found the place "where all the ladders start / In the foul rag-and-bone shop of the heart".

Q.6. Discuss the Mystical aspect of W.B.Yeats' poems and life

Or

Q. Discuss mysticism in Yeats poetry

The main themes William Butler Yeats treated in his poems are Irish nationalism, Celtic mythology, love, ageing and mysticism. But the last mentioned seems to be interpenetrating all his work. Just as Yeats himself once said: "The mystical life is the centre of all that I do and all that I think and all that I write." Besides the poems this theme is elaborated in the best way in Yeats' book *A Vision*, and also greatly revealed in his *Essays* and dramas. In this paper I would like to describe Yeats' mystical opinions and to present parts of his poems where the mystical and occult occur.

For better understanding of Yeats' choose to write about mystics it would be good to mention some facts and backgrounds which formed his mind. His mother's family, the Pollexfens, were known for their eccentricities manifested by, for our example, an interest in astrology and magic. The unbelief and arguments of Yeats' father against Christian belief led Yeats to investigate informal and exotic ones. He welcomed any teaching which spoke of supersensual experiences, or gave him a background for the visions which came to him " from beyond the mind". Aged 20 he was among the founders of a group devoted to the occult, the Dublin Hermetic Society. When the family went to London in 1887, he joined a famous mystical society of his days, the Theosophical Society. Yeats was as a visionary insisted on surrounding himself with images. Just magic and its imaginative life appealed to him. The age of science was not interesting to him, he was more attracted by astrology than astronomy. He began to study such visionary traditions as the Platonic, the Neoplatonic, the Swedenborgian, the alchemical, the Tibetan Mysteries, Buddhism and other beliefs.

He was not only a theoretic reader but he was also eager to verify many supernatural phenomenas. He had experimented with telepathy and clairvoyance with his uncle George Pollexfen. In 1890 Yeats joined Hermetic Order of the Golden Dawn, the organisation which incorporated traditional European Cabalistic Magic and astrology. This society enabled him constant experimentation and expression. He was learning magical and esoteric symbols, creating interrelationships between the seasons, various parts of body, the five elements, numbers, etc. Yeats combined this knowledge with his own experiences and poetic genius and made his own system of symbols. Finally, he was able to express in writing what he was envisioning. He treats such themes as questions of life and death, eternity, immortality, change and changelessness of things and all the world.

As mentioned, Yeats was a visionary so we can look at first to the places in the poems where he speaks directly about his visions and dreams. There are various kinds of these visions, some come out from the history, some speak about the life after death, and many reveal the images of fairies and myths form the "Great Memory". Basically, there are two types of such visions. One is when he himself wants to envision or call for it using own will (sometimes he put special flowers beside his bed). The second is when he is called or enchanted by a vision or dream practically without his will or control.

And I call up McGregor from the grave, / for in my firs hard springtime we were friends (The Tower)

I saw a staring virgin stand / Where holy Dionysus died, And tear the heart out of his side, / And lay the heart upon her hand / And bear that beating heart away (Two Songs from a Play)

When I had laid it on the floor / I went to blow the fire aflame, / But something rustled on the floor, / And someone called me by my name: / It had become a glimmering girl / With apple blossom in her hair / Who called me by my name and ran / And faded through the brightening air. (The Song of Wandering Aengus)

It was the dream itself enchanted me / Character isolated by a deed / To engross the present and dominate memory. (The Circus Animals' Desertion)

The dews drop slowly and dreams gather: unknown spears / Suddenly hurtle before my dream-awakened eyes, / And the clash of fallen horseman and the cries / Of unknown perishing armies beat about my ears. (The Valley of the Black Pig).

Suddenly I saw the cold and rook-delighting heaven / That seemed as though ice burned and was but the more ice, / And thereupon imagination and heart were driven / So wild that every casual thought of that and this / Vanished, and left but memories, that should be out of season (The Cold Heaven)

Numerous visions were connected with Yeats' leading idea of "gyres", the cones that spiral together and symbolise objectivity and subjectivity of the world. These idea was practically collaborated with his wife through her automatic writing and connection with a ghost named Leo Africanus. The gyres give the image of a single circle when looking down on them. This circle represents the moon and the twenty-eight phases of the moon which are closely related to the progression of time and world history. The new and full moon are the periods where time begins end ends. However, it is not an end in the right sense of the word, it is actually a beginning of a new cycle. The phases in between are the growth and evolution of the human soul over time. The cycle lasts two thousand years and each period is dominated by a single civilization and its own prevailing myth. The present one begun with the birth of Christ and now, as Yeats says, is already in the period of disintegration. Thus the end of our cycle will come in the year of 2000. He calls this time "The Second Coming". It might remind us the currently appearing ideas of the suggested coming of the age of "Aquarius". In *Per Amica Silentia Lunae,* Yeats says that the motion of gyres and therefore the fate of a man or the world is mathematically predestined. He also adds that therefore the coming of such personalities as Buddha, Christ or Napoleon could have been predicted. All these ideas are mainly worked out in *A Vision* but, of course, they also appeared in the Yeats' poems:

Though I had long perned in the gyre,/ Between my hatred and desire,/ I saw my freedom won/ And all laugh in the sun. (Demon and Beast)

The darkness drops again; but now I know / That twenty centuries of stony sleep / Were vexed to nightmare by a rocking cradle, / And what rough beast, its hour come round at last, / Slouches toward Bethlehem to be born ? (The Second Coming) but man's life is thought, / And he, despite his terror, cannot cease / Ravening through century after century /... / Egypt and Greece, goodbye, and good-bye, Rome ! (Supernatural Songs)

The Gyres ! the gyres ! Old Rocky Face, look forth; / Things tought too long can be no longer thought, / For beauty dies of beauty, worth of worth (The Gyres)

All things fall and are built again, / And those that build them again are gay. (Lapis Lazuli)

Together with the idea of cyclic history comes to Yeats the idea of cyclic repeating of life and death, the reincarnation of souls. He also speaks about what happens after death, describing the process of return of the soul to the cosmic trance (Yeats also calls it Anima Mundi or "artifice of eternity"), from which it sprang. The body is looked on as an animal part of a man full of desires which should be purified (this purification is symbolised by a "sages standing in God's holy fire" who "consume" desires "away").

O sages standing in God's holy fire /.../ Consume my heart away; sick with desire / And fastened to a dying animal / It knows not what it is; and gather me / Into the artifice of eternity (Sailing to Byzantium)

Yeats shared the idea of reincarnating of a soul through all worldly things, not only within the human being. This idea actually refers to his view at the world or the universe as a view in the very modern term. It is the way of looking at the universe as a whole interconnected system of energies, always changing but never disappearing. Thus the first example below refers to that particular idea and the next ones show other parts of poems treating the cycle of life and death:

I have been a hazel-tree, and they hung / The Pilot Star and the Crooked Plough / Among my leaves in times out of mind: / I became a rush that horses tread: / I became a man, a hater of the wind (He Thinks of His Past Greatness When a Part of the Constellations of Heaven)

Many times he died, / Many times rose again. (Death)

Many times man lives and dies / Between his two eternities, / That of race and that of soul (Under Ben Bulben)

Although Yeats saw and felt around himself the unchangeable order of dying and fading of temporary things, he was looking for something what wouldn't be affected by this change, the immortality and eternity. That was the world where the imagination comes from. He said that the world of imagination is just the eternal world, in opposite to the world of reason, which is the world of lies and cheat, phantasm falling apart. It is, not surprisingly, a very similar idea to the ideas of William Blake, and also to the eastern idea of illusion of the material world (Maya). The source of all imagination was for Yeats already mentioned Anima Mundi, the eternal soul of the universe.

He also spoke about the Great Memory (or Great Mind) from which every images and truth spring. He wrote in one of his essays how surprised he was whenever he found that an image that came "out of beyond [his] mind" was already described by some previous poet or writer. Yeats said, that therefore a poet and his imagination is a medium of the truth coming from the place of wisdom to the world. For him every true poet was also a prophet. And he called together those " who have sought more than is in rain or dew" to reveal the wisdom to people. However he felt that the modern time was just against the possibility of imaginative life, what he felt as a decline and prophesied the "Second Coming".

Whose images, in the Great Memory stored, / Come with loud cry and panting breast / To break upon a sleeper's rest (The Tower)

Things out of perfection sail, / And all their swelling canvas wear (Old Tom Again)

Those masterful images because complete / Grew in pure mind (The Circus Animals'Desertion)

Though leaves are many, the root is one; /... / I swayed my leaves and flowers in the sun; / Now I may wither into the truth. (The Coming of Wisdom with Me)

Though like a road / That men pass over / My body makes no moan / But sings on: / All things remain in God. (Crazy Jane on God)

Yeats' desire and striving for knowledge and truth lasted through all his life. Although he was sceptic in belief that a man could reach the final truth or knowledge during this stage on the Earth, Yeats was vivid and enthusiastic till the end of his life. He wanted to find and know his true self, not only the "mask". It is said that many poets wrote their best poetry in their youth. However, Yeats logically, as he was progressing in the effort to be better and better, wrote many of his best poems at the end of his life. Practically, he followed the ideal pattern of human life, the idea of the wise old age.

He achieved the wished aims of his life: he became famous, had money, old house, wife, daughter, son and good friends. He envisioned much of the wisdom, he knew many of the life after death. Yet he was still awaiting something to come, he was asking "What Then ?".

" The work is done." Grown old age he thought, / " According to my boyish plan; / Let the fools rage, I swered in naught, / Something to perfection brought"; / *But louder sang that ghost, " What then ? "* (What Than ?)

And I would find myself and not an image. (Ego Dominus Tuus)

Although Yeats suffered with diseases in his old age, he was still able to look at the world with a joy. He blessed the worldly things. He was reaching the similar he liked, the life of wise and mad sages. Despite the fact, that many times in his life he was feeling sadness and suffering, his mystical attitude enabled him to attain some states of ecstasy and blissful moments.

I pray ... / That I may seem, though I die old, / A foolish, passionate man. (A Prayer for Old Age)

Know why an old man should be mad. (Why Should Not Old Men Be Mad ?)

My body of a sudden blazed; / And twenty minutes more or less / It seemed, so great my happiness, / That was blessed and could bless. (Vacillation)

We must laugh and we must sing, / We are blest by everything, / Everything we look upon is blest. (A Dialogue of Self and Soul)

The Last Poems display perfectly the unbelievable energy of this old man. This energy I think did not spring only from Yeats' mystical experiences but also from the fact that he was till the end of his life doing what he liked and ever had wished to do. He wanted to reveal his attained knowledge and wisdom more and more clearly. He belonged to a few people who do not regret their life. In his last unfinished essay he wrote:

I know for certain that my time will not be long.... I am happy, and I think full of an energy, of an energy I had despaired of. It seems to me that I have found what I wanted.

I have mentioned only a few parts concerning the mysticism of Yeats'poems and life in this essay. Anyhow, the mentioned ones are still sufficient to make the reader convinced thatYeats' entirely described will of the person, striving for wisdom, makes his poems interesting till these days. They are full of appreciating honesty and personal feelings. It is not a cheap poetry of kitsch images of nature or love, it is a poetry charged with deep thoughts, poet's personality, wisdom and an effort to transmit it to the readers. Nevertheless, despite the fact that Yeats wanted to express himself clearly, many of his ideas in the poems are sometimes hard to understand for me. I think that to a reader who is not interested in mysticism they must be (similarly to Blake's poems) quite obscure.

Q.7. One of the important themes in Yeats's writing is his exploration of the relationship between the natural and the artificial, and particularly the relationship between nature and art. With particular reference to the two Byzantium poems, describe how Yeats characterizes this relationship. Does he prefer the natural to art, or art to nature?

Because the artificial is permanent, unfading, impervious to decay, beautiful, and free of the troubles of the human heart, and because the natural is impermanent, fading, destined to decay, frequently ugly, and troubled by pain and longing, Yeats consistently finds himself attracted to the artificial, particularly when it is at its most beautiful. In the Byzantium poems, Yeats glorifies a golden bird that is the apotheosis of the relationship between nature and art: the bird takes its form from nature, but it is not bound to "the fury and the mire of human veins." It will last forever, and will never forget how to sing; and Yeats longs to become it.

Q.8. Some of Yeats's least accessible poems are his works of visionary history, which often incorporate themes from *A Vision* and seem, on the surface, thematically irrelevant to contemporary readers. How can these poems best be understood—in other words, should they be read today strictly for their magnificent language, or is there a way in which they embrace more universal elements of human experience than their occult, mythological frame of reference might imply? (Think especially about "Leda and the Swan" and "The Second Coming.")

The language of "Leda" and "The Second Coming" is certainly magnificent, but the poems' themes are also quite powerful, and remain relevant to the experience of contemporary readers. Putting aside all the mystical jargon from *A Vision,* "The Second Coming" is a brilliant evocation of chaos and primal energy, and of a kind of eerie premonition: the sphinx "slouching toward Bethlehem" can be interpreted in many ways besides that which Yeats described. And "Leda" is a wonderful document of a violent encounter with the incomprehensible, the alien, the overwhelming, and of a turning point after which nothing will ever be the same.

Q.9. If you have read John Keats's great "Ode to a Nightingale," compare it to Yeats's equally great "Sailing to Byzantium." In what ways does the Yeats poem seem designed to refute the Keats poem? How does the singing golden bird differ from Keats's singing nightingale?

Our first clue that the Yeats poem may be related to the earlier Keats poem occurs in the first stanza, when the speaker calls the birds singing in the trees "dying generations," a phrase quite similar to one in Keats's ode—"Thou wast not born for death, immortal Bird! / No hungry generations tread thee down." From that moment on, the poems are as thematically opposite as is possible for two poems glorifying art. Keats's nightingale (a natural bird) is a symbol of lyric fluidity, expressiveness, change, and union with nature; around the nightingale, Keats thinks that it would be "sweet to die" and "to cease upon the midnight with no pain." Yeats's golden bird (an artificial bird) is a symbol of permanence, knowledge, unchangeability, and a liberating separation from nature; Yeats longs to be "gathered into the artifice of eternity" precisely because he does not wish to age and to die.

Q.10. Discuss the relationship between tendency and literary style in yeats

Or

Q. Do you agree that yeats tendency is fascist

One thing that Marxist criticism has not succeeded in doing is to trace the connection between "tendency" and literary style. The subject-matter and imagery of a book can be explained in sociological terms, but its texture seemingly cannot. Yet some such connection there must be. One knows, for instance, that a Socialist would not write like Chesterton or a Tory imperialist like Bernard Shaw, though HOW one knows it is not easy to say. In the case of Yeats, there must be some kind of connection between his wayward, even tortured style of writing and his rather sinister vision of life. Mr Menon is chiefly concerned with the esoteric philosophy underlying Yeats's work, but the quotations which are scattered all through his interesting book serve to remind one how artificial Yeats's manner of writing was. As a rule, this artificiality is accepted as Irishism, or Yeats is even credited with simplicity because he uses short words, but in fact one seldom comes on six consecutive lines of his verse in which there is not an archaism or an affected turn of speech. To take the nearest example:

Grant me an old man's Frenzy,
My self must I remake
Till I am Timon and Lear
Or that William Blake
Who beat upon the wall
Till Truth obeyed his call.

The unnecessary "that" imports a feeling of affectation, and the same tendency is present in all but Yeats's best passages. One is seldom long away from a suspicion of "quaintness", something that links up not only with the 'nineties, the Ivory Tower and the "calf covers of pissed-on green", but also with Rackham's drawings, Liberty art-fabrics and the PETER PAN never-never land, of which, after all, "The Happy Townland" is merely a more appetising example. This does not matter, because, on the whole, Yeats gets away with it, and if his straining after effect is often irritating, it can also produce phrases ("the chill, footless years", "the mackerel-crowded seas") which suddenly overwhelm one like a girl's face seen across a room. He is an exception to the rule that poets

do not use poetical language:
How many centuries spent
The sedentary soul
In toils of measurement
Beyond eagle or mole,
Beyond hearing or seeing,
Or Archimedes' guess,
To raise into being
That loveliness?

Here he does not flinch from a squashy vulgar word like "loveliness" and after all it does not seriously spoil this wonderful passage. But the same tendencies, together with a sort of raggedness which is no doubt intentional, weaken his epigrams and polemical poems. For instance (I am quoting from memory) the epigram against the critics who damned The Playboy of the Western World:

Once when midnight smote the air
Eunuchs ran through Hell and met
On every crowded street to stare
Upon great Juan riding by;
Even like these to rail and sweat,
Staring upon his sinewy thigh.

The power which Yeats has within himself gives him the analogy ready made and produces the tremendous scorn of the last line, but even in this short poem there are six or seven unnecessary words. It would probably have been deadlier if it had been neater.

Mr Menon's book is incidentally a short biography of Yeats, but he is above all interested in Yeats's philosophical "system", which in his opinion supplies the subject-matter of more of Yeats's poems than is generally recognised. This system is set forth fragmentarily in various places, and at full length in A VISION, a privately printed book which I have never read but which Mr Menon quotes from extensively. Yeats gave conflicting accounts of its origin, and Mr Menon hints pretty broadly that the "documents" on which it was ostensibly founded were imaginary.

Yeats's philosophical system, says Mr Menon, "was at the back of his intellectual life almost from the beginning. His poetry is full of it. Without it his later poetry becomes almost completely unintelligible."

As soon as we begin to read about the so-called system we are in the middle of a hocus-pocus of Great Wheels, gyres, cycles of the moon, reincarnation, disembodied spirits, astrology and what not. Yeats hedges as to the literalness with which he believed in all this, but he certainly dabbled in spiritualism and astrology, and in earlier life had made experiments in alchemy.

Although almost buried under explanations, very difficult to understand, about the phases of the moon, the central idea of his philosophical system seems to be our old friend, the cyclical universe, in which everything happens over and over again. One has not, perhaps, the right to laugh at Yeats for his mystical beliefs—for I believe it could be shown that SOME degree of belief in magic is almost universal—but neither ought one to write such things off as mere unimportant eccentricities. It is Mr Menon's perception of this that gives his book its deepest interest. "In the first flush of admiration and enthusiasm," he says, "most people dismissed the fantastical philosophy as the price we have to pay for a great and curious intellect.

One did not quite realise where he was heading. And those who did, like Pound and perhaps Eliot, approved the stand that he finally took. The first reaction to this did not come, as one might have expected, from the politically-minded young English poets. They were puzzled because a less rigid or artificial system than that of A VISION might not have produced the great poetry of Yeats's last days." It might not, and yet Yeats's philosophy has some very sinister implications, as Mr Menon points out.

Translated into political terms, Yeats's tendency is Fascist. Throughout most of his life, and long before Fascism was ever heard of, he had had the outlook of those who reach Fascism by the aristocratic route. He is a great hater of democracy, of the modern world, science, machinery, the concept of progress—above all, of the idea of human equality. Much of the imagery of his work is feudal, and it is clear that he was not altogether free from ordinary snobbishness. Later these tendencies took clearer shape and led him to "the exultant acceptance of authoritarianism as the only solution. Even violence and tyranny are not necessarily evil because the people, knowing not evil and good, would become perfectly acquiescent to tyranny.... Everything must come from the top.

Nothing can come from the masses." Not much interested in politics, and no doubt disgusted by his brief incursions into public life, Yeats nevertheless makes political pronouncements. He is too big a man to share the illusions of Liberalism, and as early as 1920 he foretells in a justly famous passage ("The Second Coming") the kind of world that we have actually moved into. But he appears to welcome the coming age, which is to be "hierarchical, masculine, harsh, surgical", and is influenced both by Ezra Pound and by various Italian Fascist writers. He describes the new civilization which he hopes and believes will arrive: "an aristocratic civilization in its most completed form, every detail of life hierarchical, every great man's door crowded at dawn by petitioners, great wealth everywhere in a few men's hands, all dependent upon a few, up to the Emperor himself, who is a God dependent on a greater God, and everywhere, in Court, in the family, an inequality made law." The innocence of this statement is as interesting as its snobbishness.

To begin with, in a single phrase, "great wealth in a few men's hands", Yeats lays bare the central reality of Fascism, which the whole of its propaganda is designed to cover up. The merely political Fascist claims always to be fighting for justice: Yeats, the poet, sees at a glance that Fascism means injustice, and acclaims it for that very reason. But at the same time he fails to see that the new authoritarian civilization, if it arrives, will not be aristocratic, or what he means by aristocratic. It will not be ruled by noblemen with Van Dyck faces, but by anonymous millionaires, shiny-bottomed bureaucrats and murdering gangsters.

Others who have made the same mistake have afterwards changed their views and one ought not to assume that Yeats, if he had lived longer, would necessarily have followed his friend Pound, even in sympathy. But the tendency of the passage I have quoted above is obvious, and its complete throwing overboard of whatever good the past two thousand years have achieved is a disquieting symptom. How do Yeat's political ideas link up with his leaning towards occultism? It is not clear at first glance why hatred of democracy and a tendency to believe in crystal-gazing should go together. Mr Menon only discusses this rather shortly, but it is possible to make two guesses.

To begin with, the theory that civilization moves in recurring cycles is one way out for people who hate the concept of human equality. If it is true that "all this", or something like it, "has happened before", then science and the modern world are debunked at one stroke and progress becomes for ever impossible. It does not much matter if the lower orders are getting above themselves, for, after all, we shall soon be returning to an age of tyranny. Yeats is by no means alone in this outlook. If the universe is moving round on a wheel, the future must be foreseeable, perhaps even in some detail. It is merely a question of discovering the laws of its motion, as the early astronomers discovered the solar year. Believe that, and it becomes difficult not to believe in astrology or some similar system.

A year before the war, examining a copy of GRINGOIRE, the French Fascist weekly, much read by army officers, I found in it no less than thirty-eight advertisements of clairvoyants. Secondly, the very concept of occultism carries with it the idea that knowledge must be a secret thing, limited to a small circle of initiates. But the same idea is integral to Fascism. Those who dread the prospect of universal suffrage, popular education, freedom of thought, emancipation of women, will start off with a predilection towards secret cults.

There is another link between Fascism and magic in the profound hostility of both to the Christian ethical code. No doubt Yeats wavered in his beliefs and held at different times many different opinions, some enlightened, some not. Mr Menon repeats for him Eliot's claim that he had the longest period of development of any poet who has ever lived. But there is one thing that seems constant, at least in all of his work that I can remember, and that is his hatred of modern western civilization and desire to return to the Bronze Age, or perhaps to the Middle Ages. Like all such thinkers, he tends to write in praise of ignorance. The Fool in his remarkable play, THE HOUR-GLASS, is a Chestertonian figure, "God's fool", the "natural born innocent", who is always wiser than the wise man. The philosopher in the play dies on the knowledge that all his lifetime of thought has been wasted

The stream of the world has changed its course,
And with the stream my thoughts have run
Into some cloudly, thunderous spring

That is its mountain-source;
Ay, to a frenzy of the mind,
That all that we have done's undone
Our speculation but as the wind.

Beautiful words, but by implication profoundly obscurantist and reactionary; for if it is really true that a village idiot, as such, is wiser than a philosopher, then it would be better if the alphabet had never been invented. Of course, all praise of the past is partly sentimental, because we do not live in the past. The poor do not praise poverty. Before you can despise the machine, the machine must set you free from brute labour. But that is not to say that Yeats's yearning for a more primitive and more hierarchical age was not sincere. How much of all this is traceable to mere snobbishness, product of Yeats's own position as an impoverished offshoot of the aristocracy, is a different question.

And the connection between his obscurantist opinions and his tendency towards "quaintness" of language remains to be worked out; Mr Menon hardly touches upon it.

This is a very short book, and I would greatly like to see Mr Menon go ahead and write another book on Yeats, starting where this one leaves off. "If the greatest poet of our times is exultantly ringing in an era of Fascism, it seems a somewhat disturbing symptom," he says on the last page, and leaves it at that. It is a disturbing symptom, because it is not an isolated one. By and large the best writers of our time have been reactionary in tendency, and though Fascism does not offer any real return to the past, those who yearn for the past will accept Fascism sooner than its probable alternatives. But there are other lines of approach, as we have seen during the past two or three years.

The relationship between Fascism and the literary intelligentsia badly needs investigating, and Yeats might well be the starting-point. He is best studied by someone like Mr Menon, who can approach a poet primarily as a poet, but who also knows that a writer's political and religious beliefs are not excrescences to be laughed away, but something that will leave their mark even on the smallest detail of his work.

Q.11. Discuss the mutually interdependent relationship of Nature and Artifice in Yeats

Or

Q. Analyze the effect of dual realities in Yeats

The natural and artificial worlds have always been a source of fascination for William Yeats. Even in his early poetic career, Yeats' interest in artifice and nature were underlying subjects in his works. Along with the evolution in his critical writings, brought to a peak in *A Vision,* the development of his poetic form also reflects the budding importance of the dualistic realities. Through his portrayal of the natural and artificial worlds over the course of his poetry, it becomes more and more apparent that Yeats is not favouring one world over the other, but rather proclaiming that the two opposing worlds are mutually dependent.

Defining Terms: Nature and Artifice

The terms nature and artifice have, over time, developed distinct connotations and commonly held meanings. Presently, nature and artifice are typically differentiated by whether something exists organically in nature or is created artificially by man. Throughout Yeats' writings, the terms nature and artifice take on enduring meanings. The natural world is primarily typified by imperfection, decay, the continual impurities of desire, and the limits of time. On the other hand, artificiality is depicted as perfect, unchanging, and timeless. The idolization of artificial flawlessness permeates Yeats' writings. "The quest for an ideal moment outside of time silently generates the Yeatsian text"

Disgust/Intrigue of Natural Bodily Function

In 1927, Yeats said that "only two topics can be of the least interest to a serious and studious mind- sex and the dead". For Yeats, sexuality and the belief in an existence beyond death are fundamental to his perception of the physical and other worldly realms. Yeats' preoccupation with death is laden with the desire for something of intellectual and spiritual significance beyond corporal decay. He unearths his own quest for spirituality in "Sailing to Byzantium," (1926) the first poem in the collected works of *The Tower*. The poem distinguishes youth from old age by the formers' desire for sensual worldly pleasures and the latters' longing for timeless wisdom.

Youth, who are often clouded by sexuality and human yearnings, are archetypal of the natural realm. In the movement away from the sensuality of youth in "Sailing to Byzantium," sexual desire and decay of the body are purified, leaving the perfection of the artificial. As a product of the imagination, the artificial is eternal and without flaw. In the approach to old age, the bodily corrosion accompanying the stretch toward death is distinguished by the decline of sexual instinct and subsequent amplification of the spiritual.

As early as 1889, Yeats' preoccupations with the limits of his aging body were evident. In a letter written in 1889 to the Boston Pilot, Yeats said, "I have been very near the gates of Death, and an old man feeble and tottering, but not in spirits and life, not in the real man, the imagination which liveth for ever. In that I am stronger and stronger as this foolish body decays-". In response to the disgust of his bodily bounds, Yeats looked toward an immortal perfection for a permanent place that his mind and spirit may inhabit. Yeats discovers this undying spiritual flawlessness in his vision of the eternal city of Byzantium.

Yeats was on the threshold of old age when "Sailing to Byzantium" was written. Its composition was a way for him to recover his spirits. With the looming bodily decay that is a product of fading youth, the speaker of "Sailing to Byzantium" realises that he is caught in the land of the young (Ireland). He contrasts the futility of his own decrepit body in the land of Ireland to the youth, who are sensual, energetic, and filled with desire, by describing himself as "A tattered coat upon a stick". Feeling detached from the "sensual music" of the young, he yearns for an existence beyond the limits of his mortality. Instead of looking at life through an external viewpoint, Yeats began to turn his eyes inward. "When the senses cease to be preoccupied with the external world, and the mind turns inward to a contemplation of its own essential form, the Divine is revealed,". By relinquishing mortal desires, a fusion of the soul and body sanctioning a life of higher purpose becomes accessible.

For Yeats, the connection between sexuality and mortality lies deeper than their significance in his poetry. In both the relationship is characterized simultaneously by attraction and repulsion. The disgust that Yeats felt about his bodily decomposition in old age was similarly endured in youth in reference to his budding sexuality. He describes his experience, beginning near age fifteen, of being constantly burdened by the tortures of unfulfilled sexual desire. In "Memoirs," written between 1916 and 1917, Yeats described his relationship to his own sexuality. He asserted that it was "a continual struggle against an experience that almost invariably left me with exhausted nerves". Although his sexual encounters were infrequent, they typically were adverse experiences that left him with a feeling self-loathing. In "Sailing to Byzantium," it becomes clear that this discomfort with sexuality is reflected in the poem. In the land of sexually charged youth, there is a distinct coldness and the speaker reveals feeling unwelcome in Ireland. He longs to exist in a place of wisdom, devoid of sex, where he may once again feel at ease. The sensual music of youth is depicted negatively in that it disregards wisdom in favour of bodily pleasure. "Caught in the sensual music all neglect/ monuments of unageing intellect".

Adding to Yeats' interest in the eternal world, beyond the limits of mortality, was his arrival at a life of stimulation in old age. In the context of his recent marriage, his position as a Senator, and having been awarded the Nobel Prize in 1923, "Life was exciting, but there was the bother of old age,". Later in life, he had come to a point where he could continually reinvent and rediscover himself. With the success in his later years, Yeats defied his earlier disillusionment that was felt when he wrote that "my own life seems to me a preparation for something that never happens," In the 1920s, Yeats' efforts in early life finally came to be rewarded. His involvement in revolutionary politics led to his position as a senator, while his early interest in mysticism and theology led to his creation of *A Vision*. The richness of the works encompassed in *The Tower* was the result of the evolution of his writing style that accompanied or that coincided with his personal maturation.

Unity of Being and The Mask

Of central importance to the Yeats' comprehension of nature and artifice are the closely related concepts Unity of Being and the Mask. In the 1937 version of *A Vision*, Yeats alludes to the state of embodied Unity of Being as a divine experience, occurring fleetingly, if at all. He defines Unity of Being to be "complete harmony between physical body intellect and spiritual desire". Unity of Being is, as a rule, experienced more often in the undying confines of art than in life. "As the metaphysician decries the impossibility of unity, the poet struggles to forge a unity in which thought and passion, subject and object, the incarnate and the discarnate, natural and supernatural, particular and archetypal come together in the living lines as they cannot in the living person". Much like Yeats' assertion that man can embody truth but he cannot know it, man can encounter the eternal but cannot possess it. "We attain (the perfect moment) in the creation or enjoyment of a work of art, but that moment though eternal in the Daimon passes from us because it is not an attainment of our whole being". Hence, because Unity of Being is experienced, not acquired for ownership, it has greater potential to exist in an ageless art form. Despite the realization that the artificial realm is a sought out, passing encounter, Yeats' work on *A Vision* is pervaded by the desire to possess the artificial.

Unity of Being and Yeats' theory of the Mask embrace similar connotations. "The discarnate image, as the object of desire, is closely allied to that he calls in *A Vision* the Mask". Much like Yeats' concept of the Mask, in the case of nature and artifice, one always desires its opposite. Both the Mask and Unity of Being describe the human quest to be defined by seeking completion in the image to which we aspire to become.

Yearning for a Mask contradictory to oneself "the incarnate subject desires the unattainable". Ultimately, Unity of Being is only possible in the unification of the incarnate and discarnate. In pursuit of divine fusion "artists and visionaries are always sailing the dolphin-torn gong-tormented sea to Byzantium- and never arriving". The quest for Unity of Being through art is central to both Byzantium poems. Yeats' captivation with Byzantium stemmed in large part from the unifying quality which he saw in the city. He saw it to be a conceptual model for cultural unity.. Yeats deemed that "in early Byzantium, maybe never before or since in recorded history, religious, aesthetic, and practical life were one". In both Byzantium poems, Unity of Being is achieved through the immortal world of art. In "Sailing to Byzantium," Unity of Being is sought in the journey from the temporal world to the paradise of spiritual life. In " Byzantium," as the uncleansed icons of sensuality submit to tranquil images of spirituality, there is a progression from complexity to simplicity. Unity of Being is realised in the eternal and the time confined realms..

Passion Incited by Opposites

Oppositional forces that produce passion are necessary for the desired Unity of Being to be achieved. Opposition serves as a catalyst for provoking and fusing clashing emotions, with passion as the end result. In Yeats' final revised definition of the Mask he states that the Mask is "a form created by passion to unite us to ourselves". In the case of the Mask and Unity of Being, "passion is what the Daimon behind the vision desires of its human opposite; passion alone effects Unity of Being". Through the existence of contradictory forces, passion is incited. The spiritual entity of the Daimon is described by Yeats to be either "another mind,' or 'part of our own mind,". Each yearns for what lacks and what is seen in the other. The incarnate human desires the Daimons' capacity to attain wisdom. "For wisdom is the property of the dead,/ A something incompatible with life" (75). The disincarnate Daimon desires the potential of the living for passion. Yeats remarks on the similar ability to incite passion in the relationship between man and Daimon and that of man and woman. "Man and Daimon face each other in perpetual conflict or embrace. The relation (the Daimon being of the opposite sex to that of man) may create a passion like that of sexual love".

Conceivably, because opposites continually seek one another and Yeats writes more closely allied to the natural realm throughout most of his poetic career, the natural world is often portrayed to be inferior to the artificial. In "The Dolls" (1914), Yeats describes the experience of dolls on a shelf, looking at the natural world, embodied by a baby, with repugnance. Through the continuous portrayal of the natural world permeated by the supernatural, it grows to be apparent that Yeats is striving for an experience beyond nature, incessantly looking toward the artificial for the ageless quality deficient in human flesh. Likewise, in "Sailing to Byzantium," the reader is taken on a journey from the natural to the artificial. The voyage to Byzantium concludes in the arrival at the eternal city, however, the speaker does not actually enter it. He is filled with a wisdom brought on by old age, but his body cannot match the thriving powers of his mind. He looks to the embodiment of his opposite with admiration, seeking the ideal reality, free from the burdens of time.

He makes a seemingly inhuman wish, but justifiable in the quest of completion in a contradictory force, to enter into the emotionally devoid state of an art form. The separation from bodily drives as a result of the journey to Byzantium signifies an entrance into the spiritual. "It is but the old youthful desire to conquer bodily inclinations and live a lonely life of wisdom". Yeats' portrayal of immortality in " Byzantium" (1930) is fundamentally different from what the old man envisioned eternity to be in "Sailing to Byzantium." " Byzantium" was also written from a spell of depression as a way for Yeats to recuperate his melancholy mental state. His admiration for the artificial is still observable as he praises the eternal world. "I hail the superhuman; / I call it life-in-death and death-in-life".While man and his bodily drives are fleeting, art and ideas have the capacity for timelessness.

Much like the instinctive nature of humanity to seek completion in its opposite, in tracking the path of Yeats' poetry, it becomes more and more clear that the artificial and natural realms continually seek totality in one another. Pervasive symmetry yields a stagnant state where imbalance permeates. "Evil is the cessation of opposition; it is a world devoid of difference".

The Rose as a Symbol for Unity of Being

In Yeats' early works, such as the collected poems of *The Rose,* the converse natural and artificial spheres tend be represented in simple symbols, while more complex symbols, such as the eternal city of Byzantium, tend to be used in his later works. Yeats relied on the symbol for its capacity to fuse numerous emotions, images, and associations. "Yeats sought to attain the unity he so desired through the symbol,". At the foundation for his dependence on the symbol was the assumption of an ideal reality. From the affirmation of an ideal existence "springs a conflict between the ideal and the physical". Hence, "The rose for Yeats thus becomes a symbol of Unity of Being, Of the reconciliation and union of natural and spiritual for which the poet is striving". In "The Rose Upon the Rood of Time," published in 1893, the rose is portrayed as both eternal and earthly. "In all poor foolish things in a day,/ eternal beauty wandering on her way". Although the rose is part of the cycle of birth and death, its standing as a symbol of desire and beauty supersedes its earthly status, making it also capable of immortality. The rose is ever-present in nature, but Yeats' portrayal of the rose tinged with an element of supernatural lends it to be slightly out of reach. Hence, the rose is representative of Yeats' spiritual quest, "distinguished by his desire to cross the threshold beyond human experience".

Physical Beauty and Unity of Being

Those with the ability to unite the immortal with the mortal, attaining Unity of being, assume the form of great physical beauty. "Yeats' symbol for this spiritual perfection is superhuman physical beauty in life.". In *A Vision,* Yeats deems that the fifteenth phase of the 28 incarnations indicates great physical beauty which accompanies spiritual illumination. "Yeats numbers among those nearly perfect beings Helen (at phase fourteen); his many references to Maud Gonne too show that she represented this kind of beauty,". Like Yeats' rendering of Gonne as Helen of Troy, the beautiful Rose is another example of the human world being punctured by the world of the supernatural. The rose is observed by Yeats to be "for many centuries a symbol of spiritual love and supreme beauty.". Thus, the rose icon is both immortal and mortal, idealized for its ability to sustain timeless beauty.

The Byzantium Poems and the Central Theme of Nature and Artifice

Although nature and artifice are themes that run through all of Yeats' collected poems, they reach their height of prominence in the collected works of *The Tower* and *The Winding Stair*. Specifically, the notions of nature and artifice are imperative to the Byzantium poems. It was from his reading and his understanding of Byzantine art that Yeats constructed the concept of the eternal city of Byzantium. Although his life-long interest in Byzantine art began in the 1890s, the greater part of Yeats' knowledge of Byzantium was acquired primarily from readings that he did during the time that was consumed with writing *A Vision,* between 1917 and 1925.

Byzantium represents a timeless world of perfection and divinity amid the mortal world of decay. Yeats chose Byzantium as the destination of his journey because " Byzantium was the center of European civilization and the source of its spiritual philosophy, so I symbolize the search for the spiritual life by a journey to that city". In "Sailing to Byzantium," the understanding of the mutually interdependent relationship between the natural and the artificial, the body and the spirit, progresses further from earlier works such as *The Rose* collection. After his completion of the poem, Yeats wrote a letter to Mrs Shakespear, stating, "How well too it puts my mood between spiritual excitement and the sexual torture the knowledge that these two are somehow inseparable!".

Partially because the natural and artificial worlds continually seek one another for wholeness, " Byzantium" continues from where "Sailing to Byzantium" left off. Rather than portray the journey to the timeless city, in " Byzantium," Yeats depicts what it is to be in the city's core for the first time. On clear distinction between the two Byzantium poems is the contrast of what eternity is anticipated to be and what eternity is in actuality. This distinction is vital to the re-imagining of the eternal city. In " Byzantium," there is a reconciliation of the worlds whereby the two clearly depend upon one another. Just as life is constantly looking to art for spiritual meaning, Byzantium continually looks to a fresh supply of life in order to be art. "In our system it is a cardinal principle that anything separated form its opposite-the victory of separation-'consumes itself away.' The existence of the one depends upon the existence of the other". Although the speaker is inside Byzantium, he is clearly a guest of the eternal observing his surroundings. As a natural guest in the supernatural realm, being in the mists of both worlds, we are able to see the true interdependence of life and art. In " Byzantium," Yeats continues his progression toward the portrayal of the interdependence of the immortal and mortal realms. He calls it "death-in-life and life in death".

In " Byzantium," Yeats portrays the creatures that exist in his undying paradise. Yeats' reference to the golden tree and birds stems from his learning of a tree of gold and artificial birds that dwell in the royal palace of Byzantium. "I use it as a symbol of the intellectual joy of eternity, as contrasted with the instinctual joy of human life".

The paradise of art that is Byzantium essentially remains the same between the Byzantium poems. One plain, but notable distinction between the Byzantium poems is that Yeats writes the second poem closer to his demise and more distanced from his youth. Much like Yeats' mutual fascination and repulsion with death and sex, the Byzantium poems make it evident that at the core of Yeats' notion of the other world is a the idea that there is a mutual dependence and necessary enmity between the two opposite spheres. "Mortals need and seek spiritual knowledge (wisdom) from the other-world; Immortals lack physical substance (power) and require mortals to complete their tasks.

Yeats spent his life engulfed in his art. Hence, in dedicating his life not only to his creations, he also dedicated to the attainment of the Unity of Being. While nature and artifice have always been themes in his writings, it can be said that with age, as Yeats began to be more and more interested in his own immortality, he became closer to attaining Unity of Being and that proximity to such a Divine form is reflected in his later works. "The shift in Yeats's poetry is not so much from emphasis on the goal to the quest itself as it is from the seeker who has faith but no certain knowledge to the seeker who sees more clearly. In the early poetry, the seeker searches through the mists".

Q.12. Analyze the Tragic Joy in Yeats poetry

Or

Q. Discuss Yeats's attitude towards art in *last poems*

Irrational streams of blood are staining earth;
Empedocles has thrown all things about;
Hector is dead and there's a light in Troy;
We that look on but laugh in tragic joy.
['The Gyres']

Yeats's collection *Last Poems (1936-1939)* opens with one of his best-known poems 'The Gyres', which sets out the main theme of the collection: that our civilization is coming to an end, but it does not matter - in fact we should 'Rejoice!' Instead of despairing he finds an attitude of 'tragic joy' with which to view the decay of both the historical epoch and his own body. This essentially antithetical line of thought is expressed repeatedly throughout Last Poems, taking on many different forms and being applied to many different aspects of life. For example the decay is seen in Irish politics, the monarchy, and modern art, while the joy is seen in nature, art, dance, sensual pleasure, madness, and intoxication. The range of aspects of life Yeats deals with is matched by his range of tones, from the colloquial of 'The Old Stone Cross, to 'the prophetic of 'Under Ben Bulben'.

The states of mind Yeats adopts in place of despair are usually associated with art in one form or another, and in Last Poems we see him examining his attitude towards art, both his own art and the major world traditions of art. 'Lapis Lazuli' begins as a defence of art against the attacks of 'hysterical women'; people who respond to life in an immediate, emotional way, their minds limited to the here and now. Set against their hysterics is the noble attitude of the tragic actor:

The great stage curtain about to drop,
If worthy their prominent part in the play,
Do not break up their lines to weep.
They know that Hamlet and Lear are gay;

These actors represent the attitude of mind Yeats has found, as does the nobility of tone in such phrases as 'The great stage curtain', in contrast to the slangy colloquialism of 'Pitch like King Billy bomb-balls in'.

In the midst of this poem, separate from the rest in a short stanza on its own, we have a description of the actual work of art, the carving itself which stands unmoved by the rise and fall of civilizations around it. The calmness and objectivity of this stanza, as well as its separate place in the structure of the poem, reflect the nature of the object. The carving also has a symbol of its significance for Yeats built into it.

Over them flies a long-legged bird,
A symbol of longevity;

The image reminds us of the poem 'Long-Legged Fly' in which 'great' people are shown to have a mental faculty which Yeats calls 'silence'; an ability of the artist to look into the silent source of all things. Yeats shows how the surface of the work of art stimulates his imagination in random ways:

Every accidental crack or dent,
Seems a water-course or an avalanche,
Or lofty slope where still it snows
Though doubtless plum or cherry-branch
Sweetens the little half-way house.

These personal meanings exist only in the mind of the viewer, and Yeats's inclusion of them here strengthens, by contrast, the tone of objectivity given to the final section of the poem in which he outlines the deeper meaning of the carving.

The Chinamen climbing the mountain reflect Yeats's own climb through old age towards death, and just as Yeats has achieved a stable and final attitude of 'tragic joy', the Chinamen on the mountain stare at the 'tragic scene' while:

Their eyes mid many wrinkles, their eyes,
Their ancient, glittering eyes are gay.

Yeats sees the carving as a timeless object reflecting a timeless outlook; the creation of an artist embodying and communicating the state of mind of the artist, and simultaneously a medium for Yeats's own personal vision. As in the 'Byzantium' poems, Yeats identifies himself with both the artist and the artefact.

Yeats continually looks back to the origins of civilizations, the starting points of the gyres of history. In 'Lapis Lazuli' he refers to Callimachus, inventor of the Corinthian column from the germinal point of western culture, and representing the east the Chinese statue.

In 'The Statues' these two world traditions are taken up again and contrasts are made between the characterisations of each. Rational thought as we know it began with The Greeks, and in the first stanzas of 'The Statues' Yeats takes us back to the origins of Greek art.

In the first stanza he postulates that it was the abstract mathematical laws behind art which were the key to its beauty. The 'character', or individual personality which abstract mathematics lacks was supplied by the passions of observer.

In the second stanza he shifts the importance of the statues from the mathematical basis to the actual work of carving and creation performed by the sculptor. Both were necessary; abstract and technical skills combining to assert themselves and ensure the triumph of Greek culture over the 'vague enormities' of the east.

In the third stanza an antithesis is set up between the two cultures, and Yeats would seem to prefer the east. The image of Buddha combines with a pre-Renaissance image in the image 'round and slow' with 'Empty eyeballs'. Here the intellectual thought of The Greeks is belittled.

... Empty eyeballs knew
That knowledge increases unreality, that
Mirror on mirror mirrored is all they show. [The Statues]

The true wisdom of spiritual knowledge, needed when 'gong and conch declare the hour to bless', is found in 'Buddha emptiness'. Again this is reminiscent of that 'silence' found in great minds in 'Long-Legged Fly'.

Yeats's concept of 'tragic joy' seems to be more in tune with eastern transcendental religion than anything from western culture, yet in the final stanza it is evident that he thinks a rediscovery of Greek methods is necessary for the reconstruction of Irish art. Thus Yeats's thought embodies both western rational and eastern mystical elements.

Yeats's dislike of modern art is evident throughout Last Poems. In 'Under Ben Bulben' he says of painting:

Nor let the modish painter shirk
What his great forefathers did,
And of poetry:
Scorn the sort now growing up
All out of shape from toe to top,

Yeats believes that a new era will emerge from the modern corrupt state. In 'The Gyres' his attitude was one of objective acceptance, but in other poems his personal feelings show through clearly enough. In 'The Circus Animals' Desertion' modern culture is a 'mound of refuse'.

Old kettles, old bottles, and a broken can,
Old iron, old bones, old rags, that raving slut
Who keeps the till

This decay is not only in the rest of the world, bit is affecting him too.

I must lie down where all the ladders start,
In the foul rag-and-bone shop of the heart.

Again, and as usual in Yeats, a double attitude is maintained, for if the heart is a 'foul rag-and-bone shop' it is still, as he says in 'The Spur', the source of motivation for his art.

You think it horrible that lust and rage
Should dance attention upon my old age;
They were not such a plague when I was young;
What else have I to spur me into song?

These sensual feelings are the bass counterpart of tragic joy, and are expressed less 'horribly' in the art of dance which is referred to throughout Last Poems.

Dance is the most primitive and perhaps the oldest art form known to man. In 'Imitated from the Japanese' Yeats sounds a note of regret that he has never 'danced for joy', and in the next poem, 'Sweet Dance', he admires a girl who can escape the gloom of life through dance, which, after all, is a natural, rhythmic, cyclic action. The gyre itself is perhaps a kind of dance, and in 'A Drunken Man's Praise of Sobriety' it seems that dancing is the best way to wear out drunkenness and return to sobriety, just as the gyre will spin itself out and give rise to a new beginning.

Last Poems ends with 'Under Ben Bulben', a prophetic poem written with a conscious air of finality. The poem makes a sweep from the abstract to the concrete; from the wisdom of sages, through art, to the earth, and finally into the grave. Here again we see Yeats contemplating art, particularly in relation to tradition. 'Measurement', the abstract knowledge of The Greeks, 'began our might', and for Yeats 'our might' lasted through the Renaissance and through the seventeenth century with 'Calvert and Wilson, Blake and Claude,' but has now run itself out.

... but after that
confusion fell upon our thought.

The reason why modern art is in a state of confusion is that the artists 'unremembering hearts and heads' have lost touch with tradition. They are like the falcon in 'The Second Coming'.

Turning and turning in the widening gyre
The falcon cannot hear the falconer.

It is not only the intellectual artistic tradition which Yeats values; he finds another valuable tradition in the myths of the Irish peasantry. He reflects this interest in poems such as 'The Three Bushes', which with its simple diction, narrative structure, and repeated refrain has the tone of a folk ballad. This aspect of Irish culture, born of the peasants and their toil in the fields, is as important to preserve, in Yeats's view, as the Classical principles of art. Addressing himself, in 'Under Ben Bulben', to Irish poets of the present and future, he exhorts them to:

Sing the peasantry, and then
Hard-riding country gentlemen,
The holiness of monks, and after,
Porter drinkers' randy laughter;

The final verse takes us to the land, the actual earth of Ireland itself. Ben Bulben stands, like 'Old Rocky Face' from 'The Gyres', a symbol of our unchanging silent origins, of nature, proud and noble, which like its offspring art outlives the human tragedy. It is to his Irish roots that Yeats ultimately wants to return. He chooses his grave near a church were one of his forefathers was rector, and chooses for his grave-stone not marble, associated with the Greek culture he admires intellectually, but 'limestone quarried near the spot', to which his strongest roots are attached

Chapter 13

Critical Essays

Sailing to Byzantium: Adrift on Perfection

by Sonia Jain

In his poem "Sailing to Byzantium," Yeats rejects his perceptions of the sensual mortal world and fondly imagines a paradise of intellectual intransience in Byzantium. The impermanence of human life is recounted, for Yeats who himself is a part of the "dying generation" creates a bittersweet tone underlying the depictions of vitality and youth in the poem. Derisive words indicative of death are strategically placed to cause the literal "music" of life to be interrupted, and yet the music is described as "sensual".It is exactly this quality that lures Yeats back to the world of human condition that he himself cannot escape. In purposefully creating this poem into "the artifice of eternity" that will stand as a monument of his own "unageing intellect", Yeats attempts to create his own golden future. This is impossible however, for his intellect succumbs to the very appeals of his senses that alienate him from the "young in one another's arm" and the "song" of the "birds in the trees".

The narrator is not able to deliberately release the unexplained complexities within himself that have kept him "sick with desire", but instead focuses his attentions on the failure of his own physical body, for he repeatedly fixates on the image of his intellect "fastened to a dying animal". In this "paltry" condition, he is now able to project his illusions of perfect yet impossible visions upon this text to illuminate himself in the grandiose context of transformed "magnificence" — His transcendence into all that makes Byzantium the sacred center of intellectualism.

In the first stanza, Yeats depicts a world in which a distance exists between himself and the present reality of his mortal existence. In his "mortal dress", Yeats exists as a ragged old man who has nothing to offer the corporeal world with his physical body. In an effort to escape to a place of intellectualism that will not restrain him as his earthly "country [not] for old men" does, the poem physically progresses as Yeats' journey to Eternity occurs.

He is the sole creator of Byzantium, for his experience in this city merely exists in his own imaginings. The reader's perception of truth is simply a reflection of Yeats' fabricated truth, and is therefore rendered unreliable. Yeats yearns for the timeless and undying form, and the words he uses to diametrically oppose his two lives the one he has of ephemeral importance and the one he wants of everlasting art and intellect— exist in the very language he uses. The cycle of human life is recorded in words comprised of either one or two syllables. This creates short, choppy phrases that produce a harmony that is staccato in nature. Yeats recounts the song of "dying generations" and immediately goes on to describe the "Fish, flesh, or fowl [that] commend all summer long" whereas in describing Eternity he honors his conceptions using polysyllabic vocabulary as can be observed in the line "monuments of unageing intellect". The sensual tones flow effortlessly across the tongue, whereas in describing the reality of his present state, Yeats joins words in union that create a rough, irregular tone.

The disjointed, staccato meter produces an urgency that can only be explained in the "sick... desire" for Yeats to escape his mortal life. The music is what connects the two very different worlds of intellect and sensory, and through the structure of the poem can the reader sense Yeats' longing for Eternity. It is this ache that determines his word choice, for it is the sound that is produced from the sustained notes of polysyllabic words of passion and "desire" that resonate throughout the poem— not the author's depiction of Byzantium itself. Yeats separates himself from the physical world, and yet his soul cannot penetrate the life of Byzantium for which it lusts, for "out of nature" Yeats must fall and death must occur in order for Eternity to become his reality.

Yeats rejects his natural shape, and yet in attaining the form achieved in living in Eternity, his "monument of unageing intellect" becomes undying and his "golden bough to sing" remains fixed and unchanging. Yeats is unable to be transformed by the city, for it is Byzantium's very charm that prevents him from existing with the human conditions that are responsible for creating the intellect that Yeats now strives to preserve. Only Yeats, in a moment of artistic vision, can speak to his 'reality' of Byzantium, for the lack of metaphorical and literal progression would cause the reader, a member of the sensual world, to reject the lifeless "gold mosaic" of unfeeling, dead words. Yeats endeavors to be a "hammered gold and gold enamel[ed]" bird pleasantly amusing an Emperor, and yet the realities of existing in Eternity are that a drowsy Emperor will forever remain drowsy and not ever be excitable, as will the song Yeats sings be forever unchanging and static. Yeats shuns his mortal world because of the rejection he faces as an ageing man, and yet in Byzantium, Yeats only imagines his paradise to be a place in which he will be able to successfully appeal to the senses of others. The poem culminates in a situation in which Yeats receives attention from the ladies of Byzantium, and yet it is by alluring the senses of these ladies and the lords and the Emperor of Byzantium that Yeats imagines himself to be of a form that is not a "monument of unageing intellect" (Yeats ln 8), but simply a golden, evocative form now physically capable of engaging the sensory appeals of others.

Yeats finds himself in fully functioning form, singing in full "golden" tunes not unlike the mortal "young in one another's arms" presumably making love. In finally receiving the attention he has been alienated from since the very first stanza, Yeats finds himself "coming" but protected by the "holy fire" (Yeats ln 19). In Byzantium, hiding behind the call for lasting intellectualism, Yeats make his body unnatural relative to his former physical self, for in the human world, Yeats likens his body to that of a "dying animal". "Once out of nature I shall never take my bodily form from any natural thing" he declares, and so in images of himself in Byzantium does he envision his exterior to be physically hardened by his precious metal enameling. He transforms himself into a bird known for its golden sheen, and thus acquires a type of superficial elegance that is not a part of the intellectual appeal he once claimed to hold as his utmost priority.

In this transformation does Yeats' craving for the decadence of grandeur that appeals to the very physical senses make itself manifest, for he strives to become what as a "tattered" old man he lacks. Now he is free to compete with the music that the young lovers make, for in Byzantium, Yeats merely reinvents himself and proceeds to envision Eternity as the sensory world he once rejected. His body and soul are interconnected in Byzantium, and he calls to be physically "gathered" for his mind "knows not what [his body] is". Like a virgin, his body is at the mercy of the entity that 'gathers' him, and he is taken into the sexually charged "artifice of eternity" where he later "comes". His own song is now enough to rouse the senses of the Emperor of Byzantium as well as compete with the lovers' song. Yeats carefully chooses the words which he sings, for in specifying "what is past, or passing or to come", Yeats uses the words "past" and "passing" to create a lulling effect that can only be countered by the ending staccato pulse of the word "come." The poem culminates in this very moment, for in Yeats' literal coming, his future is a symbolic orgasm which secures his ability to be sexually satisfied.

It is as a sexually capable being that Yeats is able to secure his place in Eternity, the haven of intellectualism, and yet in gaining this fertility, he figuratively gains reproductive abilities that he is incapable of using. The dead irony of the situation is that while Yeats "sailed the seas" and quite literally 'came' in Byzantium, he is unable to release his manifest ideas that produce the intellect he wishes to preserve. In Byzantium he is set upon becoming an everlasting beauty of great thought, and yet by singing a never changing song, he will forever exist as an archaic machine of past pleasantries. In order to continually "keep a drowsy Emperor awake", change must persist, and yet change is the very quality that has not only created an aging Yeats, but has also condemned him to the human life cycle.

Yeats recounts the mortal life where "whatever is begotten, born and dies", for it is in Yeats' mortal life that he has become a part of "those dying generations". In describing Byzantium in polysyllabic phrases, Yeats creates a long, soothing tone that echoes in the music created and referred to throughout the poem2E He falls victim to this music in the same way the human world he wants to escape from does, for they too are "caught in that sensual music [where] all neglect monuments of unageing intellect". In describing that which he previously heralded as the problem of the human condition, he outlines his own failure in successfully being transformed by Byzantium, for he is unable to reject the very senses he idealizes.

He appeals to the "sages standing in God's holy fire" as one would call to a muse for inspiration and creativity, and yet despite these sages becoming the "singing-masters of [his] soul", the thoughts he gains from them can only be contained within his internal flames. This lack of expression causes his thoughts to "consume his heart away", and yet his mind, pregnant with thought, is still unable to release the complexities that exist within him. Like a "perne in a gyre" his mind is spinning around and around constantly, yet Yeats is simply a bird of "unnatural" form, producing a harmony that although may be melodious, will forever remain sterile in its ingenuity and vision.

In gaining an eternity in time, Yeats is locked mechanically into the "artifice of eternity", and Byzantium exists more as a physical process of transformation than as a "holy city" of complete intelligence. Yeats rejects the mortal, fertile world for refusing him the opportunity to symbolically 'reproduce' his art, and yet he gains virility in the intellectually sterile city of Byzantium. By the end of the poem, the tension builds between the need for the reproduction of creative expression and its impossibility, and the everlasting sense of time is strictly divided into the "past... passing" and the implied future. Byzantium cannot eternalize Yeats' genius, for the reader must envision a city so basic that the very complexities that exist as a mere byproduct of the human condition fail to exist, and it is this very anomaly that reflects in the absurdity of the old man Yeats' desire in quite literally "Sailing to Byzantium." Yeats is faced with the biggest paradox, for he wishes to become the form that is essential to perfect art, yet despises the very senses without whose perceptions, perfect art could not exist.

The Critics on Yeats and Postcolonialism

This section will provide abstracts of a selection of the major critical contributions to the question of Yeats and Postcolonialism, arranged chronologically. For more information on these texts and suggestions for further reading, please see the bibliography.

On Seamus Deane's Celtic Revivals (1985)

Seamus Deane's essays debate Yeats's position as postcolonial writer. At times Deane finds in Yeats a strong cultural nationalist, but just as often he accuses Yeats of writing out of reductive visions of Ireland. He interrogates Yeats's position in two essays in this volume, "Yeats and the Idea of Revolution" and "O'Casey and Yeats: Exemplary Dramatists." The first essay implicates Yeats in "inventing an Ireland amenable to his imagination". Deane reads the connections between death and sex in Yeats's play A Full Moon in March: "Sex and violence produce poetry. Aristocrat and peasant produce, out of a violent fusion, art". At the same time, Deane sees in Yeats's attitude towards Ireland and England a conflict that he compares to V. S. Naipaul's position on India and

England: "the English left behind in their twentieth century colonies one of their most enduring inventions-a concept of Englishness... The whole Irish Revival is a reaction against this attitude, a movement towards the colony and away from the mothercountry, a replacement of 'Englishness' by 'Irishness'". Though Deane has problems with some of Yeats's "colonialist" dramatizations of Ireland, he investigates this issue in postcolonial terms. Deane's second essay on Yeats and O'Casey finds in Yeats "a more profoundly political dramatist than O'Casey, that it is in his plays that we find a search for the new form of feeling which would renovate our national consciousness". Deane's writings explore the question of Yeats as postcolonial writer.

On Edward Said's "Yeats and Decolonization," from Culture and Imperialism (1993):

After acknowledging Yeats's position as a canonical European, modernist poet, Said introduces the notion of Yeats as an "indisputably great national poet who during a period of anti-imperialist resistance articulates the experiences, the restorative vision of a people suffering under the domination of an offshore power". Said goes on to place Ireland in the context of colonialism, and defines nationalism as the "mobilizing force that coalesced into resistance against an alien and occupying empire on the parts of people possessing a common history, religion, and language".

The essay moves towards Yeats as Said discusses the connection between geography, place names, and the decolonization of both land and language. Grouping Yeats with other English speaking African and Carribean authors, Said describes an "overlapping" between Yeats's "Irish nationalism with his English cultural heritage". After questioning nativism and negritude in terms of Yeats's writing, Said argues that "Yeats's slide into incoherence and mysticism during the 1920s" relates to a limited nativist perspective. Yeats's preoccupations with an "ideal community" and with history as "the wrong turns, the overlap, the...occasionally glorious moment," Said argues, place him in the company of "all the poets and men of letters of decolonization". Close readings of Yeats's poetry beside Pablo Neruda's follow, and Said ends by placing Yeats somewhere along the way to full postcolonialism: "True, he stopped short of imagining full political liberation, but he gave us a major international achievement in cultural decolonization nonetheless".

On David Lloyd's "The Poetics of Politics: Yeats and the Founding of the State," from Anomalous States: Irish Writing and the PostColonial Moment (1993):

Emphasizing the important political "discomfort" that Yeats's poems still cause, Lloyd explores the relationships between Yeats's poetry and Irish nationalism. Applying later Yeats to the poet's earlier work, Lloyd detects Yeats's discomfort with the nationalist force of his own drama and poetry. The famous early Yeats play, Cathleen Ni Houlihan inspired such fervent nationalism that in later life Yeats would ask: "Did that play of mine send out certain men the English shot?" In Lloyd's view, this concern is "by no means an overweening assessment of the extraordinary part his writings played in the forging in Ireland of a mode of subjectivity apt to find its political and ethical realization in sacrifice to the nation yet to be". Lloyd addresses the paradoxical emphasis on foundation and demise in Yeats's poetry. At the end of the essay, Lloyd turns to Yeats's female characters, and raises questions about "the antagonism between certain feminisms and the nationalism of the state".

On Declan Kiberd's Inventing Ireland (1995)

Kiberd spends his first chapter, "Childhood and Ireland," on Yeats, discussing the effect of the poet's Sligo childhood on both his writing and his vision of Ireland. He questions the ways that Yeats's early work, like other Revival texts, "which so nourished the national feeling, were often British in origin, and open to the charge of founding themselves on the imperial strategy of infantilizing the native culture". Kiberd weighs in with other critics on the strong connection between Yeats's writing and place: "In emphasizing locality,

Yeats, Synge and Lady Gregory were deliberately aligning themselves with the Gaelic bardic tradition of dinn-sheanchas (knowledge of the lore of places)". Kiberd offers a reading of the differences between Irish and British definitions of culture: "In (Yeats's) estimate, a true culture consisted not in acquiring opinions but in getting rid of them". "Innocence," then, "is not inexperience, but its opposite". In the next chapter, "The National Longing for Form," Kiberd argues that Yeats and Whitman, as postcolonial writers, both perform "a search for a national style". This chapter explores the relationship between the literature of the "cultural colonies" and the "parent country" (115). Kiberd then presents a fascinating argument for Yeats's (and Chinua Achebe's) search for their own style as a form of "self-conquest". Connecting literature and self, Kiberd argues that for both Whitman and Yeats "the decolonization of the body was a task almost as important as the decolonization of the native culture". Investigating ideas of culture, and arguing for the search for a new style as a quest for a new self and nation, Kiberd reveals connections between Yeats and Whitman as writers of decolonization.

On Jahan Ramazani's "Is Yeats a Postcolonial Poet?" (1998)

Ramazani's fascinating essay begins by outlining the arguments for and against Yeats's inclusion as a postcolonial writer. Acknowledging Yeats's "whiteness, and his affiliation with the centuriesold settler community of Anglo-Irish Protestants, Ramazani argues that due to his "anticolonial resistance to British cultural domination and his effort to transform the degraded colonial present by recuperating the precolonial past," Yeats warrants examination as an anticolonial writer. If we place Yeats "under the postcolonial microscope, the many different shapes and sizes of postcoloniality need to be distinguished." Ramazani then discusses postcolonialism in terms of Yeats and Ireland, arguing that the term "anticolonial" replace "postcolonial." With "influences on writers as diverse as Derek Walcott and Lorna Goodison, Raja Rao and A. K. Ramanujan, Chinua

Achebe and Wole Soyinka," Yeats belongs to the postcolonial tradition of hybridization. Ramazani continues to position Yeats with postcolonial, or anticolonial writers: "When Yeats, speaking at a political gathering in 1898, declared that the English empire 'has been built on the rapine of the world,' he anticipated Frantz Fanon's claim". In terms of Irish cultural history, Ramazani claims that through their "Revival, the poets have turned a corpselike Ireland into a living, vibrant, even awe-inspiring 'imagined community.'" Finally, Ramazani interrogates Yeats's use of Indian symbols and characters as neither completely Orientalist nor affiliating, but sees his attraction to India because it "represents the Unity of Culture he wished for Ireland." Ramzani concludes that as a nation-maker and a writer of hybridization Yeats should be considered an anticolonial writer.

The Poet As Politician - new Biography of W.B. Yeats Examines Broader Context of Poet's Life - Critical Essay

Reason, Feb, 2001 by Michael Valdez Moses

The Ideological Odyssey of W.B. Yeats

In December 1923, William Butler Yeats, the first Irish writer to be awarded the Nobel Prize for literature, seized upon the occasion of his lecture to the Royal Academy of Sweden to present his literary career in political terms. Noting with irony that an English committee had almost certainly forwarded his nomination to the academy, Yeats cast himself as a standard-bearer of Irish nationalism and a champion of Ireland's cultural independence.

"The theatres of Dublin," he recounted in his speech on "The Irish Dramatic Movement," "were empty buildings hired by the English travelling companies, and we wanted Irish plays and Irish players. When we thought of these plays we thought of everything that was romantic and poetical, because the nationalism we had called up—the nationalism every generation had called up in moments of discouragement—was romantic and poetical."

Yeats had reason to regard himself as a political figure of national, even international, importance. He was at the time of this address a senator of the newly established Irish Parliament. Moreover, he spoke not long after the conclusion of a violent guerrilla war waged by the Irish Republican Army against British imperial rule in Ireland and a subsequent civil war, fought between the newly formed army of the Irish Free State and a breakaway wing of IRA irregulars, over the terms of the peace treaty that concluded the Anglo-Irish War of 1919-21. While Yeats could not boast of having fought in the streets against the British, he nonetheless used the occasion of his literary success to claim, retrospectively, a leading role in the national campaign that led to Irish independence in 1922.

One of the many splendid qualities of Terence Brown's recent biography, The Life of W.B. Yeats, is its critical appreciation of the poet's extraordinary cultural accomplishments within the broader context of a brilliantly rendered political and social history of modern Ireland. Brown's Yeats is the consummate late romantic and modernist artist, arguably the greatest lyric poet to write in English in the 20th century and one of the most innovative playwrights of his age. (The magnitude of Yeats' poetic achievement has tended to overshadow his accomplishments as a dramatist. More's the pity. He was quite possibly the most original avant-garde Irish dramatist before Beckett.) Brown, Professor of Modern English Literature in Trinity College, Dublin, is by no means the only biographer of late to take on the life of W.B. Yeats. While neither as comprehensive nor as authoritative as Roy Foster's projected two-volume W.B. Yeats: A Life, the first installment of which has appeared, nor as salacious as Brenda Maddox's recent Yeats's Ghosts: The Secret Life of W.B. Yeats, Brown's book is nonetheless the finest single-volume biography of the Irish poet since the publication of Richard Ellmann's seminal Yeats: The Man and the Masks in 1948.

If the Yeats that Brown portrays is every inch the literary titan, he is also a man of unusual personal complexity immersed in the political, cultural, and religious controversies of the day, a figure who, despite his own occasional championing of l'art pour l'art, struggled to imbue his poems, plays, essays, and stories with political and religious, even cosmic, significance. In the course of a poetic career that stretched from the 1880s to the late 1930s, Yeats adopted many different political masks, including those of radical nationalist, classical liberal, reactionary conservative, and millenarian nihilist.

Brown's biography offers us the chance to revisit an era in which the range of political options and ideas was considerably wider than in our own day. If the poetic appeal of extremist politics was more palpable, Brown's book and Yeats' life remind us that grave risks attend the heightened drama and aesthetic appeal of an illiberal era. If we sometimes lament the colourlessness of our modern politician s, whose programmes and ideologies are as predictable as their neckwear, we might nonetheless be grateful that in our day no genius in the throes of divine madness lights our way to paradise.

In his Autobiographies, Yeats recalled an Anglo-Irish Protestant childhood set against the backdrop of Fenian (Irish nationalist) violence and the "outrages" of the Land War, agrarian agitations aimed at reforming the neo-feudal system of land tenure in Ireland. Yeats was born in Dublin in 1865, but his earliest memories are of London, and even they are haunted by the specter of violence. In one recollection, a servant warns him that the town will be blown up, and he thereafter "goes to sleep in terror."

His earliest recorded memory of the power of poetry harks back to his boyhood days in Ireland and concerns a (presumably Catholic) stable boy who introduces the future Nobel laureate to a book of "Orange rhymes," that is, a popular book of anti-Catholic and anti-Fenian political verse. Yeats recalls that shortly after his first exposure to poetry he was told of "a rumor of a Fenian rising, that rifles had been served out to the Orangemen; and presently, when I began to dream of my future life, I thought I wou ld like to die fighting the Fenians."

Constructions of History in Yeats's "Nineteen Hundred and Nineteen" and "Meditations in time of Civil War" - of Twentieth Century Literature

The one duty we owe to history is to rewrite it.

Oscar Wilde

the problem after any revolution is what to do with your gunmen as old Billyum found out in Oireland....

Ezra Pound

For those who engaged in bringing postcolonial theory to bear on Yeats studies, The Tower, a collection traditionally read within the context of "British" high modernism, offers a tempting point of entry. Published in 1928, The Tower contains poems mostly written during the nine-year period that saw the drafting of the Irish Declaration of Independence in 1919, the passage of the Government of Ireland act in 1920 and of the Anglo-Irish treaty in 1921, and the creation of the Irish Free State in 1922—a period that, viewed from one angle, marked Ireland's emergence from the shadow of imperialism into the light of postcolonial independence. Published after this supposed instant of transition, The Tower may allow critics to position Yeats as a postcolonial poet, an attractive move given the current scholarly cache attached to the postcolonial and given the potential such a characterization would afford for counterbalancing the attacks on Yeats's politics that have gained prominence since the 1980s.

Scholars who analyze Yeats and Irish literature from a historical vantage, a practice that inevitably raises issues related to British imperialism, colonization, and Irish nationalism, have, however, been correctly suspicious of the temptation to make broad-based, prematurely celebratory, postcolonial readings. Echoing the cautionary remarks of postcolonial theorists Ella Shohat, Anne McClintock, and others, they have argued that such readings, in assuming a clean break between an oppressive colonial past and a liberated "postcolonial" present, obscure the complexities and unique features of the Irish situation, fail to examine in detail the transitional period itself (one in progress to this day), and, most importantly, ignore empire's crippling economic, political, cultural, and psychological legacies, as Frantz Fanon has famously outlined. Indeed, recent Yeats scholarship has been particularly attentive to these considerations, frequently emphasizing the degree to which his verse from the 1920s and 30s remains bound in empire's Manichean logic, idealizing those aspects of Irish culture and those apparently essential qualities of the Irish race that imperial discourse had used to mark the former colony as "other." According to critics ranging from Donald Torchiana and Conor Cruise O'Brien to Terry Eagleton and Seamus Deane, Yeatsian cultural nationalism worked to romanticize, and thus to reinscribe, these outmoded forms of Irish identity, and in his late verse we can perceive Yeats liberally rewriting Irish history in the service of that end, fetishizing an eighteenth century during which peasant and Ascendancy landlord existed in supposed harmony.

Despite the emergence of counterbalancing arguments by Declan Kiberd, David Lloyd, and Edward Said, more work needs to be done responding to these criticisms and expanding the possibilities for reading Yeats through the lens of a locally engaged postcolonial theory that attends to the specifics of the Irish situation. Rather than offering a means either to celebrate Yeats as a writer whose verse somehow transcends the legacy of imperialism or to attack Yeats (again) for his admittedly aristocratic and authoritarian politics, the postcolonial affords a new vantage from which to reinvestigate Yeats's verse in light of Irish history, to uncover his complex relationship with an Ireland in transition that, as Auden has famously written, "hurt [him] into poetry".

This essay will focus on an issue often explored in postcolonial criticism: constructions of history during a period of militant nationalism. After situating my work in relation to Yeats's more hostile postcolonial critics and after briefly analyzing the discourse of Irish nationalisms in the early 1920s, I will argue that in two key poems from The Tower, "Nineteen Hundred and Nineteen" and "Meditations in Time of Civil

War," Yeats is exercising his "one duty" to rewrite history. But far from reinscribing an outmoded nationalist mindset that idealizes one form of Irish identity, eighteenth century or otherwise, Yeats pointedly challenges former and current nationalist narratives of history by focusing instead on instances of rupture and the chaos of the present. In so doing, Yeats undercuts those stable narratives of a unified heroic nation that were central to the political and cultural nationalists' agendas in the 20s and that helped to perpetuate, in Deane's words, a "colonialist mentality" even after the establishment of the Free State.

Looking broadly at Yeats's evolving project of cultural nationalism, particularly as it is represented in his most bitterly nostalgic works in the 1930s, it would be difficult to defend yeats against the claim "that he distorted history in the service of myth" and it is not my intention to do so here. Seamus Deane and Terry Eagleton are certainly correct when they argue that Yeatsian cultural nationalism was, at least in part, grounded in an ultimately conservative attachment to an idealized vision of Ireland's Ascendancy past, a romantic conception of Irish identity and Irish history that, according to Deane, "clearly harbours the desire to obliterate or reduce the problems of class, economic development, bureaucratic organization, and the like, concentrating on the essences of self, community, nationhood, racial theory, Zeitgeist". However, while I agree to some extent with their general claims, I differ with them concerning "Meditations in Time of Civil War" and "Nineteen Hund red and Nineteen." The primary point of contention involves their reliance on a traditional Marxist reading of historical false consciousness whereby these poems are viewed as expressing a retreat from the material present into an imagined past.

Rather than emphasize those historical narratives that would displace a concrete engagement with history (as if that displacement occurs seamlessly, one narrative simply erasing another), I intend, in keeping with more broad-based deployments of postcolonial theory by critics such as Homi

Bhabha, to focus on the moment of displacement itself, a transitional moment when, as Bhabha puts it, "[t]he language of culture and community is poised on the fissures of the present becoming the rhetorical figures of a national past" (142). Where a strictly Marxist reading would see a dialectical shift from an engagement with history unfolding in the present to a glorification of history in the past, our postcolonial reading will center on this ambivalent moment in war-torn Ireland when history is becoming History, when the heterogeneous scraps of individual experiences are transformed and translated through the discourses of nationalism into homogenous narratives of national history and national identity. By shifting our gaze to this transitional moment itself and to Yeats's engagement with these nationalist constructions of history as they are being formulated, we begin to perceive a more complicated Yeats whose poetic meditations on an Ireland gripped by war may not be so readily dismissed as romantic idealism or naive historical mythmaking. To establish this context for analyzing the poems we must, therefore, briefly turn to the discourses of nationalism shortly before and during "the troubles."

In the late 1910s and early 1920s, the period during which Yeats wrote "Nineteen Hundred and Nineteen," the rhetoric of Sinn Fein drew heavily on a type of nationalism popularized in the previous century by Thomas Davis (Boyce 295). Characterized by appeals to Ireland's heroic past of imperial resistance, such nationalism foregrounded both the duty of the patriot to continue that struggle and the duty of the historian and artist, in the words of Davis, to lead us into the love of self-denial, of justice, of beauty, of valour; of generous life and proud death; and to set up in our souls the memory of great men who shall then be as models and judges of our actions...." (qtd. In Thuente 44)

During their ultimately successful 1918 election bid, Sinn Fein campaigned on a platform of "separatism," the final goal being not simply home rule but a distinct, and increasingly Catholic, Irish Republic, an "imagined community" (11) sanctified through the discourse of Sinn Fein nationalism as that state for which former insurrectionists had given their lives. As historian P. S. O'Hegarty claimed in 1924: "what was sold to the electorate [in 1918], what they voted on, was not Sinn Fein, not the republic, but Easter Week" (qtd. in Boyce 318). (12) Easter Week certainly, but, more important, it was a distinctly "historical" Easter Week couched as the climactic date in a revolutionary calendar whose highlights included 1798, 1848, and 1867, and which affirmed, as the Sinn Fein General Election Manifesto (1918) proclaimed, "the fact that in nearly every generation, and five times within the past 120 years our people have challenged in arms the right of England to rule this country" (Mitchell and O'Snodaigh 48).

At the time of the election, 1916 was marked by most Republican leaders as the conclusion of violent resistance, a past that would in itself serve to invigourate a political struggle in the present, but that position changed during the years of the Anglo-Irish War, as increased violence and revolutionary resistance in what came to be known in IRA discourse as the "four glorious years" of 1918 to 1921 readily provided for, indeed demanded the articulation of, a living history of heroic struggle. Responding to this crisis, Sinn Fein obliged by again offering a narrative of the present, readily grafted upon earlier nationalist constructions, through which acts of violence—the burning of homes, the killing of "informers," the deaths of fellow insurrectionists—might be read within the context of a larger revolutionary mythology. While certainly understandable during a period of armed resistance, the continuous elaboration of a unified national history centered on a tradition of heroic sacrifice served to sup port the normalization of violence and helped, we can say with admitted hindsight, to lay the groundwork for a reactionary and an oppressive politics after liberation occurred.

The hasty execution by the IRA of accused spies and the killing of innocent civilians during surprise attacks were forgotten, while the deeds of men like Tom Barry readily became the stuff of folklore, significantly altering the landscape of nationalism for years to come and giving, in the opinion of historian D. George Boyce, "political violence a new lease of life in Ireland..." (323).

The Yeats of this period must be understood against this backdrop of nationalist sentiment. Conor Cruise O'Brien has written that the conception of history as a series of blood sacrifices enacted in every generation...is most essentially a literary invention. The great propagandist of this notion, as far as Ireland is concerned, was the poet Yeats.

(qtd. in Cullingford, Gender and History 57)

But as early as 1918 Yeats seems to have been acutely aware of the practical impact of inflaming "the old historical passion" (Letters 649), and during the debates that followed the passage of a British bill (March 1918) authorizing conscription of Irish soldiers for service in the Great War, Yeats, though publicly opposed, carefully tempered his opposition. Writing to Clement Shorter concerning an upcoming lecture on Irish poetry Yeats explains:

[T]imes are too dangerous for me to encourage men to risks I am not prepared to share or approve. If the Government go on with conscription there may be soon disastrous outbreaks....

[T]he old historical passion is at its greatest intensity (Letters 649)

As a letter to the British Lord Haldane written later that year reveals, Yeats's primary concern was not simply violence in itself but what that violence might become in both imperial and national historiography:

If conscription is imposed... [t]here will be incidents that will become anecdotes and legends.... Each side will have its wrongs to tell of and these will keep England and Ireland apart during your lifetime and mine. (qtd. in Cullingford, Yeats 104).

In "Nineteen Hundred and Nineteen" Yeats offers a response to such potential constructions of history by articulating a vision of the present that steadfastly refuses to conform to the contours of Republican historiography. This is not to say that Yeats peers through the haze of Republican nationalism to discover or articulate a "ture" history of the Anglo-Irish War, nor, as Deane would argue, does he attempt to replace one idealized history with another. Rather, as so often happens with Yeats, he begins anew. He fundamentally questions those positivistic histories developed by most forms of Irish nationalism. He indicts himself for having blindly participated in the construction of previous national histories and, in an attempt to lay the foundation for a new history of Ireland rendered in art, plunges into the "foul rag and bone shop" of war, exploding the gap, to borrow Enda Duffy's remarks on Ulysses, "between the horror of actual violence and the explanations of overtly political discourse", between the actual community and imagined community, between a history waiting to be written and a history that has been written.

"Nineteen Hundred and Nineteen," as Curtis Bradford's compilation of Yeats's manuscripts indicates, underwent numerous revisions, two of which, central to our reading, occurred after its original publication in The Dial (1921) and The London Mercury (1921): the title was changed from "Thoughts upon the Present State of the World" and the postscriptum date "1919" was added, though, as a letter to Olivia Shakespear reveals, Yeats was still working on the poem in April 1921 (Letters 668). These changes nicely highlight the issue of historiographic desire that I see at the core of the poem, as Yeats, in a move designed to heighten the poem's ultimate irony, initially seems to present a poem that will give order and meaning to history as it unfolds. The original title serves to indicate the subjective position of the author, an artist simply reflecting on a series of events passing before his eyes. In sharp contrast, both the formal title "Nineteen Hundred and Nineteen" and the postscriptum date resonate with a se nse of objective truth and the weight of history/historiography. It is as if Yeats, in the manner of the prophetic romantic artist, perceives the historical importance of that year as it happens. Furthermore, by seeming to announce the centrality of that year in his title, Yeats asks the reader to view the poem as a representation of history, a point in time that must then be considered within the context of other significant historical moments. This is true of Yeats's whole canon, as the title inevitably brings to mind other key dates such as 1913 and 1916, demanding the contextualization of the poem within, at the very least, his individual literary history and potentially suggesting an evolutionary trajectory in which the sacrifices of 1916 would be (re)validated by the revolutionary heroes of 1919. Historical contextualization is also demanded on a broader level, for, as numerous critics have noted, "Nineteen Hundred and Nineteen" signals the beginning of a new era after the Great War and, in terms of the Irish situation, clearly sets the poem within the context of the Anglo-Irish War, marking the first year of that struggle when, in January, the Dail formally declared succession from the United Kingdom. Indeed, during the 1921 treaty debates, 1919 was, according to nationalist leaders such as Eamon De Valera, the year when the Republic envisioned in 1916 actually came into being (Cronin 140).

Viewed in this light, Yeats's decision to alter the title and to add the postscriptum date would appear to support the type of reading initially advanced by Donald Torchiana: the act of grounding the poem in a historical moment that must be read within the broader context of larger historical narratives pointedly heightens the poem's fundamental irony. Rather than offering a linear progression, an unbroken positivistic history as the title might suggest, the poem turns upon itself, profoundly critiquing the present state of disorder and looking back with a mixture of bitterness and nostalgia toward an idealized ascendancy past. Yet a rejection of the present does not necessarily entail a desired return to a more stable—that is, colonial—moment in Ireland's past. Rather, the poem itself is doubly ironic in that the expected progression evoked by the date is undercut by a chaotic vision of the present, which is in turn further undercut by the poem's refusal to sanction any concrete historical narrative as a means for comprehending (and, in turn, valorizing) that present. In other words, the poem plays upon historiographic desire—the desire to use temporal markers as a means for constructing order in the present—by continually frustrating that desire, revealing that the old, particularly nationalist and imperialist modes for ordering time must be cast aside before new histories of Ireland may be articulated in this transitional period. Though direct analogy between the African and Irish colonial and nationalist situations must not be readily assumed, Fanon's words concerning the truly revolutionary national poet are applicable here:

> It is not enough to try to get back to the people in that past out of which they have already emerged; rather we must join them in that fluctuating movement which they are just giving a shape to, and which, as soon as it has started, will be the signal for everything to be called in question.

While Yeats's own earlier cultural nationalism would seem to find answers in history, in "Nineteen Hundred and Nineteen" Yeats finds only questions that all point to a profound need to (re)join the Irish people with a new, fluctuating present.

The poem opens, like Pound's Cantos, with a lamentation for what has passed, an Athenian world of artistic triumphs, "ornamental bronze and stone / An ancient image made of olive wood— / And... Phidias' famous ivories." Yet the tone is not one of nostalgia but grim acceptance; instead of a desire to return to that past (or to recreate that past in the present), there is a need to perceive the dangers of attempting to do so. With the line "We too had many pretty toys when young," the poem shifts to a more recent past, and here we begin to perceive the root of this acceptance: the compulsion to establish a seamless relationship between past and present, and to assume that the supposed greatness of the past has continued unabated into the present, has led to historical myopia, an idealization of what had gone before and naive confidence in what was to come:

> *... habits... made old wrong*
> *Melt down, at it were wax in the sun's rays;*
> *Public opinion ripening for so long*

We thought it would outlive all future days.
O what fine thought we had because we thought
That the worst rogues and rascals had died out.

"ABITS"—ESTABLISHED MODES OF READING THE PAST—HAVE SERVED TO LIMIT HISTORICAL PERCEPTION AND HAVE LED TO A BLIND FAITH IN THE STABILITY OF "FUTURE DAYS."

Elizabeth Cullingford reads this section as a bitter commentary on nineteenth-century values, faith in "Victorian stability, peace, and [a] belief in progress" (Yeats 118), and clearly the passage is designed to capture a mood of naive certainty. A trace of the Irish context, though, is recognizable in the drafts, as the lines concerning "public opinion" originally contained a more local reference: "A speedy remedy for obvious wrong; / No swaggering soldier on the public ways / Who weighed man's life lighter than a song" (Bradford 72). Likely a direct allusion to the Black and Tans (Bradford 78), the British forces sent to occupy Ireland in 1920, these lines suggest a more pointed historical narrative that would align directly with nationalist historiography.

The Victorian values espoused by British cultural imperialism—Britain as the paradigmatic modern, civilized nation fostering the evolutionary journey of the colony toward a similar state of civilization—were simply hollow rhetoric, a set of belief s no longer able to conceal during the Anglo-Irish War the true goals of imperialism: political subjugation, economic exploitation, and cultural domination. Yeats's use of the term "swaggering" would likely have had strong and direct connotations for an Irish audience all too familiar with R.I.C. and Black and Tan atrocities—the burning of Balbriggan, the sacking of Cork, and the Croke Park massacre—and with popular representations of these troops as proud, heartless, and, in the words of British Brigadier-General F. P. Crozier, "drunken and insubordinate" (Lyons, "The War" 245). Significantly, Yeats immediately does away with this image in the next draft, preferring the much more ambiguous "public opinion." In so doing, he moves from a clearly nationalistic history—one that would immediately sanctify 1919 and, by extension, the Anglo-Irish War as another chapter of heroic sacrifice—to a broader indictment of historical desire. Public opinion, be it British or Irish, has led to blind faith in histori cal progression, that which "made old wrong / Melt down," and the return of that faith leads to a state of profound violence in the present.

The two stanzas that follow look Janus-faced toward both sides of the Irish Sea. As several critics have noted, the phrase "Parliament and king" refers to the British Empire prior to the Great War, a world of imperial certainty soon to be undone, while the stanza that follows, characterized by some of the most bitter language in The Tower, centers on Black and Tan attacks during the Anglo-Irish War:

Now days are dragon-ridden, the nightmare
Rides upon sleep: a drunken soldiery
Can leave the mother, murdered at her door,
To crawl in her own blood, and go scot-free;
The night can sweat with terror as before
We pieced our thoughts into philosophy,
And planned to bring the world under a rule,
Who are but weasels fighting in a hole.

Yeats's vivid description of the murdered "mother" again smacks of nationalist historiography, of British confidence in its own evolutionary imperial project now exposed as simple tyranny, the wanton killing of an innocent woman. The mother referred to is Ellen Quinn (Cullingford, Yeats 106), a woman, as Lady Gregory's journals reveal, "shot dead with her child in her arms" in November 1920. Gregory used this incident as the basis for her Nation article "Murder by the Throat" (1920), one of many nationalistic works decrying Black and Tan atrocities. Yeats too wrote an explicitly nationalistic poem on the subject. In "Reprisals" he imagines the deceased Robert Gregory looking upon the current state of Ireland and finding that "Half-drunk or whole-mad soldiery / Are murdering [his] tenants there." The poem goes on to ask with bitterness:

Where may new-married women sit
And suckle children now? Armed men
May murder them in passing by
Nor law nor parliament take heed. (Variorum 791)

According to Jeffares, Yeats chose not to publish "Reprisals" for fear of upsetting Robert Gregory's pro-British widow. Yet the poem provides a useful context for Yeats's handling of the same incident in "Nineteen Hundred and Nineteen." In the former, agency is quite clear, as these "armed men," the minions of a coldly detached British "parliament," move about the countryside—the traditional site, understandably enough, in nationalist historiography of evictions, burning of homes, and summary executions—"murdering" the Irish peasantry, Gregory's former "Kiltartan... tenants." In the latter, though Black and Tan "murder[s]" are certainly evoked, agency is somewhat clouded.

The death of the mother is viewed as part of a more abstract whirlwind of chaos and violence, and the local Kiltartan time and setting is replaced by a broader vision of "days" that are now "dragon-ridden." More important, the pronoun "we," so rarely used by Yeats, abounds in this section, suggesting no clear demarcation b etween Irish victim and British aggressor. The two, bound together in their desire to find stability in time and to discover in the past validation for deeds in the present, whether in service of an imperial or a national cause, have tragically failed to perceive the violent ends of such desires: "We pieced our thoughts into philosophy, / And planned to bring the world under a rule, / Who are but weasels fighting in a hole."

Sections two and three are less overtly concerned with specifically nationalist or imperialist narratives of time, but they too play upon historiographic desire. The poem's second section, beginning with "Loie Fuller's Chinese dancers," would seem to anticipate a high-modernist move—practiced by Pound and at times by Yeats—in which a Western present looks for a structuring aesthetic in an Eastern past. This expected focus, though, is displaced by a much broader vision of history: "So the Platonic Year / Whirls out new right and wrong, / Whirls in the old instead." The compulsion to find order in the past leads only to an awareness of time as profoundly uncontrollable, of a Platonic year of 25,000 years in which the planets return to their original positions, of change without change, of the whirling of Fuller's dancers replaced by the whirling of time itself in which "All men are dancers and their tread / Goes to the barbarous clangour of a gong." This move into a more abstract understanding of time is itself undercut, as Yeats plays ironically upon his own "platonic" sense of history. The "solitary soul" is compared to "a swan," recalling Yeats at a slightly earlier stage, the "moralist or mythological poet" who, in The Wild Swans at Coole, first wrote poems based on the visionary system he derived from automatic writing sessions with his wife. In the eponymous opening poem of that collection, swans "All suddenly mount / And scatter wheeling in great broken rings / Upon their clamorous wings"—a figure for cyclical history, the wheeling of gyres whose true nature the poet in his tower, as Robartes sees in "The Phases of the Moon," "seeks in book or manuscript" but "shall never find."

In "Nineteen Hundred and Nineteen," in time of war, such attempts to garner a broader comprehension of history have taken on an added sense of urgency. Yet here again the fulfillment of historiographic desire never occurs: time viewed politically, artistically, or, in this case, philosophically remains profoundly uncontrollable. History whirls onward, "A man" remains "lost amid the labyrinth that he has made / in art or politics," while the dreams of those, including the poet, who sought "to mend / Whatever mischief seemed / To afflict mankind" have gone unfulfilled:

The swan has leaped into the desolate heaven:
That image can bring wildness, bring a rage
To end all things, to end
What my laborious life imagined, even
The half-imagined, the half-written page:
O but we dreamed to mend
Whatever mischief seemed

To afflict mankind, but now
That winds of winter blow
Learn that we were crack-pated when we dreamed.

The swan has departed, fading, as with all things in this poem, into a whirlwind of dust and chaos, a "desolate heaven." Such knowledge tempts the poet to despair, "to end / What my laborious life imagined," yet that individual sense of bitterness is again linked with a broader "we," a people on both sides of the Irish Sea whose faith in history as evolutionary is now revealed as "crack-pated."

Section four seems to address the confident mindset of the British (and perhaps the Anglo-Irish) prior to the Great War:

We, who seven years ago
Talked of honour and truth,
Shriek with pleasure if we show
The weasel's twist, the weasel's tooth.

"[S]even years ago," though certainly evocative of prewar Britain, speaks equally to Ireland's recent past. The years 1912-1914, alluded to in "Easter, 1916" ("For England may keep faith / For all that is done and said"), marked a period of debate concerning the final prerevolution Home Rule Bill introduced to the British Parliament in April 1912. That bill, designed to grant Ireland a separate parliament with jurisdiction over internal affairs, was, after two years of heated Parliamentary argument, placed on the statute books in 1914 but not enacted because of the outbreak of war. The subsequent Easter Rising, the British government's hardline response and its later attempts to conscript Irish forces, all led to a climate in which support for constitutional home rule in Ireland gave place to more extreme demands for complete autonomy.

In this context, the section tantalizingly evokes a pointedly nationalist reading of history: imperial commitments, talk of "honour and truth," have given way to the reassertion of imperial might. Yet the pronoun "we" is again of central importance. Like most nationalists (Lyons, "The Developing" 144), Yeats supported the 1912 bill, and it is particularly telling that he referred to the weight of history when expressing that support to a group of southern Protestants: "The clear verdict of the history of civilised nations in modern times is that the responsibilities of self- government and the growth of political freedom are the most powerful solvents for sectarian animosities" (qtd. in Cullingford, Yeats 86). Adopting a key trope of imperialist historiography—"the history of civilised nations" as the field from which "clear" historical truths may be harvested-Yeats recasts the evolutionary certainties of the modern imperial nation in Irish terms, establishing those certainties as the basis of his faith in m oderate constitutional nationalism.

In "Nineteen Hundred and Nineteen" such faith is dismissed as another component of the labyrinth, a historical myopia pervading both sides of the colonial binary; however, rather than replicate that binary by simply attacking imperialism's rhetoric of "honour and truth" and by positioning himself as an Irish nationalist who perceives clearly the betrayal that imperial discourse would belie, Yeats indicts all who have participated in the construction of sanctioning historical narratives. What remains is not the aloof comfort of gazing upon a historical narrative proved false but the bitter "shriek" of "pleasure" that comes with perceiving the hollow core of historiographic desire.

In the poem's concluding section Yeats moves quickly from a chaotic present in which there are no heroes (the "few... handsome riders... break and vanish"), no clear villains, only "Violence upon the roads," to a vision of the distant past, a final ironic play on historiographic desire: But now wind drops, dust settles; thereupon

There lurches past, his great eyes without thought
Under the shadow of stupid straw-pale locks,
That insolent fiend Robert Artisson
To whom the love-lorn Lady Kyteler brought
Bronzed peacock feathers, red combs of her cocks.

These lines look back to "The Second Coming," with Robert Artisson—a fourteenth-century "evil spirit" from Irish folklore (Yeats's note in Collected Poems 461)—occupying the same position as the "rough beast," a pitiless figure who, gazing "without thought," does not trouble to look upon unimportant local human time, his visage "stupid" because he is simply an agent of cyclical history This section, however, is not without a local Irish trace. In Raphael Holinshed's The Historie of Ireland (1577), Artisson is the spirit with whom the witch, Dame Alice Kyteler, "was charged to haue nightly conference... [and] to whom she sacrificed in the high way ix red cockes, and ix peacocks eies" (Yeats's note in Collected Poems 469).

The image of a "love-lorn" woman making a sacrifice functions as a bitter trope in Yeats, with women such as Maud Gonne and Constance Gore-Booth represented as sacrificing all (or what Yeats considered as "all") to the cause of extreme nationalism. For such women, "Too long a sacrifice," as Y eats wrote in "Easter, 1916," "Can make a stone of the heart." In "Nineteen Hundred and Nineteen," as so often occurs in Yeats, woman becomes a figure of Yeats's own nationalist desires and frustrations. The desire to find a structuring object in Ireland's folk past and to construct a homogenous narrative of an Irish history that might evoke an Ireland worthy of sacrifice meets with its ironic, frustrating fulfillment. If blood sacrifice is the ultimate goal of cultural nationalism, blood sacrifice is what Yeats discovers in this journey back into Ireland's folk past, but in this poem it is a sacrifice utterly devoid of heroism: the sacrifice of animals to an evil spirit, a fitting commentary on an Ireland where human lives continue to be sacrificed for historical causes.

The postscriptum date that follows these lines is thus entirely ironic. The historical certainty that it seems to evoke, the historiographic desire to order time in an evolutionary manner, has been foreclosed in the poem proper. Confidence i n linear history, be it in the service of imperial or national programme, has produced days that are "dragon-ridden" and a world in which men and women have, like Dame Kyteler's peacocks, lost their eyes, their capacity to see the violence that history has produced. For the cycle to break—for 1919 to not be read as simply another "glorious year"—history, in the fluctuating world of a colony becoming nation, must be viewed anew.

As with "Nineteen Hundred and Nineteen," "Meditations in Time of Civil War," a sequence of poems Yeats composed while residing in his tower during the summer and autumn of 1922, may be productively studied in light of nationalist discourse, particularly in light of Republican and Free State appeals to Ireland's noble past during the Anglo-Irish Treaty debates and ensuing civil war. Not surprisingly, both groups adopted the rhetoric of preindependence nationalism, though with different ends in mind.

While Free State supporters tended to promote the treaty as the climactic moment in a centuries-old struggle, an ultimate validation of the heroic actions undertaken by previous generations, Republicans characterized the treaty as a fundamental betrayal, "a surrender" according to Republican leader Eamon De Valera, "of the ideals for which the sacrifices of the past few years were deliberately made and the sufferings of these years consciously endured" (qtd. in Cronin 154). Following the Republican seizure of the Four Courts, the act that precipitated the civil war, De Valera issued an "Easter Proclamation," a revolutionary declaration designed to construct a clear historical trajectory extending from 1916, through the current "uprising," and toward the imagined future republic, "the destiny God has in mind for Ireland the fair, the peerless one" (qtd. in Coogan 314). The Free State responded in kind:

> Under [the] Treaty the government and control of your own country and its resources have been surrendered back to you after centuries of usurpation. You are asked to reject this surrender and engage in a hopeless and unnecessary war with Great Britain. The people in the Four Courts say they are fighting for a Republic. In reality they are fighting to bring the British back.
>
> (qtd. in Cronin 153)

Here the weight of history is brought to the fore, though the emphasis is on a highly specific historical narrative. The agreed return to Ireland of limited political and economic control is characterized as a British "surrender," a term designed expressly to position this "victory" within a nationalist tradition of armed resistance, heroic sacrifice, and martyrdom, as opposed to a more moderate tradition of constitutional nationalism.

Accused by Republicans of securing merely a "political" triumph akin to the supposed triumph of the 1914 Government of Ireland Act, this Free State pronouncement places the treaty within history as the end for which previous generations had given their lives. To reject the treaty would amount to an invalidation of those sacrifices and a return to a "hopeless" war against the British, a curious twist of logic given that the British had apparently "surrendered."

Written in the whirlpool of violence that followed the treaty split, "Meditations in Time of Civil War" engages these competing narratives of an Irish present and past. Again, though, it is important to recognize the fundamental instability of these ideologically driven narratives. As both Fanon and Bhabha emphasize, the articulation of a new national history along a progressive linear axis necessarily remains an ongoing and essentially temporal process. Throughout that process fissures are constantly erupting as the national "intellectual" is called to graft the amorphous, uncertain, and chaotic present of which he or she is a participant onto nationalism's more stable master narratives. This, explains Bhabha, is the central difficulty facing those who would write the history of a people:

> The present of the people's history, then, is a practice that destroys the constant principles of the national culture that attempt to hark back to a "true" national past, which is often represented in the reified forms of realism and stereotype. Such pedagogical knowledges and continuist national narratives miss [in the words of Fanon] the "zone of occult instability where the people dwell."

Like other public figures struggling to articulate a unified, stabilizing vision of a new Irish nation during the profound instability of the civil war, Yeats, as his critics have suggested, did much to promulgate a brand of nationalism intent on "hark[ening] back to a 'true' national past," a desirably premodern Ireland set against a present driven by self-interest and hatred. In "Meditations in Time of Civil War," however, we find a more complicated engagement with nationalism. Writing in the "zone of occult instability" that was the civil war, Yeats attempts to construct a space in which a new vision of Ireland might emerge and in which the deeds of the present—Irish turned against Irish, violence now bereft of the sanction of imperial resistance—cannot be and must not be contained by or reconciled with what had been sustaining nationalist narratives. As with other more recent postcolonial writers who focus on time, Yeats questions stable narratives of and from the past that can be controlled by any one nationalist (or imperialist) agenda; emphasizes violence as rupture, moments to be understood, not as the culmination of a series of past events but as profoundly engendering the unknowable (or for Yeats partially knowable) future; and, most importantly, confronts his reader with the senseless violence of the living present.

Yeats opens "Ancestral Houses" by positing a split between a supposedly culturally unified Ireland in the past and a fundamentally debased Ireland in the present, but this section, as with the opening of "Nineteen Hundred and Nineteen," is less a call for a return and more a meditation on the viability of deploying narratives derived from that past as a means for comprehending the present. Here, unlike the remaining poems, the focus of historiographic desire is initially not a nationalist past but a distinctly Anglo-Irish past in which cultural unity, "The sweetness that all longed for night and day," emerges ironically from "violence" and "bitterness." Yeats wrote in 1910 that "all noble things [including "great nations and classes"] are the result of warfare" (Essays 321), but in 1922, a time saturated with violence, that possibility seems foreclosed from the start, the product of an utterly naive idealism. The age of noble ancestral homes has ended. The "abounding glittering jet," an image of the "selfdeli ght[ing]," creative spirit of that age, has dried, leaving only "some marvellous empty sea-shell /... which / Shadows the inherited glory of the rich." In every home once occupied by a great man resides "the great-grandson of that house" who, for all the "bronze and marble" of his surroundings, is "but a mouse," a useless creature living among halls constructed by men long since dead. The "levelled lawns and gravelled ways," physical reminders of individuals who tamed their natural surroundings, remain merely for "slippered Contemplation....," reminders that the present is devoid of both greatness and bitterness.

With violence on all sides, why has not the spirit of Ireland's Anglo-Irish past been reawakened? A letter written in October 1922 from Yeats to Olivia Shakespear holds one possible clue:

> I spent the summer correcting proofs and writing a series of poems called "Meditations in time of civil war" which I shall send to the Mercury.... The situation here is very curious—a revolt against democracy by a small section.... I have met some of the ministers who more and more seem too sobre to meet the wildness of these enemies; and everywhere one notices a drift towards Conservatism, perhaps towards Autocracy. I always knew that it would come, but not that it would come in this tragic way.... Perhaps there is nothing so dangerous to a modern state, when politics take the place of theology, as a bunch of martyrs. A bunch of martyrs (1916) were the bomb and we are living in the explosion. (Letters 690)

This is Yeats the privately outspoken Free State supporter (he was less so in public and when addressing his more Republican-leaning friends such as Lady Gregory), and his words provide an important and more local context for reading "Ancestral Houses." The current Free State leaders of Ireland, unlike their mythical predecessors of "a haughtier age" are "too sobre to meet the wildness of these enemies." At the same time, what Yeats goes on to emphasize is not the cowardice of such individuals but the very pervasiveness of violence, the seemingly inevitable slide toward "Autocracy" in an Ireland where political agendas, on both sides, are advanced with religious fervor, an Ireland "living in the explosion" of revolution.

This contrast between a past in which violence leads to greatness and a present in which violence yields only further violence, is evident in the opening stanza. The spirit of Ascendancy Ireland is characterized as a jet of water that "rains down life," choosing "whatever shape it wills / And never stoop[ing] to a mechanical / Or servile shape, at others' beck and call." In an Ireland gripped by civil war, those who embrace violence and bitterness, certainly do so in a "mechanical" manner, obeying the "beck and call" of their Republican leaders with the blind zeal of martyrs. But this awareness of the gap between past and present offers little comfort, only the knowledge, as the poem's closing lines suggest, that Anglo-Ireland's noble past cannot be recreated in the present: "What if those things the greatest of mankind / Consider most to magnify, or to bless, / But take our greatness with our bitterness?"

Marjorie Howes, discussing the previous stanza, suggests that the verb "take" in the phrase "But take our greatness with our violence?" holds two possible connotations: "take away" and "take on" The same holds true for the closing stanza, though here the focus is very much historiographic desire. Those who would "magnify" or "bless" the outward trappings of Ascendancy Ireland and would retreat from the everencroaching chaos of the present into "great chambers and long galleries, lined / With famous portraits of our ancestors," "take away" greatness with bitterness. "[P]acing to and fro on polished floors," they remain caught in comfortable, impotent nostalgia, failing, like the leaders of contemporary Ireland, to take decisive action in the present—while those who perceive the necessary link between violence and greatness and who comprehend fully the root of Anglo-Irish greatness are faced with an awareness that the past contained the seeds of its own demise. A world built from bitterness and violence has regressed into violence, the past has again yielded its ironic harvest, and the speaker is left to confront a present in which the choice to "take on" further violence will merely perpetuate the cycle.

In the second poem, "My House," Yeats turns to the tower itself, a hybrid image—derived in typical Yeats fashion from British literary culture ("Il Penseroso's Platonist toiled on / In some like chamber") and Irish local culture —that might serve as a physical reminder of some preexisting unity, a period in Yeats's own past when a strategic blending of imperial and colonial traditions provided the basis for a vibrant cultural nationalism. Struggling against the ever-impinging real, Yeats opens each of the first two stanzas by detailing the physical characteristics of the tower, "A winding stair, a chamber arched with stone, / A grey stone fireplace with an open hearth," as it to rebuild the tower in art, to create a monument linking past and present. But the "wall is loosening." The tower is crumbling, the civil war is at hand, and, as Yeats writes in a letter from 1922, One wonders what prominent man will live through it. One meets a minister at dinner, passing his armed guard on the doorstop, and one feels no certainty that one will meet him again. We are entering on the final and most dreadful stage. (Letters 690).

Evidence of that final stage is what Yeats finds as he gazes from the tower. Here again the emphasis is on the drive to graft an unstable present on a more stable past, and the regressive practical effects of attempting to do so. This accounts in part for the oddly "dated" reference in the first stanza to the surrounding "acre of stony ground / Where the symbolic rose can break in flower." Drawing on a symbol from his earliest phase of cultural nationalism, Yeats aligns his own personal "literary" history with that of the nation. Just as Davisite nationalism had sought to find deeds in the past that, correctly "magnified" and "blessed," would serve to energize a popular front in the present, Yeats in poems such as "To Ireland in the Coming Times" had adopted the rose as a symbol of, among other things, a once and future Ireland, a symbol designed to evoke an Irish state always poised to be again. Indeed, the rose continued to serve as a standard trope in more directly political nationalist art, the red rose o f Ireland blooming from a ground soaked by the blood of martyrs. Thus proclaimed Joseph Plunkett in "The Little Black Rose Shall Be Red At Last," a poem written on the night before his execution in 1916: "Praise God if this my blood fulfills the doom / When you, dark rose, shall redden into bloom" (qtd. in Lyons, Ireland 335).

In "The Rose Tree," published in 1920, Yeats imagines Patrick Pearse expressing the identical sentiment: "There's nothing but our own red blood / Can make a right Rose Tree." In "Meditations" this tradition of martyrdom is evoked, the "Old raged elms" and "old thorns innumerable" suggestive of Christ-like sacrifice, but the repetition of "old" and the use of "innumerable" suggest a fundamental need to question that tradition, in which violent death has led to a sterile cycle of further violence. The rose, too, functions quite differently, as Yeats now draws our attention not to what might be evoked but to the very process of evocation, not to what might be signified but to the "artifici al" operation of the signifier-the rose marked as the "symbolic" rose, the rose of sacrifice become tired cliche. The ambiguous verb "break"—suggesting both the difficult birth of a rose and the destruction of a flower already in bloom—highlights the gap between past and present. Those who would assert the will, in this case the poetic will, are called to embrace violence, the repetition of an "act of founding" that, writes Marjorie Howes, "does not institute a self-sustaining genealogy" but only further blood sacrifice; while those who see the ironic return of a past are left to confront a present in which the rose of independence has given way to the thorns of war.

Yeats gazes from his tower, hearing, in a line that echoes "A Prayer for My Daughter," the "sound / Of every wind that blows," and seeing a "stilted water-hen / Crossing stream again / Scared by the splashing of a dozen cows." Like the water-hen disturbed by a herd of cows, the solitary "stilted" artist—"stilted" distinguishing him from those taking direct action—is left behind in the wake of change, searching tirelessly for some clear evidence of purposeful bitterness, some mode of representing the present in history that moves beyond the cycle of blood sacrifice and that might sustain future generations, some "Befitting emblems of adversity" hammered into history that "My bodily heirs may find, / To exalt a lonely mind."

On Yeats's table rests one such emblem, "Sato's gift, a changeless sword?' At once an art object and an instrument of war, the sword represents an Eastern past like the previously envisioned Anglo-Irish past in which greatness is born from violence and bitterness, "a changeless work of art" produced by "an aching heart." The sword, one of many "marvellous accomplishment[s]" passed "From father unto son," sparks a renewed desire for historical continuity, but such hopes are quickly dashed: "it seemed / Juno's peacock screamed." In the 1925 version of A Vision, the scream of Juno's peacock is linked with the full expansion of the primary gyre and the inevitable slide of civilization as a whole, signaled by the abandonment of individual thought, toward mob rule: "The loss of control over thought comes towards the end; first a sinking in upon the moral being, then the last surrender, the irrational cry, revelation, the scream of Juno's peacock" (qtd. in Unterecker 179). Though Yeats's esoteric claims are, in A Vi sion, applicable not simply to the history of Ireland but to history in general, the stanza that follows in "Meditations" immediately shifts the focus to a more local Irish context:

Life scarce can cast a fragrance on the wind,
Scarce spread a glory to the morning beams,
But the torn petals strew the garden plot;
And there's but common greenness after that.

We are again in the garden of the Big House, a garden littered with "torn petals," confirmation that the rose of Ireland has indeed been broken. The closing image comments ironically on "Easter, 1916," where the heroes of revolution, "Now and in time to be, / Wherever green is worn, / Are changed, changed utterly." Though by no means devoid of irony itself, "Easter, 1916" presents violent historical change as a "terrible beauty," the flowering of independence from the graves of martyrs. Here we have violence without growth, a landscape scene in which an image of temporal progression, dawn, gives way to "common greenness."

In "The Road at My Door," Yeats, for the first time in the poem, meditates directly on the civil war itself:

An affable Irregular,
A heavily-built Falstaffian man,
Comes cracking jokes of civil war
As though to die by gunshot were
The finest play under the sun.

Here Yeats ironically evokes a British theatrical tradition in order to indict a Republican ideological project, a project built upon nationalist dramatic representations of the noble, self-sacrificing Irish soldier. The reference to Falstaff evokes the braggart soldier, yet it falls somewhat short of outright condemnation, expressing rather a curious mixture of tragedy and farce. In a letter from December 1922, Yeats adopts the same tone to describe the burning of a friend's home:

I have just heard that when Mrs. Campbell's house was burnt... she appealed to the irregulars not to turn her children out in the night. The irregulars cried but said they could not help themselves, the new orders. Presently one of them went up stairs with Mrs. Campbell to fetch down—the house was I think already burning—the children's Xmas toys. (Letters 695)

In each case, the Irregular—a figure who might easily have been deployed as the embodiment of heartless cruelty, the callous burner of homes—is rendered with surprising sympathy, less a political dissident to be executed by the Free State government and more a deluded follower. The true focal point of the stanza is thus the capacity of nationalist rhetoric to render violence as heroic, killing as fulfillment of a cause, death as noble sacrifice, duty as blindly following "the new orders." It points to Falstaff's primary flaw, his ability to exploit those inexperienced soldiers for whom war has been represented as glorious, and to the Irregular's own tragic belief that "to die by gunshot were / The finest play under the sun."

Indeed, by emphasizing the theatrical,Yeats roots the return of colonial violence in a supposedly "liberated" Ireland precisely in a nationalist Republican project that would represent war as heroic theater. Yeats, in the aforementioned letter, touches on this when he continues: "Strang e tragedy of thought that creates for such men such crimes but I don't suppose that these men were conscripted rebels." The men who burned his neighbour's home were not conscripted, but they were fired by the same passion that fuels Yeats's "affable Irregular' that fueled Plunkett to write "The Little Black Rose," that fueled, to take an example from nationalist drama, Patrick Pearse's revolutionary hero in his play The Singer: "One man can free a people as one man redeemed the world.

I will take no pike. I will go into battle with bare hands. I will stand up before the Gall as Christ hung naked before men on a tree" (qtd. in Kiberd 201). The call to suffer and die for the cause of Ireland, for each individual to become a Christ, had produced revolution, but in the transitional moment of the civil war Yeats challenges his readers to reconsider that narrative and to imagine an Ireland in which such calls are recognized as simply words designed to perpetuate bloodshed.

Yeats turns, in order "To silence the envy in my thought," from this world of violence toward the solitude of the tower. The poet's envy is directed at a "moor-hen" who "guides" her chicks "upon the stream," an image of natural harmony set in contrast to Ireland's self-destructive present, and, ironically, toward the soldiers themselves, men capable of action because, unlike the contemplative Yeats, they remain happily and dangerously true to nationalisms' progressivist myths. For Yeats, "caught / In the cold snows of a dream," forced to fully confront violence simply as violence, such comfort is impossible.

The tower in the next poem has become a prison: "the key is turned / On our uncertainty...."Violence reigns on all sides, "somewhere / A man is killed, or a house burned," but this is violence without meaning, unjustified by history's structuring myths: "no clear fact [can] be discerned." Indeed, the plea for "honeybees" to "Come build in the empty house of the stare" merely high-lights the divide between the natural world, where decay and death give way to growth and rebirth, and Ireland's "empty" present where Yeats is forced to bear witness to the surrounding violence: "Last night they trundled down the road / That dead young soldier in his blood."

John Unterecker suggests that Yeats is referring here to a soldier who "had actually been dragged... down a nearby road, his body so battered that his mother could recover only his torn disembodied head". Yeats does mention such an incident, complete with the gruesome detail of the head, in an October 1922 letter to J. C. Grierson, but there Yeats is describing previous Black and Tan violence. A more plausible reference is the death of a "National soldier," described in a letter to T. Sturge Moore written while Yeats was working on the "series of poems about this Tower and on the civil war," which would become "Meditations": "A motor has just passed with a National soldier and a coffin up on end and what I suppose were the relatives of the dead man" (W. B. Yeats and T. Sturge Moore 46). In either case, what is important is the absence of agency in the poem itself, the refusal to identify the soldier's affiliation and thus the affiliation of his killers.

For Yeats, tempting as it may be, this momen t must not be made into another tale of heroic martyrdom readily inscribed into a Republican narrative designed to further revolutionary bloodshed, or a Free State narrative designed to justify reprisal violence. Rather, this is meaningless violence served to a people who, including the poet, "had fed the heart on fantasies." To represent this death as part of a broader fantasy of heroic sacrifice would be to contribute further to a current state in which "The heart's grown brutal from the fare; / More substance in our enmities / Than in our love...."

"Meditations in Time of Civil War" concludes with images of chaos and violence that abruptly shift the setting from civil war Ireland to eighteenth-century France, as cries now resound calling "For vengeance on the murders of Jacques Molay." Generally regarded as an emblem of the coming apocalypse that Yeats dramatized in "The Second Coming," outlined in A Vision, and saw proof of in world events such as the Bolshevik revolution, few critics, with the notable exception of Elizabeth Cullingford, have analyzed this section at any length in light of the local Irish context. A Grand Master of the Knights Templar, Jacques de Molay was executed, with the tacit approval of Pope Clement V, by Philip the Fair of France in 1314. During the eighteenth century, French Free Masons, a society at odds with both the Catholic Church and the French monarchy, symbolically linked their ancestral founder, Hiram Abif, executed for refusing to divulge the society's secrets, with Molay. From the perspective of anti-Masonic Fren ch historians, the desire of Masons to avenge the death of Molay helped to fuel the antimonarchy and anti-French church sentiments of the French revolutionaries, the "class-hatred" Yeats cryptically refers to in his note on Molay in "Meditations". But the poem itself sees vengeance as anything but clear:

The rage-driven, rage-tormented, and rage-hungry troop,
Trooper belabouring trooper, biting at arm or at face,
Plunges towards nothing, arms and fingers spreading wide,
For the embrace of nothing.

According to Cullingford, this concluding section, which seems to move us beyond the local Irish context, is in fact a fitting commentary on the civil war: "What began as the struggle to avenge a genuine wrong, and to gain Ireland's independence from England, has degenerated into fratricidal strife".

To this perceptive claim I would add that the stanza is not concerned merely with violence born from "revenge" but with the core ideological component driving the compulsion for revenge in civil war Ireland: nationalist historiographic constructions of martyrdom. According to Yeats's note, "A cry for vengeance because of the murder of the Grand Master of the Templars seems to me a fit symbol for those who labour from hatred, and so for sterility in various kinds" (Collected Poems 460-61).Vengeance for Molay is a "fit symbol," but it is so because Molay has himself been appropriated symbolically within Masonic historiography as an emblem of all who have given their lives to combat the influences of secular and religious tyranny, the foundational martyr whose death, so to speak, "pre-sanctions" subsequent extremism and unchecked violence. If, as I have suggested, "Meditations in Time of Civil War" functions to disrupt precisely those same types of constructions in Republican and Free State discourse, narratives spawned during a colonial period to counterbalance imperial versions of history and the tyranny they would legitimate, these "Monstrous familiar images [that] swim to the mind's eye" are more than fitting, more than "familiar." They provide a tale of chaotic violence and hatred that imprisons the present in the past, a tale by which a transitional Ireland ceaselessly replicates the initial wrongs of colonialism, a newly liberated Ireland struggling to become a truly postcolonial Ireland.

Bibliography

A Vision. London: Macmillan, 1937.

Andrew Motion & T. Morrisson Penguin Book of Contemporary British Poetry (Penguin).

Anthony Bradley Contemporary Irish Poetry (California Press).

Brendan Kennelly The Penguin Book of Irish Verse (Penguin).

Explorations. Selected by Mrs. W. B. Yeats. New York: Macmillan, 1962.

Frank Ormsby Poets from the North Of Ireland (Blackstaff)

Frank Ormsby The Hip Flask: Short Poems from Ireland (Blackstaff).

Gerald Dawe The New Younger Irish Poets (Blackstaff).

Gerald Dawe The Younger Irish Poets (Blackstaff).

Jeffares, A. Norman, and Knowland, A. S. *A Commentary on the Collected Plays of W. B. Yeats*. London: Macmillan, 1975.

Jeffares, A. Norman. *A New Commentary on the Poems of W. B. Yeats*. Stanford, Calif.: Stanford University Press, 1984.

John Montague Bitter Harvest, an anthology of Irish Poetry (Scribners).

Keith Tuma Anthology of Twentieth-Century British and Irish Poetry (Oxford).

Mythologies. New York: Macmillan, 1959.

Niall MacMonagle Off the Wall (Marino).

Niall MacMonagle Real Cool: Poems to Grow Up With (Marino).

Patrick Crotty Modern Irish Poetry: An Anthology (Blackstaff).

Paul Muldoon Faber Book of Contemporary Irish Poetry (Faber).

Peter Fallon & Derek Mahon Penguin Book of Irish Contemporary Poetry (Penguin).

S. Armitage & R. Crawford The Penguin Book of Poetry from Britain and Ireland since 1945 (Penguin).

Sean O'Brien The Firebox: Poetry in Britain and Ireland after 1945 (Picador).

The Collected Plays of W. B. Yeats. 1952. Reprint, London: Macmillan,1982.

The Collected Poems of W. B. Yeats. 1950. Reprint, London: Macmillan, 1982.

Thomas Kinsella New Oxford Book of Irish Verse (Oxford).

Wade, Allan. *A Bibliography of the Writings of W. B. Yeats*. Rev. Russell K. Alspach. London: Hart-Davis, 1968.

WJ McCormack Ferocious Humanism Anthology of Irish Poetry from before Swift to Yeats and After (Dent).

Yeats, W. B. *Autobiographies*. London: Macmillan, 1956.